Letters from Mafeking

Letters from Mafeking

*Eyewitness Accounts from the Longest
Siege of the South African War*

Edward M. Spiers

FRONTLINE
BOOKS

Letters From Mafeking
Eyewitness Accounts from the Longest Siege of the South African War

First published in Great Britain in 2018 by Frontline Books,
an imprint of Pen & Sword Books Ltd, Yorkshire - Philadelphia

Printed and bound by TJ International Ltd, Padstow, Cornwall

Pen & Sword Books Ltd incorporates the imprints of Frontline Books, Pen & Sword
Archaeology, Air World Books, Atlas, Aviation, Battleground, Discovery, Family History,
History, Maritime, Military, Naval, Politics, Social History, Transport, True Crime,
Claymore Press, Praetorian Press, Seaforth Publishing and White Owl.

For a complete list of Pen & Sword titles please contact:

PEN & SWORD BOOKS LTD
47 Church Street, Barnsley, South Yorkshire, S70 2AS, UK.
E-mail: enquiries@pen-and-sword.co.uk
Website: www.pen-and-sword.co.uk

Or

PEN AND SWORD BOOKS,
1950 Lawrence Road, Havertown, PA 19083, USA
E-mail: Uspen-and-sword@casematepublishers.com
Website: www.penandswordbooks.com

Contents

List of Illustrations

List of Maps

Acknowledgements

I should like to thank Baron Baden-Powell for permission to quote from the staff diary of Colonel R. S. S. Baden-Powell in the National Army Museum; Dr Alastair Massie for permission to quote from other collections in the same museum; the Warden and Scholars of New College Oxford for permission to quote from the papers of Alfred, Viscount Milner, and the Bodleian Libraries, University of Oxford for access to these papers; James and Pamela Nicholson, Woodcott House, Upper Woodcott for permission to consult and quote from the Nicholson papers; Ms Joanna Simmons to quote from the Wolseley Collection, Brighton & Hove City Libraries, Brighton & Hove City Council; and Mrs Jennifer Kimble for permission to quote from papers in the Brenthurst Library, Johannesburg.

I should also like to thank the following archivists and librarians, namely Colin Harris and Oliver House, Bodleian Libraries; Mrs. Jennifer Thorp, New College, University of Oxford; Alastair Massie and Robert Fleming, National Army Museum; Alison Metcalfe, Angus Wark and Miss Moray Hannah Teale, National Library of Scotland; David Oswald, Aberdeen Local Studies Library; Mrs Jennifer Kimble, Brenthurst Library; Jean Wooler, Mukund Miyangar, Debbie Horner, Sue Waterhouse, Kathryn Mouncey, British Library; Tim Wright, Inter-Library Loans, University of Leeds; and Major Graeme Green (retd.), Royal Dragoon Guards, York Army Museum.

I am particularly grateful to Emeritus Professor Fransjohan Pretorius for all his assistance, encouragement, and hospitality during my South African visit; David Appleyard, an independent cartographer for his map-making skills; Sello Mashile for an image from the Mafikeng Museum; and Peter Harrington for images in the possession of the Anne S. K. Brown Military History Collection, Brown University, Rhode Island.

For all their assistance during a visit to the Brenthurst Library, Johannesburg, I am indebted to Ms Sally Roberts, Mrs Jennifer Kimble, and Ms Fylyppa Meyer of the Library. I also benefited from the support of colleagues in the School of History, University of Leeds, namely Professors Graeme S. Loud, Simon Hall and Simon Ball, as well as Associate Professor Rachel E. Utley.

I also appreciate the willingness of Martin Mace of Frontline Books to commission this work and enable me to complete the trilogy on Boer War sieges. I am particularly grateful to Stephen Chumbley for his professional advice in the copy-editing of this work.

As ever, I remain very grateful for the support and tolerance of my work on this book from Fiona, my wife, and Robert and Amanda, my two children.

Edward M. Spiers
April 2018

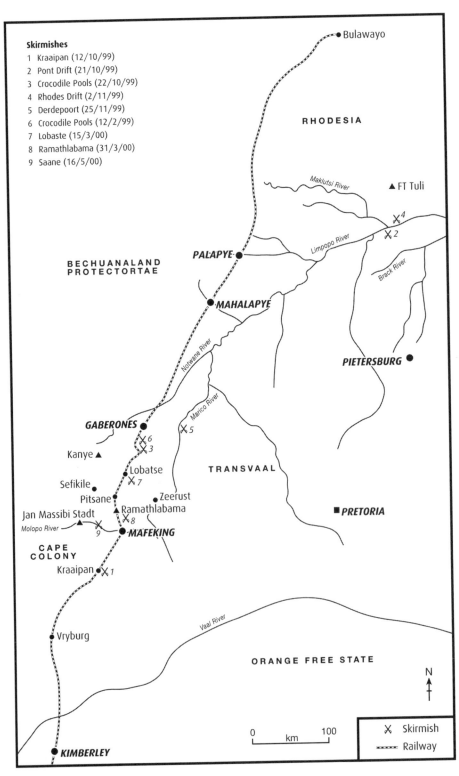

Skirmishes
1 Kraaipan (12/10/99)
2 Pont Drift (21/10/99)
3 Crocodile Pools (22/10/99)
4 Rhodes Drift (2/11/99)
5 Derdepoort (25/11/99)
6 Crocodile Pools (12/2/99)
7 Lobaste (15/3/00)
8 Ramathlabama (31/3/00)
9 Saane (16/5/00)

Bulawayo

RHODESIA

▲ FT Tuli

Maklutsi River

✗ 4
✗ 2

Limpopo River

Brack River

BECHUANALAND
PROTECTORTAE

PALAPYE

MAHALAPYE

Notwane River

PIETERSBURG

Marico River

GABERONES

✗ 5

Kanye ▲

✗ 6
✗ 3

TRANSVAAL

Lobatse
✗ 7

Sefikile
Pitsane

Zeerust

Jan Massibi Stadt
▲ Ramathlabama
✗ 8

■ PRETORIA

Molopo River
▲
✗ 9
MAFEKING

CAPE
COLONY

Kraaipan ✗ 1

Vryburg

Vaal River

ORANGE FREE STATE

N
↑

0   km   100

✗ Skirmish
╌╌╌ Railway

KIMBERLEY

Map 1 The Mafeking Theatre

Chapter 1

Mafeking and its Siege Histories

'Mafeking is a very ordinary-looking place', wrote Major-General Robert S. S. Baden-Powell,[1] 'Just a small tin-roofed town of small houses in rectangular streets, plumped down upon the open veldt close to the Molopo stream, and half a mile from the native town – better known as the "stadt" – consisting of red-clay circular huts with thatched roofs, housing about seven thousand natives [Barolongs]. All around', he observed, 'is open, undulating, yellow grass prairie.'[2] Mafeking was even more vulnerable on account of its frontier location in the far north of Cape Colony, about 1,400 km by rail from Cape Town and 13 km from the Transvaal border. With the approach of war in 1899, the population of Mafeking had changed dramatically; at least 170 women and children had left Mafeking by train but another 630, including refugees, remained within a European population of varying backgrounds and nationalities of about 1,700.[3] While every able-bodied man in the town,

---

1   Robert Stephenson Smyth Baden-Powell, the first Baron Baden-Powell (1857–1941) was an army officer and founder of the Boy Scouts and Girl Guides. Born the sixth son of the Reverend Baden Powell (1796–1860) and his third wife, Henrietta Grace, he was known as 'Stephe', pronounced Steevie, or B-P. Sent to Charterhouse School in 1870, he played football in the school Eleven, and developed his talents for acting, mimicry, and sketching and drawing ambidextrously. As a cavalry officer, he demonstrated skills in mapping, sketching, and reconnaissance work before commanding a native levy in the Anglo-Asante War (1896), and then serving as chief staff officer in the suppression of the Matabele (Ndebele) rebellion in Rhodesia (1896). He wrote *Reconnaissance and Scouting* (1883), accounts of both African campaigns, and acted as the *Daily Chronicle*'s special correspondent during the Asante war and sent sketches to the *Graphic*. Promoted lieutenant colonel in February 1897, he commanded the 5th Dragoon Guards in India before being selected for special duties in South Africa (July 1899). As commander-in-chief, north-west forces, Baden-Powell raised 500 irregulars and commanded the garrison in Mafeking (Mafikeng). After a siege of 217 days, he was promoted major general, the youngest general in the army at 43 years of age.
2   Major-General R. S. S. Baden-Powell, *Sketches in Mafeking & East Africa* (London: Smith, Elder & Co., 1907), p. 25.
3   The post-siege reports of Major-General R. S. S. Baden-Powell and Lieutenant-Colonel Courtney B. Vyvyan state that Mafeking had a population of 1,074 white men, 220 white women, 405 white children and 7,500 'natives', The National Archives (TNA), WO 105/7, Roberts Mss., Maj.-Gen. R. S. S. Baden-Powell to Lord Roberts, 18 May

and 'some who were very far from able bodied',[4] had enrolled in the Town Guard (six officers and 296 men), another single officer and 115 armed men served in a railway division, and a further 700 'trained men' composed the remainder of the 1,200-man garrison.[5] Meanwhile 2,000 blacks had entered the town to live in 'locations' on the south bank of the stream and eastwards of the stadt; these included Bangwaketse, Bakwena, Zulus, Zambesians and Shangaans, who were refugees from the Johannesburg mines, and Fingoes (Mfengu) and 'Cape Boys' (coloureds) driven from the surrounding district when the Boers burnt their villages and looted their cattle. Many of these people served in an armed capacity. Even if their exact number is unknown 300, as acknowledged by Baden-Powell, served as armed cattle guards, and over the course of the siege, possibly 400 Tshidi-Barolongs, 200 'Black Watch' (Mfengu) and 68 Cape Boys served among 750 blacks.[6]

The recent history of Mafeking partially explained why it became so important as to warrant a siege, an importance missed by those who dismiss it as merely 'dusty, insignificant Mafeking'.[7] Both the town and its surrounding country had been contested ever since Boer farmers from the western Transvaal began raiding the territory of the Bantu tribes across their border. These raids continued until 1868, when President Marthinus W. Pretorius claimed the entirety of Bechuanaland as far west as Lake N'Gami to be within the South African Republic (Transvaal). The local Tshidi-Barolong people, whose headquarters were in Mafeking, known as the 'Place of Stones', appealed to the British for protection. In 1871, the Keate award determined that Mafeking was outside the limits of the republic but the burghers never acknowledged this ruling. After the Transvaal recovered its independence (Pretoria Convention, 3 August 1881), freebooters moved into the disputed

---

1900, which was published as 'Major-General Baden-Powell's official report on the Siege of Mafeking', *London Gazette*, 8 February 1901, pp. 890–903 at p. 891, hereafter 'B-P's report', with a résumé in *South Africa Despatches*, Vol. 1, Cd 457 (1901), pp. 101–22 and TNA, WO 108/284, Lt.-Col. Courtney B. Vyvyan, 'The Defence of Mafeking', n.d.

4   General Sir Alexander Godley, *Life of an Irish Soldier* (London: John Murray, 1939), p. 72.

5   Major-General Sir Frederick Maurice and M. H. Grant, *History of the War in South Africa 1899-1902*, hereafter *Official History*, 4 vols (London: Hurst and Blackett, 1906–10), vol. 3, p. 145 and L. S. Amery (general editor), *The Times History of the War in South Africa 1899-1902*, 7 vols (London, Sampson, Low, Marston & Co., 1900–09) vol. 4 ed. by Basil Williams, p. 572.

6   Tim Jeal, *Baden-Powell* (New Haven and London: Yale University Press, 2001), pp. 281 and 620n15; Amery, *Times History*, vol. 4, p. 573; *Official History*, vol. 3, p. 145; TNA, WO 108/294, Vyvyan, 'The Defence of Mafeking', n.d.; J. Angus Hamilton, *The Siege of Mafeking* (London: Methuen & Co., 1900), p. 55.

7   Michael Rosenthal, *The Character Factory: Baden-Powell and the Origins of the Boy Scout Movement* (London: Collins, 1986), p. 30.

territory, offering assistance to the competing Griqua and Tswana peoples in exchange for promises of farms for themselves. Although the British checked their own freebooters, Boer adventurers established the independent republics of Stellaland at Vryburg and Goshen at Rooi Grond, only about 10 km from Mafeking, both of which President Paul Kruger[8] tried to annex as part of the Transvaal in 1884.

The Gladstone government, which had signed both the Pretoria Convention (1881) and then the London Convention (1884), described Kruger's action as a contravention of the London treaty. Kruger withdrew his proclamation, but the British government despatched Major-General Sir Charles Warren, RE, as a special commissioner with 4,000 men, to evict the Goshenites and Stellalanders and restore order. In a bloodless campaign Warren never encountered resistance and declared the whole of Bechuanaland to be a British protectorate. Thereafter he established Mafeking as the seat of the resident commissioner, and authorized the digging of wells, building of forts, and the layout of what would eventually become a township of about 1,000 yards [914m] square, with streets at right angles.

As a market town and starting-point for hunting expeditions into the Kalahari Desert, the settlement expanded steadily, gaining a major boost when it became connected by railway with Vryburg and Kimberley in 1894. Although it soon lost its advantage as a railway terminus when the railway was extended to Bulawayo in 1897, the railway remained a large employer of labour, and the town continued as 'a thriving commercial centre and a considerable railway depot'.[9] In its short history, first as the administrative centre for the protectorate, and then for the Mafeking district of Cape Colony after its incorporation into the colony in November 1895, Mafeking acquired all the appurtenances of a municipal and administrative centre.

Laid out round a large market square, the town had municipal and government offices in the centre; it also had a library, gaol, courthouse, several schools, Anglican, Dutch and Wesleyan churches, Dixon's Hotel and several

---

8   President Stephanus Johannes Paulus (Paul) Kruger (1825–1904) was the last president of the South African Republic (Transvaal), who spent half a century militarily and politically upholding the state's struggle for independence. After the Jameson Raid (1895–6), he imported vast amounts of modern armaments into the Transvaal, concluded an alliance with President Marthinus T. Steyn of the Orange Free State (1897), and in subsequent negotiations with the British at the Bloemfontein conference (May–June 1899), made only minor concessions before delivering an ultimatum (9 October 1899) and launching invasions of Natal and Cape Colony on 11 October 1899. After defeat at Bergendal (21–27 August 1900), Kruger fled to Europe where he failed to raise support for the Boer republics. He died in Switzerland.

9   Amery, *Times History*, vol. 4, pp. 568–70; see also TNA, WO 108/284, Vyvyan, 'The Defence of Mafeking'.

others, a Masonic Hall, a branch of the Standard Bank, Messrs Weil's store, and a local newspaper, the *Mafeking Mail and Protectorate Guardian* (established in May 1899). It also had a cricket ground and a racecourse nearby. The station and railway workshops lay on the north-west corner, while the Victoria Hospital and a convent were due north. Of the local accommodation, only the convent had more than one storey,[10] and Mafeking remained small and extremely isolated. As Lady Sarah Wilson observed, having ridden across the country that surrounded the town,

> where no tree or hill obscures the view for miles . . . one then realised what a tiny place the seat of government of the Bechuanaland Protectorate really was, a mere speck of corrugated iron roofs on the brown expanse of the burnt-up veldt, far away from everywhere.[11]

The incorporation of Mafeking within Cape Colony in November 1895 earned the town its pre-war notoriety. It provided cover for the final secret arrangements in connection with the ill-fated Jameson Raid. This was a scheme taken up by Cecil John Rhodes[12] to achieve a *coup d'état* within the

---

10   Hugh and Mirabel Cecil, *Imperial Marriage: An Edwardian War and Peace* (London: John Murray, 2002), p. 133; Brain P. Willan (ed.), *Edward Ross, Diary of The Siege of Mafeking, October 1899 – May 1900* (Cape Town; van Riebeeck Society, 1980), pp. 6–7; Louis Creswicke, *South Africa and the Transvaal War*, 6 vols (Edinburgh: T. C. & E. C. Jack, 1900), vol. 2, p. 55.

11   Lady Sarah Wilson, *South African Memories: Social, Warlike & Sporting* (London: Edward Arnold, 1909), p. 77. Lady Sarah Isabella Augusta Wilson (née Spencer-Churchill) (1865–1929) was the first woman war correspondent. The youngest of the eleven children of John Spencer-Churchill, 7th Duke of Marlborough, she was an aunt of Winston L. S. Churchill, who also served as a war correspondent in the South African War. After the capture of the *Daily Mail's* correspondent, Alf Hellawell, she was appointed as his replacement at a time when she had just left Mafeking, where her husband, Captain Gordon C. Wilson, was serving as Baden-Powell's aide-de-camp. In trying to return to the town, she was captured by the Boers and exchanged for a horse thief and suspected Boer spy.

12   Cecil John Rhodes (1853–1902) was a British imperialist, statesman and financier, who made his fortune from the diamond fields of Griqualand West and later from deep-level mining when gold was discovered on the Witwatersrand in 1886. He had a political power base in the Cape House of Assembly, becoming prime minister of Cape Colony in 1890. His imperialist ambitions focused upon the northward extension of British territory, playing a part in the Warren expedition that established the Bechuanaland Protectorate (1885) and, with the aid of the British South Africa Company, took possession of the country north of the Limpopo (1890), which came to be called Rhodesia. When he eventually realized that this territory would not become a second Witwatersrand, he turned his thoughts to removing Kruger and securing access to the gold fields through a British federation, incorporating the Transvaal. After the fiasco of the Jameson Raid, he resigned as Cape premier but remained a wealthy and influential figure.

Transvaal. It involved the launching of a flying column from the Bechuanaland Protectorate to trigger a revolt by leaders of the *Uitlanders*[13] in Johannesburg. Rhodes, Dr Leander Starr Jameson[14] and others had planned to avoid overtly embroiling the British government by raising the invading force from staff of the British South Africa Company and the Bechuanaland Border Police, whose headquarters were in Mafeking. By covertly stocking arms and equipment in Mafeking, Jameson planned to launch his column of 510 police and volunteers, with eight Maxims and three field pieces, from Pitsane in the Bechuanaland Protectorate. Although the Johannesburg plotters decided to postpone the rising on 28 December 1895, and Rhodes wanted to follow suit, a breakdown in communications resulted in Jameson launching his raid on 29 December. It proved a complete fiasco, leading to the surrender of Jameson and his men on 2 January 1896, and left a lasting sense of grievance among the Boers, 'who made no distinction between the imperialist ideals of Rhodes and the British government'.[15]

Kruger spent the ensuing years buying modern weapons in case of a conflict with Britain, while Mafeking remained, in Baden-Powell's words, 'a bone of contention between Boers and British'.[16] This applied not only to Boers on the western border but throughout the country, lest Mafeking again be used as a base from which to threaten Pretoria. Mafeking also held railway supplies and materials (valued in excess of £120,000),[17] although these never compared with similar stocks in Ladysmith, a larger railway junction, or the

---

13 *Uitlanders* ('Outlanders' or foreigners in Afrikaans) were white people who flocked to the Witwatersrand from outside the Transvaal after the discovery of gold in 1886. When some of them agitated for a shortening of the eligibility period for enfranchisement, which Kruger had extended from 5 to 14 years in 1890, their grievances were embraced first by the architects of the abortive Jameson Raid and then by Sir Alfred Milner, the British high commissioner in South Africa. Milner launched a diplomatic offensive against the Transvaal in the late 1890s.

14 Dr Leander Starr Jameson (1853–1917) was born in Edinburgh, studied in London and practised medicine in Cape Colony from 1878. A devoted friend of Rhodes, he served as a magistrate and administrator in Rhodesia before leading the disastrous raid into the Transvaal. Handed over by Kruger, he was tried by the British authorities under the Foreign Enlistment Act of 1870 and sentenced to 15 months' imprisonment in July 1896. He was released on account of ill health in the following December, and stayed out of politics until July 1896 when he supported Milner's diplomatic offensive. During the war he served as a doctor in the siege of Ladysmith.

15 Fransjohan Pretorius, *The A to Z of the Anglo-Boer War* (Lanham, Md.: Scarecrow Press, 2009), p. 195.

16 Baden-Powell, 'Narrative of Organization of Frontier Force' in *Minutes of Evidence taken before the Royal Commission of the War in South Africa*, hereafter *RCWSA*, vol. 2, Cd 1791 (1900–09), XLI, p. 424.

17 Brenthurst Library (Bren. L), Vyvyan Mss., MS. 147/5/1/40, J. R. More, 'Siege of Mafeking, 1899 – 1900', hereafter 'Railway Report', n.d., p. 3.

economic riches of Kimberley. Location may have been more tempting since the Boers feared lest Mafeking arm, and encourage blacks in the Bechuanaland Protectorate to invade the Transvaal, for which the garrison neither gave any justification nor possessed the resources to do so.[18]

Once the war erupted, Mafeking remained a potential threat to any line of communications whether the Transvaalers struck north towards Rhodesia or south towards Kimberley. Mafeking became a siege because the Boers, whatever their aims, chose to invest the town and sustain this undertaking, albeit with significantly reduced numbers, over 217 days. They could have been forgiven for thinking that Mafeking, so obviously vulnerable and bereft of natural defences, regular soldiers or effective artillery, was an easy target to overcome. Rumours circulated within Mafeking that local Boers had boasted that they could capture the town before breakfast. Doubtless their failure to do so, and the ensuing resilience of the defenders, boosted morale among the besieged in mid-October.[19] Conversely, the failure of the Boers to seize Mafeking after 217 days not only caused unprecedented scenes of frenzy and jubilation across the United Kingdom and the English-speaking empire but also represented 'one of the greatest humiliations of the war on the Boer side'.[20] Accordingly, the siege of Mafeking has attracted a remarkable volume of commentary.

Siege Histories

In his essay on the historiography of the Mafeking siege, and the many biographies of Baden-Powell, Christopher Saunders characterizes the writing before the mid-1960s as sustaining 'the myth of Mafeking' by presenting it as 'a heroic and glorious episode, a centre-piece of the South African war that had symbolized all that was best in the British character'.[21] He criticises this work because it was based on a narrow, largely British, source base and 'was not the work of scholars'. Only after the last survivors of the siege had passed away, was it possible, he avers, for a more cynical critique of the siege to emerge, one that was less interested in political and military matters than upon the lives of ordinary people, both black and white, utilizing a wider range of

---

18   Fransjohan Pretorius, 'The Besiegers' in Iain R. Smith (ed.), *The Siege of Mafeking*, 2 vols (Johannesburg: Brenthurst Press, 2001), vol. 1, pp. 63–107, at p. 66.

19   J. Emerson Neilly, *Besieged with B.-P.: A Full and Complete Record of the Siege* (London: C. Arthur Pearson, 1900), p. 47; on the strategic value of Mafeking, see Baden-Powell, 'Narrative of Organization of Frontier Force' evidence before the *RCWSA*, vol. 2, p. 424; Amery, *Times History*, vol. 4, p. 570; and *Official History*, vol. 3, p. 143.

20   Pretorius, 'The Besiegers', in Smith (ed.), *Siege of Mafeking*, vol. 1, p. 104.

21   Christopher Saunders, 'The Siege in History' in Smith (ed.), *Siege of Mafeking*, vol. 2, pp. 475–93, at p. 481.

sources.[22] Tim Jeal, the author of a magisterial biography of Baden-Powell, broadly agrees that the revisionism, or vigorous 'debunking' of the 1960s onwards, followed 'more than fifty years of hagiographical publications'.[23]

The first of these hagiographies appeared in 1900. W. F. Aitken had his book on 'the Hero of Mafeking' ready for publication as soon as news of the relief reached Britain, but before any reports on the last few months of the siege had arrived.[24] Another three books appeared in the same year, all written by war correspondents, who had reported from Mafeking throughout the siege. Far from being purely eulogistic works, they each included material that had either been excised in Mafeking, where Major the Hon. Algernon H. C. Hanbury-Tracy acted as censor, or had not been published by their newspapers. In his otherwise fairly conventional narrative, based on his diary, Major Frederick D. Baillie of the *Morning Post* revealed that Baden-Powell had armed Barolongs, 'supplemented by two squadrons of ours', to greet the Boer attack on 25 October 'with a heavy fire, killing many'.[25] J. Angus Hamilton of *The Times*, who antagonized both his editor, Moberly Bell, and Baden-Powell, wrote the most critical of the siege histories, nearly half of which never appeared in his printed articles. He referred to doubts, uncertainty and grumbling amongst the townspeople (and not simply their bravery and resilience); the shortcomings of the defences, medical provisions, and troops (describing the Protectorate Regiment was an 'ill-assorted assembly of adventurers'); and alluded to armed blacks serving alongside Protectorate troops and the Bechuanaland riflemen as well as the need to keep the 'native arms . . . more under control'. He composed, too, a pen portrait of Baden-Powell that appealed to subsequent critics as it depicted him as a solitary, calculating man, consumed with ambition, even if his energy and resourcefulness had given 'Mafeking a complete and assured security' (very different from the laconic and heroic commander in Baillie's commentary). Finally, Hamilton dwelt at length upon the food rationing, commending the

---

22 Ibid.

23 Jeal, *Baden-Powell*, preface p. ix.

24 On the timing of the publication, see the editorial, *Manchester Guardian*, 19 May 1900, p. 9; the early biographies were W. Francis Aitken, *Baden-Powell, The Hero of Mafeking* (London: S. W. Partridge & Co., 1900) and Harold Begbie, *The Story of Baden-Powell: The Wolf that Never Sleeps* (London: Grant Richards, 1900); and on the time-lag in the reporting, see Jacqueline Beaumont, 'Reporting the Siege Under the Union Jack', hereafter 'Reporting the Siege', in Smith (ed.), *Siege of Mafeking*, vol. 2, pp. 329–57, at pp. 339–40.

25 Major F. D. Baillie, *Mafeking: A Diary of the Siege* (London: Archibald Constable & Co., 1900), p. 34; see also Baden-Powell, 'Preparations for Siege', evidence before the *RCWSA*, vol. 2, p. 424.

stockpiling of Weil & Co. while castigating Baden-Powell for his illiberal treatment of the blacks.[26]

J. Emerson Neilly of the *Pall Mall Gazette* produced a volume that veered between the extremes of the other two; it commended the gallantry, loyalty and industry of the blacks, who dug trenches, ran despatches through enemy lines, raided Boer cattle and served as riflemen but suffered terribly when 'hunger had them in its grip'. It acknowledged, too, that white citizens were prone to grumble at times, and that the defenders' pluck, 'great and heroic' though it was, did not save Mafeking: 'The cowardice of the enemy saved us . . . .' Neilly's account differed from Hamilton's, nonetheless, by lauding Baden-Powell as 'a man in a thousand' or 'the Wolf that never sleeps', who watched from his rooftop by day and prowled the veld by night, and who provided soup for the blacks, only requiring payment from those employed on the works, 'the remainder, who were in the majority, obtained it free'. Baden-Powell, he argued, employed 'the most refined tricks and artifices of war' yet boosted civilian morale by his confident demeanour, his messages to the Boers and his appearance or participation in the sports, games, exhibitions and concerts organized each Sunday: 'He was the right man for the work.'[27]

Although Saunders commended these accounts and the memoirs of Lady Sarah Wilson, published in 1909,[28] as 'valuable primary sources', he implied that their main shortcoming was to regard the siege as 'a significant event'.[29] This was hardly surprising as the writers were siege participants but Neilly maintained that the siege was strategically important as it distracted the Boers from venturing northwards towards Rhodesia, with the possible assistance of an armoured train, and prevented the loss of all the resources in Mafeking.[30] Arthur Conan Doyle, who was in South Africa during the siege and wrote the first history of the war, described the town 'as a bait to the Boers, and occupied a considerable force in a useless siege at a time when their presence at other seats in the war might have proved disastrous to the British cause'.[31] His commentary was much more perceptive than the cynical critique of Michael Davitt, a pro-Boer and former Irish Nationalist MP, who deprecated Baden-Powell's use of blacks in the siege and wrote of the 'farcical character'

---

26   Hamilton, *Siege of Mafeking*, pp. 50, 75, 93, 97, 114–16, 125, 192–5, 204–6, 249–50; see also Beaumont, 'Reporting the Siege' in Smith (ed.), *Siege of Mafeking*, vol. 2, pp. 337–9.
27   Neilly, *Besieged with B.-P.*, pp. 95–6, 164–7, 200–1, 214–15, 226–32, 238–9, 252–3, 283 and 295.
28   Lady Sarah Wilson, *South African Memories*.
29   Saunders, 'Siege in History' in Smith (ed.), *Siege of Mafeking*, vol. 2, p. 478.
30   Neilly, *Besieged with B.-P.*, pp. 290–3.
31   A. Conan Doyle, *The Great Boer War* (London: Smith, Elder & Co., 1900), p. 404.

of the operations during the siege itself.[32] As Conan Doyle observed, the siege had detained four or five thousand Boers in 'the all-important early month', and later when the bulk of these men departed, it detained a more numerous enemy with eight guns, including one of the four big Creusots, when they could have been used to support operations elsewhere. The defenders paid a heavy price in over 200 fatalities but owed much to their accomplished commander, who 'was as difficult to outwit as it was to outfight him'. If the subsequent 'enthusiasm in the empire' seemed excessive, argued Conan Doyle, 'at least it was expended over worthy men and a fine deed of arms'.[33]

This measured assessment seems somewhat at odds with the 'mythical' categorization of Saunders, as does the first of the siege diaries, published admittedly for private circulation in 1901. Charles James Weir, an accountant in the Standard Bank and a member of the Town Guard, proffered interesting insights on both the vanishing currency within Mafeking and the strains of trench duty. He recorded how his spirits oscillated during the siege, leaving him reliant upon his deep religious convictions. Although Weir always retained the 'fullest confidence in' Baden-Powell, and praised him repeatedly, he thought that the Colonel 'might have done more to save the lives of the natives'. Nevertheless, he reserved his wrath for a 'brutish' enemy that had shelled women and children, and he emerged from the siege with his imperial convictions enhanced.[34]

Another two major accounts of the siege and relief[35] appeared in this period, namely the fourth volume of *The Times History of the War in South Africa* (1906) and the third volume of the officially-produced *History of the War in South Africa* (1908). By interviews with serving officers, and access to official reports, both volumes cover the military aspects of the siege in exceptional detail. *The Times* volume affirmed that 'Baden-Powell justly gained immense credit for his plucky defence . . . as an example of what can be accomplished in war by ingenuity and a bold front, this defence was worth accomplishing'.[36] Meanwhile the official history conceded that

---

32 Michael Davitt, *The Boer Fight for Freedom* (New York: Funk and Wagnalls, 1902), pp. 438 and 440.

33 Conan Doyle, *Great Boer War*, pp. 404 and 422.

34 Charles J. Weir, *The Boer War: A Diary of the Siege of Mafeking* (Edinburgh: Spence & Phimister, 1901), pp. 32, 37, 47, 49, 56, 60, 63–4, 76, 86, 105–7.

35 Two correspondents wrote accounts of the relief but purely from the perspective of the southern column: Filson Young, *The Relief of Mafeking: How It was Accomplished by Mahon's Flying Column; with an Account of Some Earlier Episodes in the Boer War of 1899-1900* (London: Methuen & Co., 1900) and Major A. W. A. Pollock, *With Seven Generals in the Boer War: A Personal Narrative* (London: Skeffington & Son, 1900).

36 Amery, *Times History*, vol. 4, p. 597.

the siege of Mafeking had not been able to absorb sufficient numbers of the enemy to retard seriously the course of the main Federal campaign . . . it had yet retained many, and had in short justified every reason which had induced Baden-Powell originally to resign himself to it.[37]

Subsequent writing on Mafeking, often overshadowed by very different forms of warfare, or perspectives on war, tended to fit more neatly into the 'mythical' and 'heroic' imagery. During the First World War, George Tighe, a former town guardsman, described the siege as 'probably the best remembered event in the South African War', involving 'the prolonged and stubborn holding of an isolated town against an overwhelmingly superior enemy'.[38] Dwarfed by comparison with the challenges and sufferings of the Great War, reflections upon Mafeking would soon be considered as an episode in 'the last of the gentleman's wars'.[39] The heroic imagery would be evoked again during the early years of the Second World War, when a booklet on the *Defence of Mafeking* was distributed to boost popular morale.[40] Ernest E. Reynolds, who had gained access to some of Baden-Powell's papers, wrote another biography in 1942, justifying wartime censorship, as in Mafeking 'since correspondents could not have possession of all the facts'. He insisted that the siege, though not 'of major military importance' as 'B-P himself maintained', boosted 'the morale of the natives' while depressing that of the Boers. 'The gay audacity of the besieged', wrote Reynolds, 'came as the one gleam of encouragement during a series of disasters'.[41]

Post-war writing continued in a similar vein for another two decades. Duncan Grinnell-Milne's study of *Baden-Powell at Mafeking* (1957), marking the centenary of Baden-Powell's birth, repeated the comparison with the 'siege of Britain'. It also contained a foreword from General Sir Alexander Godley, who had distinguished himself at Mafeking. He asserted that 'If ever the right man was sent to the right place, if ever square peg was put into square hole, that man, that "peg", was B-P at Mafeking.'[42] Another largely

---

37 *Official History*, vol. 3, p. 184.
38 George Tighe, 'How we defended Mafeking' in W. Woods (ed.), *Marvellous Escapes from Peril, as told by survivors* (London; Blackie & Son, 1915), pp. 167–79, at p. 167.
39 J. F. C. Fuller, *The Last of the Gentleman's Wars: A Subaltern's Journal of the War in South Africa, 1899-1902* (London: Faber & Faber, 1937).
40 Wilfrid Robertson, *The Defence of Mafeking* (London: Oxford University Press, 1941).
41 Ernest E. Reynolds, *Baden-Powell: A Biography of Lord Baden-Powell of Gilwell* (London: Oxford University Press, 1942), pp. 100 and 113.
42 D. Grinnell-Milne, *Baden-Powell at Mafeking* (London: Bodley Head, 1957), pp. vii and 221.

uncritical biography followed in 1964, written by William Hillcourt and the devoted widow of Baden-Powell, Olave. They maintained that the Colonel had decided to counter the Boers 'with two specialities of his own: bluff and boldness', and quoted from his diary that even the first sortie of the armoured train 'will have a great and lasting moral effect on the enemy'.[43] Uncritical commentary reappeared in the contemporary histories of the war. Rayne Kruger's *Goodbye Dolly Gray*, which went through six editions between 1959 and 1967, was the most widely read of these works, and was notable for its description of the Mafeking celebrations in the United Kingdom and across the empire. Kruger referred to 'the magical way the crowds appeared as if at the touch of a conjurer's wand, and on the complete spontaneity of the nation's unprecedented outburst'.[44]

Revisionism, though, appeared from the late 1960s onwards in keeping with the popular themes of a post-colonial and anti-heroic era. In writing *Mafeking: A Victorian Legend* (1966), Brian Gardner led a wave of critics, determined to debunk the myths and legends of previous generations. Having found new material in the papers of Benjamin Weil and in the War Office records, he broadened his critique beyond the military significance of the siege to include many of its social aspects. Unfortunately Gardner diminished the value of his research by making assertions without evidence, using inadequate referencing, and by following a single-minded approach that created its own mythology.[45] In discrediting the siege, Gardner emphasized Mafeking's abundance of supplies, the supposedly porous nature of the investment, and the tepid and casual conduct of the defence, 'so that at times it hardly took on the characteristics of a siege at all'.[46] Baden-Powell, he described, as 'one of the most ambitious officers in the British Army', who had seized 'the chance of a lifetime'. B-P, he asserted, had ignored orders by choosing to defend the town, and had committed 'a classic military blunder' of guarding his supplies rather than conducting mobile operations against the Boers. While praising the showmanship of Baden-Powell in sustaining civilian morale, Gardner accredited any military successes to his junior officers, blamed the Colonel

---

43 William Hillcourt and Olave, Lady Baden-Powell, *Baden-Powell: The Two Lives of a Hero* (London: Heinemann, 1964), pp. 173–4.

44 Rayne Kruger, *Goodbye Dolly Gray: The History of the Boer War* (London: NEL MENTOR, 1963), p. 296.

45 Saunders excuses Gardner for his sparse footnotes because he was writing for a 'popular audience', Saunders, "Siege in History' in Smith (ed.), *Siege of Mafeking*, vol. 2, p. 481, but Gardner repeatedly made allegations of internal grumbling about B-P's command, which undoubtedly occurred, but without proffering evidence to support his claims, Brian Gardner, *Mafeking: A Victorian Legend* (London: Cassell, 1966), pp. 76, 83 and 88.

46 Gardner, *Mafeking*, pp. 31–2, 42, 54, 98–9, 132–4, 198.

for the 'fearful mistake' of attacking Game Tree Fort (26 December 1899), and for remaining 'supine for months at a time', as the blacks suffered from starvation and disease. More positive assessments of the siege, such as that of the *Official History*, he dismissed as 'double-talk'.[47]

Radical and revisionist historians developed this critique. Richard Price, Piers Brendon and Michael Rosenthal agreed that Baden-Powell had been tactically naive in allowing himself to become entrapped and in requiring the diversion of valuable troops to rescue him. 'Seldom', wrote Price, 'has one man ever built such a successful career on incompetence.'[48] Rosenthal, who quoted selectively from Hamilton to suggest that the siege was a relatively benign affair, characterized the event as a 'most peculiar confrontation between two blundering foes, neither of whom had any good reason to be doing what they were doing'. Following Gardner's lead, he questioned the number of Boers detained by the siege and doubted that the Boers, after the departure of Cronjé, ever constituted 'a formidable threat'.[49] 'Boredom', conversely, 'constituted the gravest danger to the white inhabitants of Mafeking', and it was 'in repelling boredom that Baden-Powell was at his cheery best'.[50] Brendon accepted that Baden-Powell possessed a 'tactician's craft' but one that 'smacked more of the showman's stage than the theatre of war'. Nevertheless, in reviewing the casualties at Game Tree Fort, and in the final Boer assault on 12 May, he accepted that the siege was 'far from being, as B-P's modern critics suggest, a luxurious picnic'.[51]

In his major history, *The Boer War* (1979), Thomas Pakenham confirmed that the siege had been 'no picnic', that it had been nearly double the length of the sieges of Kimberley and Ladysmith, and that proportionately the casualties were much heavier, both from shelling and from raids on the enemy's lines. The siege was important, he argued, as the first month of the war represented the Boers' 'greatest strategic opportunity of the war', yet Mafeking remained the 'exposed nerve' of their 'political consciousness'. That 'a dozen imperial officers' and hundreds of 'loafers' were able to entice away 'nearly eight thousand Boers' was crucial: 'Arguably B-P's antics saved South Africa for

---

47 Ibid., pp. 31–2, 39, 42, 54, 73, 82–3, 112, 128–9, 134, 212–13, 218.
48 Richard Price, *An Imperial War and the British Working Class: Working-Class Attitudes and Reactions to the Boer War 1899-1902* (London: Routledge & Kegan Paul, 1972), p. 132; see also Piers Brendon, *Eminent Edwardians* (Harmondsworth, Middlesex: Penguin, 1981), pp. 226–7 and Rosenthal, *Character Factory*, p. 30.
49 Rosenthal, *Character Factory*, pp. 35–7; the critics are correct that Baden-Powell, in various accounts of the siege, inflated his estimates of the Boers from 8,000 initially in his report to Lord Roberts to 12,000 by his *African Adventures* (1937), see Jeal, *Baden-Powell*, pp. 244–5 and Gardner, *Mafeking*, p. 230.
50 Rosenthal, *Character Factory*, pp. 37–8.
51 Brendon, *Eminent Edwardians*, pp. 227–8 and 231.

the British'.[52] Pakenham also insisted that it was 'easy to underrate a man whose contemporary reputation was so oversold'. B-P may have erred over the attack on Game Tree Fort but overall his 'remarkable professionalism – the will to win, hidden behind the mask of good clean fun', had ensured that Mafeking did not surrender. This achievement may have aroused 'hysterical, euphoric relief' but only because 'Colonel B-P had given back the other B-P, the British Public, its faith in itself', and had dealt the Boers 'a crushing psychological blow': 'No other British commander in the war had done so much with so little.'[53] More controversially, Pakenham claimed that he had found evidence in Baden-Powell's confidential staff diary that B-P sought to conserve food supplies by forcing the 2,000 black refugees to choose between leaving Mafeking (and risk being shot by the Boers) or starve: 'There was to be no other choice.'[54]

More prominence had already been accorded the role of blacks in the siege through the discovery of the remarkable diary of Sol T. Plaatje, the only account of a black participant known to survive. Throughout the siege Plaatje acted as the official interpreter to Mafeking's resident magistrate, Charles G. H. Bell, who as the town's civil commissioner had responsibility for the welfare of blacks. Plaatje also officiated in the Court of Summary Jurisdiction, set up in November 1899 to try offences in connection with martial law, over which Lord Edward Cecil[55] presided. Plaatje's diary, annotated by the anthropologist John L. Comaroff, illuminated the many contributions of the Barolongs during the siege. It provided a vivid account of what life was like for blacks and whites during the siege, without criticising the British or Baden-Powell, including his policy of trying to remove the black refugees from Mafeking. Unfortunately the diary finishes at the end of March 1900.[56] Brian Willan and Peter Warwick both used Plaatje's diary to illustrate aspects of their writing on Mafeking; the former in the first account of social conditions

52 Thomas Pakenham, *The Boer War* (London: Weidenfeld & Nicolson, 1979), pp. 397 and 399.
53 Ibid., pp. 398, 400, 405, 416–17.
54 Ibid., pp. 406–8.
55 Lord Edward Cecil (1867–1918), the fourth son of Robert Cecil, the third marquess of Salisbury, who was the British prime minister during the South African War. Lord Edward had served in the Grenadier Guards and as ADC to Lord Wolseley before seeing active service in the Sudan. While he served as B-P's chief staff officer in Mafeking, his wife, Violet, had an affair with Sir Alfred Milner, governor of Cape Colony and high commissioner for South Africa, whom she would marry after Edward's death.
56 John L. Comaroff (ed.), *The Boer War Diary of Sol T. Plaatje: An African at Mafeking* (London: Cardinal, 1976), pp. 124–5 and 140.

within the siege and the latter in his pioneering study of blacks in the war as a whole.[57]

If Plaatje's diary remained the 'best-known' of the siege diaries,[58] many more appeared as printed primary sources, often with scholarly editing and annotation. John F. Midgley edited the letters of Ada Cock, a young mother in Mafeking, in 1974; Willan, the diary of Edward Ross, the town auctioneer, in 1980; and Arthur Davey, the diary of Samuel Cawood of the Town Guard in 1983. Of these works, Midgley proffered a 37-page critique of Gardner's book, demolishing *inter alia* the myth that Baden-Powell had a viable mobile option without guns or transport. He is much more critical of Gardner's work than Colonel A. S. Hickman, who wrote a history of the Rhodesian forces in the South African War.[59] Midgley's criticisms, though, would soon be eclipsed by the forensic analysis of Tim Jeal in his biography, *Baden-Powell*, which first appeared in 1989.

Having spent years of research in a wide array of published and unpublished materials, uncovering a range of previously unused sources, Jeal described the many difficulties that Baden-Powell encountered in South Africa. These included the obstructionism of Lieutenant-General Sir William F. Butler, the commander-in-chief at the Cape, who feared provoking the Boers; the 'inferior quality of his recruits' raised for the Protectorate Regiment, some of whom could barely ride or shoot; and the limited support of Butler's successor, Sir F. W. Forestier-Walker, namely the provision of 100 Cape Police and two guns that proved to be obsolete. By securing belated approval for the garrisoning of Mafeking, and so stationing irregular cavalry within raiding distance of Pretoria, he had provided bait that would attract a significant body of Boers and thereby fulfilled his instructions in a reasonable way. Jeal argued, too, that the revisionist critics were guilty of selective quotation: Rosenthal's claim that the defenders 'did not have much to do' came from one despatch by Hamilton, but not its successor on 'Shells and Slaughter'. Similarly, Jeal described Gardner's jibe that Kruger had dismissed Mafeking as not worth

57 Brian Willan, 'The Siege of Mafeking' in Peter Warwick (ed.), *The South African War: The Anglo-Boer War 1899-1902* (London: Longman, 1980), pp. 139–60 and Peter Warwick, *Black People and the South African War 1899-1902* (Cambridge: Cambridge University Press, 1983), pp. 30–8.

58 Saunders, 'The Siege as History' in Smith (ed), *Siege of Mafeking*, vol. 2, p. 483.

59 John F. Midgley, *Petticoat in Mafeking: The Letters of Ada Cock* (Kommetjie, C.P.: private, 1974), pp. 104–41, at pp. 115–18 and 125, and Colonel A. S. Hickman, *Rhodesia Served The Queen*, 2 vols (Salisbury: Government Printer, 1970), vol. 1, 'Rhodesian Forces in the Boer War 1899-1902', pp. 79–81, 85 and 353; see also Ross, *Diary of the Siege of Mafeking* and Arthur Davey (ed.), *The Defence of Ladysmith and Mafeking: Accounts of two sieges, 1899 to 1900, being the South African War experiences of William Thwaites, Steuart Binny, Alfred Down and Samuel Cawood* (Johannesburg: The Brenthurst Press, 1983).

fifty Boer lives, as only hearsay by a cynical trooper in the relief column. It was hardly in accord with Kruger's approval of the attack led by Field Cornet Sarel Eloff, his grandson, upon the town on 12 May.[60]

More importantly, Jeal refuted Pakenham's assertion that Baden-Powell had starved the blacks in the interests of the whites by showing the effects of a misquotation from Neilly's history. B-P, Jeal demonstrated, had not knowingly sent blacks from Mafeking 'without first establishing staging-posts where they could be fed', and far from requiring all blacks 'to pay, and pay handsomely for their food', as Pakenham alleged, B-P had opened a free soup kitchen in the stadt by the end of February, feeding at least 1,500 people a day.[61] Jeal admitted, nonetheless, that the Colonel was guilty in subsequent reports, and in evidence before the Royal Commission on the South African War, of minimising the contribution of armed blacks to the siege. In this testimony he more than halved their real numbers of about 750; rebranded the Cape Boy Contingent as a 'Colonial Contingent', so concealing their 'coloured' composition; and claimed that blacks were only used in defensive operations. If this cohered with his claims in letters to Cronjé, and his successor, General J. P. Snyman, that blacks had only taken up arms in defence of their homes and cattle, it also buttressed official policy that this was a 'white man's war'. This was a posture riddled with mutual hypocrisy, since Lord Kitchener employed armed blacks extensively and Snyman armed some 180 blacks in the laagers outside Mafeking.[62] Baden-Powell, doubtless concerned about his future military career, fell into line with official policy but he still lobbied, albeit unsuccessfully, for the award of medals or a gift of 200 oxen for the Tshidi-Barolongs. His statements, admitted Jeal, may have been 'dishonest and self-interested' but they were not derived from 'malevolence or any animus against the blacks'.[63] In one respect, though, Jeal concurred with many of B-P's critics, where they claimed that 'Baden-Powell was Mafeking': Jeal agreed that B-P was so much the hero of the hour that 'nobody in Britain seemed to want to know about Plumer's regiment, or Mahon's column'.[64]

Jeal's scholarship and measured arguments had a generally positive effect: their conclusions were broadly endorsed by two military historians, Malcolm

---

60 Jeal, *Baden-Powell*, pp. 213–15, 221–3, 237 and 251; see also Rosenthal, *Character Factory*, p. 37 and Gardner, *Mafeking*, p. 70.

61 Jeal, *Baden-Powell*, pp. 266–7; see also Pakenham, *Boer War*, p. 407.

62 Pretorius, 'Besiegers' in Smith (ed.), *Siege of Mafeking*, vol. 1, p. 96; Jeal, *Baden-Powell*, pp. 281–5.

63 Jeal, *Baden-Powell*, pp. 284–5.

64 Rosenthal, *Character Factory*, p. 31 and Jeal, *Baden-Powell*, p. 301. Lieutenant-Colonels Herbert C. O. Plumer (1857–1932) and Bryan T. Mahon (1862–1930) both enjoyed distinguished military careers. Plumer would forever be associated with the victory over the Germans at the Battle of Messines (1917); in 1919, he was promoted to the rank

Flower-Smith and Edmund Yorke, in their *Mafeking: The Story of a Siege* (2000), and Pakenham withdrew his starvation charge from one of his essays in the splendid two-volume work, *The Siege of Mafeking* (2001), edited by Iain Smith and produced by the Brenthurst Press. Among the many excellent essays in the Brenthurst volumes are studies of the war correspondents in Mafeking by Jacqueline Beaumont, the role of women by Elizabeth van Heyningen, the Mafeking celebrations by Pakenham, and an excellent account of the Boer besiegers by Fransjohan Pretorius. The editors of more recently published Mafeking diaries produced their material without excessive concerns about historiography, although P. Thurmond Smith supplied a helpful literature review in editing the diaries of a boy soldier in the Bechuanaland Rifles, Frederick Saunders.[65] Conversely, in a post-apartheid work, *The Boy: Baden-Powell and the Siege of Mafeking* (1999), Pat Hopkins and Heather Dugmore returned to the polemical barricades. By only using evidence that suited their purposes, and by ignoring most of the counter-arguments in Jeal's work, they celebrate the achievements of the Tshidi-Barolongs during the siege, which is perfectly reasonable, but insist upon juxtaposing this material with charges that Baden-Powell 'committed gross crimes against humanity'. They assert that he prolonged the siege for his own ambition, and repeat accusations that he promoted a 'leave-or-starve policy' for the black refugees. Dubbing him ungracious and dishonest in post-war testimony, they accuse Baden-Powell of 'racist crimes, omissions, excesses and inhumanity'.[66]

Fortunately subsequent writing has not followed in this vein. In *Imperial Marriage* (2002), Hugh and Mirabel Cecil acknowledge the value of Jeal's 'balanced and scholarly biography', and utilize a wide array of sources to contradict Pakenham's aspersions upon 'poor Lord Edward [Cecil]'. They

---

of field marshal and created Baron Plumer of Messines and of Bilton. Mahon, who had served in the Sudan and later in Gallipoli, Salonika and Palestine, was appointed as the commander-in-chief, Ireland in 1916. He became both a general in the British army and a senator in the Irish Free State (1928–30).

65 Frederick Saunders, *Mafeking Memories*, ed. by P. Thurmond Smith (Cranbury, N. J.: Associated University Presses, 1996); Grant Christison (ed.), 'Lord of Hosts on our Side' *Mafeking Siege Diary of Sarah Dixon Gwynne* (Pietermaritzburg: Little Orbi Press, 1996); John Bottomley (ed.), 'The Siege of Mafeking and the Imperial Mindset as Revealed in the Diaries of T. W. P. (Tom) Hayes and W. P. (William) Hayes, District Surgeons', *New Contree*, no. 41 (1997), pp. 25–161 and 'A Scots "Salvationist" Perspective of the Siege of Mafeking: The Diary of Thomas A. Young', *New Contree*, no. 45 (1999), pp. 217–51; Robin Drooglever (ed), *"A Monument to British Pluck" Captain Herbert Greener's Journal of the Siege of Mafeking* (Honiton, Devon: Token Publishers, 2009).

66 Pat Hopkins and Heather Dugmore, *The Boy: Baden-Powell and the Siege of Mafeking* (Rivonia: Zebra, 1999), pp. 154, 158, 181–2. For a more measured account of the black contribution to the siege, see Tabitha Jackson, *The Boer War* (London: Channel 4 Books, 1999), pp. 33–45.

address Pakenham's claims that Lord Edward went to Mafeking distraught over his wife's love for Alfred Milner, and that B-P 'was able to give him a task in which he could do no great harm – looking after an improvised cadet corps'.[67] However, Hugh and Mirabel Cecil demonstrate that Lord Edward, though often ill, was brave, cheerful, and socially adept as a chief of staff, who worked with a wide cross section of the town, including Ben Weil (with whom he had provided a guarantee of £500,000 for the supplies to be brought to Mafeking before the siege). He also intervened successfully in securing the exchange of Lady Sarah Wilson for a Boer prisoner and presided over the proceedings of the Court of Summary Jurisdiction. Lord Edward had much more to do than simply organize the Mafeking cadet corps.[68] Finally, Edmund Yorke has written another succinct account of the siege, *Mafeking 1899-1900* (2014), which is nicely illustrated, rooted in British and South African sources, and focused upon the battle story.[69]

The Current Volume and its Methodology

Like its companion volumes on the sieges of Ladysmith and Kimberley,[70] this volume will focus upon eyewitness accounts of the siege of Mafeking and its relief, mainly letters but also interviews, sermons, and diaries published in the metropolitan and provincial press. None of this material suffered at the hands of censors, other than self-censorship, as displayed by Corporal Gilbert (Protectorate Regiment) when he informed his mother, 'I cannot give you any news in case this letter should fall into the hands of the enemy.'[71] Fortunately from an historical perspective such discretion was rare, and the publication of more informative letters reflected the enormous and enduring interest in this siege. This interest was rooted in the Victorian fascination with sieges in general (Chapter 2) and was compounded in Mafeking's case by the splendidly laconic pronouncements of its commanding officer: after the initial shelling

---

67   Pakenham, *Boer War*, pp. 118 and 403.
68   Cecil, *Imperial Marriage*, pp. 136–42 and Viscountess Milner, *My Picture Gallery 1886-1901* (London: John Murray, 1951), pp. 125–6. For a contemporary appreciation of Cecil's achievements, see 'Lord Edward Cecil', *Manchester Evening Chronicle*, 19 May 1900, p. 4.
69   Edmund Yorke, *Mafeking 1899-1900* (Stroud, Glos.: History Press, 2014).
70   Edward M. Spiers (ed.), *Letters from Ladysmith: Eyewitness Accounts from the South African War* (Barnsley: Frontline Books, an imprint of Pen & Sword, 2010) and Spiers (ed.), *Letters from Kimberley*; see also Fransjohan Pretorius, 'Another gem from a masterful military historian Edward M Spiers, Letters from Kimberley: Eyewitness Accounts from the South African War', *Historia*, vol. 59, issue 2 (2014), pp. 397–400.
71   'Letters From Local Men at the Front', *Tunbridge Wells Gazette*, 27 June 1900, p. 4.

Baden-Powell wrote, 'All well. Four hours' bombardment. One dog killed.'[72] Compared with the elderly and hesitant Sir George White, V.C., who had to be invalided home after Ladysmith, and the reserved, inarticulate Lieutenant-Colonel Robert G. Kekewich, who struggled to cope with Rhodes, an imperial icon, in Kimberley, Baden-Powell possessed a charisma that kept attention focused on Mafeking. It was not the case, as Jacqueline Beaumont claims, that 'very few newspapers had much to say about the siege [of Mafeking] before 1900':[73] if the Mafeking correspondents sometimes failed to get their copy through in a timely manner, reports appeared periodically in the influential metropolitan dailies, and more coverage appeared in the provincial press, courtesy of the news agencies. The 'one dog' story was reported widely,[74] Baden-Powell's 'amazing combination of daring and ingenuity' gained currency by early November,[75] the revelation of 500 armed blacks fighting for Mafeking found its way into the *Morning Post* of 2 November 1899,[76] and the attractive writings of Lady Sarah Wilson reached beyond the *Daily Mail*, with its readership of nearly one million and rising.[77]

Mafeking had an appeal that the other sieges lacked, despite (or perhaps because of) the wealth of Kimberley's diamonds and the strategic significance of the large British garrison trapped in Ladysmith. Yet when relief arrived, and B-P became the hero of the hour in the frenzied celebrations that followed, Jeal and other commentators err in claiming that he eclipsed interest in all other aspects of the siege. The *Derby Daily Telegraph* of 22 May 1900 maintained that

> There is a great deal that we all want to know concerning Colonel Mahon's brilliant march . . . how he managed to join hands with Col. Plumer . . . [and] how touch was first established with the garrison . . . Public anxiety on these points is very keen.[78]

---

72 Hillcourt, *Baden-Powell*, p. 175.

73 Beaumont, 'Reporting the Siege', in Smith (ed.), *Siege of Mafeking*, vol. 2, p. 351.

74 'Mafeking Bombarded', *Northampton Mercury*, 3 November 1899, p. 3; 'The War', *Lincoln, Rutland and Stamford Mercury*, 3 November 1899, p. 3; 'Mafeking Still Game', *Western Gazette*, 3 November 1899, p. 3; 'The War', *Jackson's Oxford Journal*, 4 November 1899, p. 3; 'Mafeking', *Essex County Standard*, 4 November 1899, p. 7; 'The War', *Leicester Chronicle and the Leicestershire Mercury*, 4 November 1899, p. 3.

75 'Dr Rutherfoord Harris at Newport', *Western Mail*, 8 November 1899, p. 6, 'Baden-Powell and Mafeking', *Western Gazette*, 3 November 1899, p. 5 and 'Western Frontier', *Yorkshire Herald and York Herald*, 6 November 1899, p. 5.

76 As Major Baillie's report of 6 October pre-dates the war, this was possibly pre-censored copy, 'Mafeking Day by Day', *Morning Post*, 2 November 1899, p. 3.

77 'A Plucky Lady War Correspondent', *(Dundee) Evening Telegram,* 3 November 1899, p. 5.

78 *Derby Daily Telegraph*, 22 May 1900, p. 2.

In the provincial press, such interest partly reflected concern about the experiences of ordinary citizens with local connections. Among the besieged in Mafeking were two sons of the late Charles Grenfell of Gulval, Cornwall; James Woodthorpe, who had left Peterborough to become an inspecting engineer on the Bechuanaland Railway; another engineer, Alexander Moffat of Lochee; and Mrs Rayne and her children, originally from Arbroath, who were refugees from Pretoria and her brother-in-law, Charles Rayne, who was trapped in Mafeking when travelling to Bulawayo.[79] Provincial newspapers relished, too, whenever they could record the exploits of local soldiers, and their linkages with Mafeking, through headlines such as 'A Forest Hill Man in Mafeking' or 'A Derby Man Dead at Mafeking'.[80]

Methodologically, finding correspondence from these soldiers and citizens proved far more challenging than from Ladysmith or Kimberley. In the first place, the white community in Mafeking, including the garrison, was far smaller than the corresponding communities in the other towns, barely one sixth of the 13,000 whites in the swollen population of Kimberley and one-ninth of those invested in Ladysmith, including over 12,500 soldiers. The population bases of these larger communities produced samples of over 250 letters, diaries and interviews apiece from 99 and 78 metropolitan and provincial newspapers respectively, so Mafeking required a much more extensive search in over 178 newspapers.[81] Secondly, the pool of potential correspondents dwindled further in Mafeking by virtue of its 400 children – one-fifth of the white community – and the larger proportion of fatalities in Mafeking than in the other towns. Thirdly, the European population in Mafeking, as in Kimberley and Ladysmith, was quite diverse, encompassing many 'widely varying backgrounds and nationalities'.[82]

While this ethnic and national diversity failed to hamper the search for material from the two larger besieged communities, and from their much larger, and predominantly regular, relief forces, it reduced the potential base of correspondence from Mafeking. The town also included a community of Boers; English settlers like Sarah Dixon Gwynne, who were born and brought up in South Africa (and so unlike first generation migrants may not have had family and friends to correspond with in the United Kingdom);

79   'Our Friends and Neighbours in the War Theatre', *Cornishman*, 2 November 1899, p. 2; 'About Town and Country', *Northampton Mercury*, 3 November 1899, p. 5; 'Lochee Man at Mafeking', *(Dundee) Evening Telegram*, 28 May 1900, p. 5 and 'Shut Up In Mafeking', *(Dundee) Evening Telegram*, 26 May 1900, p. 3.
80   *Kentish Mercury*, 11 May 1900, p. 3 and *Derbyshire Advertiser*, 24 February 1900, p. 5.
81   Spiers (ed.), *Letters from Kimberley*, pp. 1 and 166 and Spiers (ed.), *Letters from Ladysmith*, pp. 1 and 168.
82   Willan, 'Prelude' in Ross, *Diary*, p. 6.

Irish nationalists like the station master, Jimmy Quinlan, who were hardly supportive of the siege; and a Protectorate Regiment that included twenty-seven Dutchmen, fifteen Arabs and Indians, six Russians, five Norwegians, four Americans, four Germans and two Swedes (Appendix A).[83]

Of the trained men engaged in the siege only twenty were regular officers, and of the combined relief forces only 200 were regular soldiers in Mahon's column, half drawn from the Royal Horse Artillery and the other half infantry, composed of twenty-five fusiliers from each of the four nations, England, Scotland, Wales and Ireland. So in finding material from Mafeking, the well-honed techniques of identifying the recruiting areas of specific regiments, or places of departure of military units from Britain, and then finding letters by consulting their respective local newspapers, supplemented by a sample of the press from urban areas,[84] barely applied. They helped in locating a few letters from the fusiliers but generally the unearthing of new Mafeking material required as comprehensive a sweep as possible of the metropolitan, provincial and colonial press. The aim was to find material from a wide range of sources, both soldier and civilian, as the diaries of individuals were limited in their perspectives. Nurse A. M. Crauford, for example, who kept a diary used in many accounts of the siege, agreed that 'nurses usually saw very little of what was going on' but she was involved in one of the critical incidents of the siege, when Eloff's forces seized Colonel Hore's fort, only 274 m from the hospital.[85] Similarly Samuel Cawood, who kept a diary while spending many weary hours in the trenches, had to find information from the *Mafeking Mail* and army orders to supplement the events he actually saw.[86]

Accordingly, this account has sought to supply a broad range of insights upon the siege, mainly gathered from letters and diaries in the metropolitan and provincial press.[87] It covers the pre-war preparations for the siege

---

83   Christison (ed.), '*Lord of Hosts*', p. 3; Lady Sarah Wilson, *South African Memories*, p. 79; and the Protectorate Regiment included 'a few Americans, some Germans and Norwegians', Hamilton, *Siege of Mafeking*, p. 93. On B-P's claim that he had 'forty Fenian prisoners', see 'The Siege of Mafeking', (Gloucester) *Citizen*, 9 February 1900, p. 3.

84   Edward M. Spiers, 'Military correspondence in the late nineteenth-century press', *Archives*, vol. 32, no.116 (2007), pp. 28–40.

85   'Nursing in Mafeking. A Talk with Miss Crauford', *Pall Mall Gazette*, 7 August 1900, p. 3 and A. M. Crauford, 'A Nurse's Diary in Besieged Mafeking', *Crampton's Magazine of Fiction*, vol. 17 (1901), pp. 290–2 and 396–8. Lieutenant-Colonel Charles O. Hore commanded the Bechuanaland Protectorate Regiment during the siege of Mafeking.

86   Davey (ed.), *Defence of Ladysmith and Mafeking*, p. 124.

87   In the referencing, editorials will be given with only the title, date and pagination of the newspaper concerned but letters and articles in newspapers will include their titles, and, in subsequent commentary, where the titles are the same in differing newspapers, full references will be given.

(Chapter 3) and the early phase of its defence, characterized by an 'aggressive defence' (Chapter 4). Two chapters then follow on the 'Long Siege', covering rationing, trench warfare, civil-military relations and Eloff's attack, before Chapters 7 and 8 on the subsequent relief and celebrations. This analysis follows a contextual Chapter 2 on the Victorian fascination with sieges in order to explain the depth of popular interest and anxiety about the fate of Mafeking. It will also help to understand the extraordinary scenes that swept across most of the United Kingdom and the empire after Mafeking's relief (Chapter 8), and the continuing interest in written and material curios from the siege (Chapter 9), all part of the siege's remarkable legacy.

Chapter 2

The Victorians and Sieges

In reflecting upon the siege of Mafeking, the *Manchester Courier* was only one of many newspapers that compared it with the 'famous sieges' of the nineteenth century. It referred to the great Crimean sieges of Sevastopol and Kars; the 'desperate defence' of the Lucknow Residency, which followed the fateful siege of Cawnpore (both in 1857); the 11-month siege of Khartoum (1884–5), involving the martyrdom of Major-General Charles 'Chinese' Gordon; the more recent 'heroic defence' of Chitral fort (1895); and several sieges from the Franco-Prussian War (1870–1), the Great Siege of Gibraltar (1779–83), the less well-known African sieges of Eshowe (1879) and Potchefstroom (1880–1) and sieges from the Peninsular War, notably the investment of Badajoz (1812). Like many newspapers it emphasized that Mafeking had held out for 217 days, much longer than the contemporary sieges of Kimberley (124 days) and Ladysmith (118 days), and compared this length of endurance with the duration of other sieges.[1] The *Courier* concluded that 'in modern times, at any rate, famine rather than the strength of the enemy was the real conqueror of besieged towns'.[2]

Setting Mafeking in a broader historical context reflected the Victorian fascination with sieges both when they occurred and in retrospect. Nor was this a matter of distant memory; within five years of the outset of the siege of Mafeking several sieges had been commemorated, one had been contested, and another avenged. During the renewed celebration of Waterloo and the military exploits of the Duke of Wellington in the 1890s, Richard Caton Woodville had depicted the duke in his painting, *After the Storming of Badajoz 1812* (1894). Standing by a breach in the walls of a captured city, a traditional siege image, the Iron Duke is seen reflecting upon the costly assault, namely the loss of some 5,000 British and allied soldiers, and not the wanton sacking of Badajoz, when British troops

---

1   'Some Famous Sieges', *Daily Chronicle*, 19 May 1900, p. 6; 'Some Famous Sieges', *Yorkshire Telegraph and Star*, 19 May 1900, p. 3; *Manchester Guardian*, 19 May 1900, p. 9; 'Some Famous Sieges', *Sheffield and Rotherham Independent*, 21 May 1900, p. 6; 'Some Famous Sieges', *Cheltenham Chronicle*, 26 May 1900, p. 6 and 'Some Famous Sieges', *Lurgan Times*, 26 May 1900, p. 4.
2   'Some Famous Sieges', *Manchester Courier*, 23 June 1900, p. 2.

engaged in mass rape, slaughter and pillage.[3] An even more dramatic image appeared in the following year when Vereker M. Hamilton painted his life-size *Storming of the Cashmere Gate*, commemorating a memorable scene, based on contemporary sketches, from the siege of Delhi (1857).[4]

In March 1895, the Chitral siege began when the British agent, Surgeon-Major George Scott Robertson, had sought to protect the Chitral's ten-year-old ruler and about a hundred civilians in the fort. The image of a small garrison, with a few British officers and loyal Indian soldiers, holding out against overwhelming odds, evoked comparisons with Khartoum, and enabled Frank Younghusband, an imperial traveller and former political agent in the Chitral, to campaign successfully for a relief action. Frank and his brother George accompanied one of the two relief forces, reporting on behalf of *The Times*. They chronicled the hard-fought engagements of Sir Robert Low's relief force, and although the other, much smaller relief force raised the siege, their best-selling account of the enterprise, *The Relief of Chitral* (November 1895), sold out two editions within a fortnight.[5] Finally, even if Lord Salisbury's cabinet acted out of strategic calculations in approving the invasion of northern Sudan in 1896, the subsequent extension of the mission via the construction of the Sudan Military Railway, and the eventual crushing of the Khalifa's forces at Omdurman (2 September 1898), carried overtones of vengeance and restitution. Gordon, as Douglas Johnson argued, had become 'a symbol of the rightness and righteousness of imperialism', and his death had placed the national honour at stake.[6] The Christian martyr had to be avenged, and, in describing his memorial service after the battle, George Warrington Steevens of the *Daily Mail*, wrote 'We came with a sigh of shame: we went away with a sigh of relief. The long-delayed duty was done . . . Gordon had his due burial at last. . . . We left Gordon alone again – but alone in majesty under the conquering ensign of his own people.'[7]

---

3   J. W. M. Hichberger, *Images of the Army: The Military in British Art, 1815-1914* (Manchester: Manchester University Press, 1988), pp. 104–5; Paul Usherwood, 'Officer material: Representations of leadership in late nineteenth-century British battle painting' in John M. MacKenzie (ed.), *Popular imperialism and the military 1850-1950* (Manchester: Manchester University Press, 1992), pp. 162–78, at p. 172.

4   Peter Harrington, *British Artists and War: The Face of Battle in Paintings and Prints, 1700-1914* (London: Greenhill Books, 1993), pp. 175–6.

5   Patrick French, *Younghusband: The Last Great Imperial Adventurer* (London: HarperCollins, 1994), pp. 114–16 and 130; Edward M. Spiers, *The Scottish Soldier and Empire, 1854-1902* (Edinburgh: Edinburgh University Press, 2006), pp. 118–20.

6   Douglas H. Johnson, 'The Death of Gordon: A Victorian Myth', *Journal of Imperial and Commonwealth History*, vol. 10 (1982), pp. 285–310, at pp. 301–4.

7   George W. Steevens, *With Kitchener to Khartum* (Edinburgh: Blackwood, 1898), pp. 315–16.

Sieges as self-contained, intensely dramatic events, often infused with high degrees of risk to women and children as well as the isolated garrison, fascinated Victorians. They only happened when challenges erupted from within or without the empire, prompting outbursts of popular imperialism, laced with assertions of Anglo-Saxon racial superiority. Sieges, as Arthur Davey, argued, had 'arresting characteristics'; they had a definite time span, a comprehensible arena, a diverse array of challenges that the besieged leader had to address and a set of shared experiences that bound the besieged more intimately together than campaigners would ever experience in open warfare. The form of conflict, too, was distinctive, with the contesting forces often engaged in an evolving pattern of investment, with the sapping of trenches, bombardments and periodic assaults offset by resolute defence and periodic sorties by the beleaguered. Sieges often involved ingenious attempts to communicate with the outside world, and diplomatic exchanges between the opposing forces, interspersed with forms of psychological pressure and exhortations to surrender. Waiting for relief added an extra imponderable; would such forces be authorized and assembled in time, could they break the siege cordon, and would they arrive in time? Quite often the siege experience moved towards a climax, which marked 'the dividing line between successful endurance and parleys for capitulation'.[8]

Yet all sieges were distinctive; if they involved long periods of watchfulness, patience and boredom, they had varying moments of uncertainty, alarm and tension. Some of these factors were affected by differences in geographical location, the size of the besieged communities and the investing forces, and the quantity and quality of their supplies, especially water which, if untreated, could spread all manner of water-born diseases. Of the three South African sieges, Ladysmith, which possessed the largest garrison of regular troops, was surrounded by hills and suffered from poor water.[9] Kimberley, like Mafeking, was located on open veld, but was a very much larger and richer community, with all the resources of the De Beers mining company at the disposal and direction of Cecil John Rhodes. All the communities were mixed: with the smallest proportion of blacks and Indians, about 13 per cent, in Ladysmith; over 60 per cent blacks, and another 15 per cent Indians and 'coloureds', in Kimberley's swollen population in excess of 50,000; and 5,000 Barolong and another 2,000 black refugees alongside the 2,000 whites in Mafeking.[10]

---

8   Davey (ed.), *Defence of Ladysmith and Mafeking*, p. 11.
9   'A Lance-Corporal and the Relief of Mafeking', *Cheshire Observer*, 25 August 1900, p. 7.
10   As population numbers differ from source to source, and varied considerably during the course of each of the sieges, I have given rough proportions to make the point about their mixed compositions. For other estimates, see Pretorius, *A to Z of the Anglo-Boer War*, pp. 236, 212 and 256; Iain R. Smith, 'Introduction' in Smith (ed.), *Siege of Mafeking*, vol. 1, pp. 1–21, at pp. 10 and 15; Cecil, *Imperial Marriage*, p. 134.

This qualifies somewhat John Peck's argument that the 'centrality of the siege in the Victorian period' involved small groups of British soldiers finding themselves 'surrounded and outnumbered', and that the threat was 'always from the indigenous population'. The colonial pattern of siege warfare, he argues, featured 'a small British enclave defending not just itself but the very idea of the English way against everything that is unEnglish'.[11] Undoubtedly many British observers perceived colonial sieges in this manner, and expressed such sentiments when Mafeking was relieved.[12] They also understood the role of protecting loyal 'natives' under the notion of *noblesse oblige* and the chivalrous code of gentlemanly behaviour 'affecting the way in which the Empire was run'.[13] Such perceptions cohered with claims of an almost umbilical cord, linking the British response to siege situations from the Indian Mutiny to the South African War. Mafeking, asserted the *Wharfedale and Airedale Observer*, was 'the Lucknow of South Africa'[14] or as Alfred Austin, the Poet Laureate, proclaimed in his somewhat pedestrian poem, 'Mafeking' (1900):

> Then, when hope dawned at last,
> And fled the foe, aghast
> At the relieving blast
> Heard in the melley, –
> O our stout, stubborn kith!
> Kimberley, Ladysmith,
> Mafeking, wedded with
> Lucknow and Delhi![15]

British forces were not supposed to become besieged. Although the Royal Engineers were perfectly able to construct redoubts and entrenchments, erect observation posts, alarm systems and field telegraphy, and emplace mines or appear to do so, British forces, whenever engaged in small colonial wars, were expected to assume the offensive and bring the enemy to battle. As Colonel Charles E. Callwell explained in his major treatise *Small Wars* (first published in 1896), these wars were first and foremost 'campaigns against

---

11 John Peck, *War, the Army and Victorian Literature* (Basingstoke: Macmillan Press, 1998), p. 165.
12 For example 'Mafeking Relieved', *South Wales Daily News*, 19 May 1900, p. 4; 'Mafeking', *Kilmarnock Standard*, 26 May 1900, p. 4 and *Macclesfield Courier and Herald*, 26 May 1900, p. 4.
13 Mark Girouard, *The Return to Camelot: Chivalry and the English Gentleman* (New Haven and London: Yale University Press, 1981), p. 224.
14 'The Hero of the Hour', *Wharfedale and Airedale Observer*, 23 May 1900, p. 3.
15 'The Poet Laureate and Mafeking', *Wigan Observer and District Advertiser* (hereafter *Wigan Observer*), 25 May 1900, p. 8.

nature', as distinct from wars against hostile armies. Given the uncertainties of supply, and the enemy's advantages of local knowledge, intelligence and tactical mobility, the overriding aim of an expeditionary force must be 'to prosecute the war with vigour'. It had to maintain the initiative and dominate the enemy, and, even if forced onto the defensive, it must not adopt a 'passive defensive' response. The essential aim, Callwell affirmed, was 'to fight, not to manoeuvre, to meet the hostile forces in open battle'.[16] Even in the third edition, published in 1906, where Callwell updated his text to refer to the Boer generals Christiaan De Wet, Jacobus (Koos) de la Rey and Louis Botha under guerrilla warfare, he neither drew any lessons from Ladysmith, Kimberley or Mafeking, nor included a section on siege warfare.[17]

Lord Wolseley, who was the commander-in-chief when the South African War erupted, promoted a very similar perspective. In his *Soldier's Pocket Book*, which was regularly updated after its first publication in 1869, and distributed to every soldier, he never referred to being besieged, only to the 'defence of posts'. Should a commander find himself compelled to defend a position, Wolseley urged that he must 'show' resistance 'as long as [it] can be offered'. 'Even at the last moment', he contended, a beleaguered commander 'if he still commands a disciplined body of men who are in good heart, he may perhaps hope to cut his way out and join his armies in the field.'[18]

Cawnpore (1857) cast a long shadow over British siege memories. The treachery of Nana Sahib, in inducing surrender with the offer of safe passage, eclipsed the folly of Major-General Sir Hugh Massy Wheeler, who had moved out from the centre of the city and its well-stocked magazine, all of which fell to the rebels. Having chosen to shelter his forces and the European residents within a temporary bastion, behind a hastily-erected mud wall less than a metre high in places, the siege lasted a mere three weeks. After Wheeler surrendered and received an offer of safe conduct from Sahib, the latter promptly reneged on the offer and ordered the massacre of Wheeler and his 200 officers and men when they were attempting to board boats on the River Ganges at Satichaura Ghat (27 June). He later ordered the hacking to death of the 197 surviving women and children, whose naked bodies were thrown down a well (15–16 July).[19] By demonstrating the risks of surrender, this atrocity

16   Colonel Charles E. Callwell, *Small Wars: A Tactical Textbook for Imperial Soldiers* (London: H.M.S.O., 1906, reprinted by Greenhill Books, 1990), pp. 44, 52–4, 57, 73, 75–7, 91.

17   Ibid., p. 126.

18   General Viscount Wolseley, *The Soldier's Pocket Book for Field Service* (London: Macmillan, 1886), pp. 302 and 406.

19   Saul David, *The Indian Mutiny 1857* (London: Penguin, 2003), pp. 182–6, 213–19, 253–4.

caused outrage in Britain, with many fearing that some of the women had suffered a fate then deemed as worse than death. Among the women forced into concubinage was Margaret, the missing daughter of General Wheeler, and the legend rapidly developed that she had killed her abductor and herself. This became the subject of numerous theatricals and mutiny engravings,[20] while Nana Sahib and his presumed lust for a white woman, Ophelia, became the subject of a rare imperial ballet, *Nana Sahib* (1872).[21] Nor were memories of Cawnpore cast into the recesses of distant history. Even if the Boers as a white, Christian enemy were never thought capable of such an appalling collective atrocity, when their shells pounded the well-marked laager for the women and children in Mafeking, killing a 'little girl' and mortally wounding an eight-year-old boy, the outrage evoked comparisons. As J. Emerson Neilly, of the *Pall Mall Gazette*, observed, 'The excuse of heathenism can be held out for Nana Sahib; the Mahdi was a religious fanatic; the Red Indians of the plains were steeped in dark ignorance; but these Boers read the Bible and sang psalms.'[22]

More immediately, the Cawnpore massacres aroused a massive desire for vengeance, both among the British at home and the soldiers who learned of the outrages in India or, in many cases, visited the site of the second massacre at Bibighur barracks.[23] Soon cast in a starkly religious light as the massacre of Christians by non-Christians, the episode underpinned a developing sense of Christian militarism[24] and raised the stakes for the contemporary siege at the Residency of Lucknow (30 June – 17 November 1857). The small relief force, commanded by Major-General Henry Havelock, absorbed popular attention as it battled to reach the residency in time. Ultimately, with the 78th Highlanders (Ross-shire Buffs) exploiting a breach in the enemy lines, the column entered the Residency on 25 September 1857. Although it would require another relief force under Sir Colin Campbell to raise the siege on 17 November 1857, and permit the evacuation of the women, children, sick and

---

20   In fact Margaret became a concubine and only revealed her identity on her deathbed fifty years after the mutiny. Ibid. pp. 221–2; see also Gregory Fremount-Barnes, *The Indian Mutiny 1857-58* (Oxford: Osprey, 2007), p. 51.

21   Jeffrey Richards, *Imperialism and Music: Britain 1876-1953* (Manchester: Manchester University Press, 2001), p. 252.

22   Neilly, *Besieged with B.-P.*, pp. 173–4. During the siege of the Foreign Legations in Peking later in 1900, Sir Claude Macdonald, the British Ambassador, would cite memories of Cawnpore to explain his reluctance to accept the offer of escort to Tientsin, 'London Letter', *Western Times*, 15 August 1900, p. 3 and Diana Preston, *The Boxer Rebellion: The Dramatic Story of China's War on Foreigners That Shook the World in the Summer of 1900* (New York: Berkley Books, 2000), p. 80.

23   Spiers, *Scottish Soldier*, p. 7.

24   Peck, *War, the Army and Victorian Literature*, pp. 72–3.

wounded, the devout Havelock, who was knighted just before his death from dysentery after the siege, became revered as a Christian hero.[25]

Once again the plight, and possible fate, of the British women and children during the siege in Lucknow had caused widespread anxiety. The risks and relief were impressed upon Scottish popular consciousness through the ballads and songs about the 'dream' of Jessie Brown, who was purportedly a corporal's wife in the besieged Residency. Her experiences were captured in a drama in four acts, a painting by Frederick Goodall, and several ballads, including 'Jessie's Dream at Lucknow', where she first hears the pipes playing 'The Campbells Are Coming' and gives thanks to 'Brave Havelock and his Highlanders/The bravest of the brave'.[26]

A plethora of plays, novels, sermons, memoirs and poems expressed the popular reaction to the human tensions of both sieges, including Mrs. J. A. Harris, *Lady's Diary of the Siege of Lucknow* (1858), Mowbray Thompson's *Story of Cawnpore* (1859), Dion Boucicault's *The Relief of Lucknow* (1858) and Alfred Tennyson's 'Havelock' (1857) and 'The Defence of Lucknow' (1879). Among the memorable paintings and prints was Joseph Noel Paton's *In Memoriam* (1858), depicting a group of English ladies in a room at Cawnpore – one holding a Bible, another kissing her baby – as sepoys enter through a rear doorway. T. J. Barker's *The Relief of Lucknow* (1859), showed another memorable meeting between the three heroes of the relief, Havelock, Campbell and Sir James Outram, which was incorporated 'into the national mythology as an example of British *sang-froid*'.[27]

So when commentators compared the relief of Mafeking with that of Lucknow, as even the forty surviving veterans of Lucknow were proud to do at their annual 'defence dinner' in the Holborn Restaurant, London, on 6 June 1900,[28] they were not simply referring to the similar periods of investment: 217 days for Mafeking, 140 days for Lucknow. They were comparing events that gripped popular attention in the United Kingdom, involving the protection of a civilian community, if not from the threat of deliberate massacre in Mafeking then from the risk of injury and death from shot and shell, losses from sickness and disease, and the privations of a protracted siege. They were aware, too, that the conduct of sieges and their

25 Richards, *Imperialism and Music*, p. 59; Graham Dawson, *Soldier Heroes: British adventure, empire and the imagining of masculinities* (London and New York: Routledge, 1994), pp. 96–9.
26 'Jessie's Dream at Lucknow', http://digital.nls.uk/broadsides/broadside.cfm/id/15105 (accessed 21 November 2010); see also Harrington, *British Artists and War*, pp. 163–4.
27 Hichberger, *Images of the Army*, p. 61; see also Harrington, *British Artists and War*, pp. 165–7 and 169–70 and Peak, *War, the Army and Victorian Literature*, pp. 80–1.
28 'The Defence of Lucknow', *Standard*, 7 June 1900, p. 3.

relief required leadership, self-sacrifice and gallantry, and upon their outcome rested a challenge to the national honour. In his refrain for the 'Defence of Lucknow', Tennyson proclaimed: 'And ever upon the topmost roof our banner of England blew', a refrain reiterated by the *Yorkshire Telegraph and Star* when it described 'the spectacle of Colonel Baden-Powell and his handful of men, ill-armed, half-trained, and half starving, heroically keeping the flag of England flying'.[29]

More prosaic matters also contributed to the success of sieges, as occurred during the ten-week siege of the Eshowe mission (23 January – 3 April 1879) during the Anglo-Zulu War (1879). Colonel Charles K. Pearson, commanding a force of 1,300 European troops and some 400 black auxiliaries, became stranded at the mission. Unlike Rorke's Drift, which had just ended (22/23 January 1879) in which about 140 British soldiers had fought off attacks by over 4,000 seasoned Zulu warriors, Pearson was never heavily pressed by local Zulus. He simply fortified the mission, employed four field pieces and one Gatling gun as powerful weapons of defence, and mounted various patrols, skirmishing with the enemy and destroying a kraal. Within the mission morale deteriorated amid the cramped and often sodden conditions as rations were cut, and fever and dysentery swept through the camp, but the siege remained a largely passive affair until the relief force appeared. As the column, led by the 91st Argyllshire Highlanders, approached the mission, Charles L. Norris-Newman, of the London *Standard*, followed by two other special correspondents arrived first. Even this largely uneventful siege, though bereft of dramatic incident, had attracted a smattering of press attention. Norris-Newman was delighted to beat his rivals and exclaim: 'First in Eshowe'.[30]

Paradoxically, although seven sieges took place during the ensuing Anglo-Transvaal War (1880–1), they received scant coverage in the British press. The eruption of hostilities over Boer demands for a restoration of their independence both surprised and divided British opinion. The small force of 1,800 British soldiers in the Transvaal found itself hopelessly dispersed, defending the capital, Pretoria, and the small townships of Rustenburg, Lydenburg, Marabastad, Standerton, Wakkerstroom and Potchefstroom. In the largely hostile town of Potchefstroom two companies of the 2/24th (Royal Scots Fusiliers), and a score of artillerymen with two 9-pounder guns, began to construct a makeshift fort to protect forty-eight civilians and

---

29 Christopher Ricks (ed.), *The Poems of Tennyson* (London and Harlow: Longmans, Green & Co., 1969), p. 1251; "'And Ever Upon the Topmost Roof, Our Banner of England Flew'", *Yorkshire Telegraph and Star*, 19 May 1900, p. 2.
30 Edward M. Spiers, *The Victorian Soldier in Africa* (Manchester: Manchester University Press, 2004), pp. 45–6; Donald R. Morris, *The Washing of the Spears* (London: Sphere Books, 1968), pp. 421–30 and 456–8.

sixty-one blacks (15 December 1880). After the ambush of another British column at Bronkhorst Spruit five days later, a humiliating series of military reverses followed, as the British relief force from Natal foundered at Laing's Nek, Schuinshoogte and most disastrously on the summit of Majuba Hill (27 February 1881). Only three special correspondents arrived in time to report on the final battle, which involved the death of Major-General George Pomeroy Colley and the rout of his force. From their reports a famous sketch of the débâcle appeared in *Illustrated London News*, which shocked domestic opinion by depicting Gordon Highlanders fleeing down the hillside.[31]

The remainder of the press arrived after the battle and could only report upon the armistice negotiations, which brokered a truce (6 March) followed by a peace agreement on 23 March 1881, approved by the Liberal government of William E. Gladstone. Massively controversial, this denouement outraged many Conservatives, English-speaking settlers and military commanders eager to avenge the stain of Majuba.[32] None of the special correspondents travelled into the Transvaal to report upon the sieges and only one despatch from the garrison at Lydenburg reached the outside world. The sieges lasted for about three months, and, with one exception, the British garrisons resisted the long-range rifle fire of the enemy (and use of elderly cannon in four sieges), and mounted the odd sortie in reprisal. Consequently the writings of the besieged – a couple of memoirs and a few letters – all published a month or longer after the war ended, hardly became the stuff of imperial legend.[33]

Potchefstroom, though, was an exception. The small garrison of 180 soldiers, bereft of any local support, defended a poorly-fortified and ill-provisioned position. Outnumbered by 1,500 Boers under the determined leadership of General Piet A. Cronjé, the garrison soon lost most of its black drivers and white townsfolk (only thirty-three remained until the end). As casualties mounted, the survivors saw their numbers diminish from disease (dysentery, scurvy, typhoid and enteric fever). Under intense pressure from rifle fire, sapping, and desultory shelling, they also faced psychological pressure, as Cronjé sent copies of the republican gazette, the *Staats Courant*, into the fort, chronicling the litany of British defeats and hence the unlikelihood of

---

31 'The Transvaal War: Sketches by Our Special Artist', *Illustrated London News*, 23 April 1881, p. 413.

32 Joseph P. Lehmann, *The First Boer War* (London: Buchan & Enright, 1972), pp. 266–81; Spiers, *Victorian Soldier*, pp. 61–73; Ian Bennett, *A Rain of Lead: The Siege and Surrender of the British at Potchefstroom* (London: Greenhill Books, 2001), pp. 21–3 and 228.

33 Lehmann, *First Boer War*, Ch. 7; and for letters missed in the standard accounts, see Spiers, *Victorian Soldier*, pp. 71–3.

any relief. The Boer general then deceived the garrison by refusing to pass on news about the truce and the associated promise of a convoy of provisions for each garrison. By 19 March thirty-five soldiers were dead, including six from disease (and another two died on 23 March), and with rations extremely low, Lieutenant-Colonel Richard W. C. Winsloe surrendered the fort. After two days of negotiations, he yielded his two field guns and rifles (but not their ammunition) to Cronjé. Officers were allowed to keep their personal property and swords, and to march out with honours, while the Boers provided medicine, foods, ambulances and waggons for the fifty-six wounded. On 23 March, the same day as the peace agreement, the British garrison and its civilians left Potchefstroom and began their march over 402 km to Ladysmith, Natal.[34]

Although the Boer leaders, in seeking a final agreement with Britain (eventually the Pretoria Convention of 3 August 1881), agreed to cancel the capitulation and return the surrendered material, the damage had been done. The surrender became the lasting memory of the sieges, graphically depicted in a sketch in the *Penny Illustrated*, and reproduced in subsequent engravings. The scene of disconsolate British officers and men moving past triumphant Boers may have been fictional (the British are depicted carrying cased regimental colours whereas they were allowed to leave with flags flying) but it captured the ignominy of surrender for a Victorian audience.[35] Potchefstroom demonstrated that the risks of siege warfare in an Anglo-Boer context could be political and psychological but also potentially strategic, depending upon the location of the siege. They could, too, damage both British prestige and relations between the Dutch- and English-speaking communities.

These risks were as evident in 1899 as they had been nearly twenty years earlier. The siege histories of Potchefstroom and Mafeking overlapped directly as Cronjé assumed command of the Boer forces at Mafeking, at least in the opening weeks when Mafeking was at its most vulnerable. Cronjé had emerged from the Potchefstroom siege as the most formidable of the Boer commanders in British eyes, and as someone who had a reputation for deceit and treachery. He had achieved international fame by the capture of Dr Jameson and his 510 men during their ill-fated raid into the Transvaal in January 1896. At the outset of the South African War in 1899, when he was stout, stubborn, and sixty-three years of age, Cronjé was again appointed as the assistant commandant-general of the Transvaal. This may have been more of a political than a military appointment, as Cronjé's command at

34 Bennett, *Rain of Lead*, pp. 127, 182, 203–4, 207–11, 242–5; Lehmann, *First Boer War*, p. 286.
35 'The Last Act of the Transvaal War: Surrender', *Penny Illustrated*, 9 April 1881, p. 232; see also Bennett, *Rain of Lead*, pp. 215 and 223.

Potchefstroom remained controversial in Boer circles (that is, by disobeying orders, he had complicated the peace negotiations, and ended the siege by subterfuge).[36] For British commentators, though, the 'treachery and cunning' displayed by the 'crafty Cronje' lingered long in the memory, despite their readiness to acknowledge that he had 'undoubtedly showed great military skill in the conduct of the siege'.[37] Nor were the links between the two wars limited to the sieges; the role of the Gladstone government in not seeking retribution for Majuba was remembered bitterly. 'It was one of the cruel ironies of history', wrote the *Brighton Gazette*, that on Saturday, 19 May 1900, when 'the whole Empire' was celebrating the relief of Mafeking, 'a statue of Mr. Gladstone, the most active contributor to the South African tragedy, was being unveiled in the House of Commons'.[38]

However partisan this impression, it paled by comparison with Gladstone's role in the next siege controversy, probably the most contentious of the late Victorian era. The Mahdist revolt against Egyptian suzerainty in the Sudan threatened all the Egyptian garrisons in the country, including the well-armed forces in the capital, Khartoum. This threat to the Sudan, and potentially Egypt, became all the more pressing after the annihilation of an 11,000-man, Egyptian army, commanded by a retired Indian Army officer, Colonel William Hicks, at El Obeid (5 November 1883). The Gladstone government faced an acute dilemma as it had recently crushed a nationalist revolt in Egypt, and established a 'temporary' occupation of the country, bolstering the khedive while protecting Britain's financial interests, including the Suez Canal. Instinctively the prime minister sympathized with the Sudanese as a 'people struggling to be free, and they are struggling rightly to be free',[39] but his cabinet felt that it had to respond to the public outcry after El Obeid. These protests, fanned by the influential *Pall Mall Gazette*, focused upon sending Gordon, already an imperial legend and a former governor-general of the Sudan, up the Nile to Khartoum. Ordered to 'consider and report' on the military situation, particularly the prospects for evacuating Egyptian soldiers and civilians, Gordon soon exceeded his orders. He tried to arrange a political successor to oppose the Mahdi, and once in Khartoum began organizing the

---

36 Bennett, *Rain of Lead*, Ch. 17; see also Pretorius, 'The Besiegers' in Smith (ed.), *Siege of Mafeking*, vol. 1, pp. 63–107, at p. 73 and Pretorius, *A to Z of the Anglo-Boer War*, pp. 110–11.

37 'The Ablest Boer General', *Manchester Courier*, 3 March 1900, p. 3; see also Charles Lowe, 'Chronicle of the War', *Graphic*, 3 March 1900, p. 16 and 'The Transvaal Garrisons and the Boers', *(Dundee) Courier & Argus*, 5 April 1881, p. 2.

38 'Mafeking and After', *Brighton Gazette*, 24 May 1900, p. 4 and *Berkshire Chronicle*, 26 May 1900, p. 2. For a more measured reflection on the previous war, see 'The Last Boer War', *Lloyd's Weekly Newspaper*, 5 November 1899, p. 14.

39 *Parl[iamentary] Deb[ates]*, third series, vol. 288 (12 May 1884), cols. 54–8.

evacuation of sick and wounded Egyptian troops and civilians. He evacuated about 2,000 refugees before the Mahdi cut off any escape route north by seizing Berber on 13 May 1884.[40] Thereafter while thousands of Egyptians and their families remained in Khartoum, controversy and anxiety raged over the relief of Gordon, as it would to a lesser extent over the relief of Mafeking.

Gladstone was reluctant to become involved politically or militarily in the Sudan and resisted pleas to send an expedition to extricate the Egyptians and uphold the nation's honour. Gladstone's reticence, coupled with a protracted debate, known as the 'battle of the routes', over the best method to despatch a relief force, and a belated Vote of Credit on 5 August, sowed the seeds of the subsequent recriminations.[41] These political consequences duly followed when news reached London on 5 February 1885 that a steamer, carrying the leading group from the relief force, had reached Khartoum on 28 January 1885, two days after the sack of the city and the massacre of thousands of its inhabitants. Gordon's fate, though initially uncertain, became the 'all-engrossing topic of the day'.[42] When his death was confirmed, the outcry engulfed the nation with a tidal wave of newspaper, poetic, musical, literary, religious and dramatic commentary. 'Too Late!' bewailed the *Essex Standard*, a theme taken up in the music halls by N. G. Travers, *Too Late!* and by G. H. MacDermott, *Too Late, Too Late*, stressing Gordon's 'commitment to service, duty and the protection of the native races'.[43] The siege disaster spawned a profusion of poems, plays, sermons and souvenirs, venerating Gordon as 'an uncalendared saint, a Christian hero and martyr', whose noble death had shamed the nation.[44] Robert Louis Stevenson wrote of 'these dark days of national dishonour',[45] and Edward Elgar, despite never completing his

---

40 Fergus Nicoll, *Gladstone, Gordon and the Sudan Wars: The Battle over Imperial Intervention in the Victorian Age* (Barnsley: Pen & Sword, 2013), pp. 68 and 80–1; see also H. C. G. Matthew, *Gladstone 1875-1898* (Oxford: Clarendon Press, 1995), pp. 143–6; Earl of Cromer, *Modern Egypt*, 2 vols (London: Macmillan, 1908), vol. 1, p. 443.

41 Nicoll, *Gladstone, Gordon and the Sudan Wars*, pp. 70–104; Frank Power, *Letters from Khartoum* (London: Sampson Low et al, 1885), p. 107; Johnson, 'Death of Gordon', p. 302; Adrian Preston (ed.), *In Relief of Gordon: Lord Wolseley's Campaign Journal of the Khartoum Relief Expedition 1884-1885* (London: Hutchinson, 1967), pp. xxviii–xxxii; Julian Symons, *England's Pride: The Story of the Gordon Relief Expedition* (London: Hamish Hamilton, 1965), pp. 65–72.

42 'The Crisis in the Soudan', *Falkirk Herald,*, 11 February 1885, p. 2.

43 Richards, *Imperialism and Music*, p. 331; *Essex Standard*, 7 February 1885, p. 5; Dave Russell, '"We carved our way to glory" The British soldier in music hall song and sketch, c. 1880-1914' in J. M. MacKenzie (ed.), *Popular Imperialism and the Military 1850-1950* (Manchester: Manchester University Press, 1992), pp. 50–79, at p. 66.

44 Richard Hill, 'The Gordon Literature', *The Durham University Journal*, vol. XLVII, no. 3 (1955), pp. 97–103, at p. 99.

45 Robert L. Stevenson to S. Colvin, 8 March 1885, in B. A. Booth and E. Mehew (eds),

'Gordon Symphony', incorporated many of its ideas and emotions into other works, not least *The Dream of Gerontius*.[46]

Khartoum demonstrated that the risks of a siege were not simply confined to the besieged inhabitants but that a siege disaster could have far-reaching political consequences. Anguish over the death of Gordon soon turned to anger, as people hissed at Gladstone in the streets and changed his nickname from GOM (Grand Old Man) to MOG (Murderer of Gordon). Liberals rallied round their embattled prime minister, maintaining that the relief force was sent when needed (as Gordon was still claiming that Khartoum was all right as late as 14 December), and that the city fell by treachery, which could have occurred at any time.[47] Yet the discovery of Gordon's Khartoum journals by the relief force, and their subsequent editing and publication by Egmont Hake during the second half of 1885, kept the controversy alive.[48] Fundamentally, Gordon's death transformed the impact of the siege. Just as the fallen hero had demanded a relief force to uphold the national honour, his death demanded vengeance to restore the national honour. The government responded by promising to 'smash' Mahdism and began building a railway across the Eastern Sudan. Within a few months, however, in May 1885, it abandoned this project when more pressing matters arose in Afghanistan. Gordon now seemed 'both betrayed and sacrificed'.[49]

As a pall of martyrdom began to cloak his legacy, Gordon's reputation as a siege commander underwent a steady transformation. No longer were his practical achievements sufficient whether as an administrator, who organized the evacuation of refugees and later the rationing of supplies, or as an engineer, who improvised unorthodox defences and mined the approaches to the city, or as a commander, who conducted an active defence by mounting sorties and sending his steamers up and down the Blue and White Niles. In numerous sermons and pamphlets Gordon was dubbed a *Christian Hero*, a *Hero and Saint*, *The Forsaken Hero*, *The Youngest of the Saints*, and in this context, as John MacKenzie has argued, Gordon appeared 'as a lonely traveller fulfilling God's will before finding his final martyrdom'.[50] Even the manner

---

The Letters of Robert Louis Stevenson, 8 vols (New Haven and London: Yale University Press, 1995), vol. 5, pp. 79–81.

46 Richards, *Imperialism and Music*, pp. 60–1.

47 'Party and Patriotism', *North-Eastern Daily Gazette*, 25 February 1885, p. 2 and 'The Soudan', *Perthshire Advertiser,* 25 February 1885, p. 2.

48 Nicoll, *Gladstone, Gordon and the Sudan Wars*, pp. 132–41.

49 Johnson, 'Death of Gordon', p. 302.

50 John M. MacKenzie, 'Heroic Myths of Empire' in MacKenzie (ed.), *Popular Imperialism*, pp. 109–38 at p. 126; for evidence that his practical skills as a commander were once recognized, see 'How Gordon Reached Khartoum. History of the Mission', *Aberdeen Journal*, 6 February 1885, p. 5.

of his death, about which there was no conclusive evidence, became a crucial component of the Gordon myth. Of all the many images of Gordon in the illustrated press, statues, lantern shows, and *tableaux vivants*, none compared with the imaginative painting of George William Joy, *The death of General Gordon, Khartoum, 26th January 1885* (1894). This image of an unarmed and dignified Gordon, standing alone at the top of a flight of stairs in the palace of Khartoum, unresisting as he faced a prospective black assassin, encompassed all the virtues expected of a Christian hero about to meet a noble death.[51]

Gordon may have been unique, but the way in which Victorians interpreted his death, ascribed character traits to him, and sustained a controversy over the failed relief expedition, testified to how they viewed sieges. They recognized that sieges could impose strains and challenges, and that the risks of disaster could have profound consequences. They realized, too, that the length of sieges mattered, and that the longer a siege had to be endured without the prospect of relief, so it compounded the strains upon the besieged – soldiers and civilians alike – and augmented the burden of leadership to maintain a degree of collective resolve. Even the *Edinburgh Evening News*, a rabidly pro-Boer newspaper, recognized that sieges had their own internal dynamic, and that the conduct of the siege at Mafeking meant that it would take 'its place beside Lucknow, Jallalabad and Khartoum'. Indeed the editor observed that

> It had almost seemed at times as if 'too late' would be written against Mafeking as it was recorded against Khartoum; but whenever a period of despair came it was quickly ended by some resolute act which would have lent lustre to any campaign. If there was at any time despair at home, there was never any at Mafeking.[52]

Magnifying the achievements at Mafeking was the perception that the town, 'composed of frail mud-bricked tin-roofed houses',[53] lacked any natural defences and was 'wholly unfitted by its position, out on an unsheltered plain, to stand the rigours of a siege'.[54] Compounding these inherent difficulties were the small size of Mafeking's population base, its lack of resources (in all respects save provisions, which had been pre-stocked in lavish amounts),

---

51 Some accounts suggest that Gordon may have been shot, see Johnson, 'Death of Gordon', pp. 302–07; Charles Chenevix Trench, *Charley Gordon: An Eminent Victorian Assessed* (London: Allen Lane, 1978), pp. 290–1; Henry Keown-Boyd, *A Good Dusting: A Centenary Review of the Sudan campaigns 1883-1899* (London: Leo Cooper, 1986), p. 73.
52 *Edinburgh Evening News*, 19 May 1900, p. 2; on the political affiliations of this newspaper, see Spiers, *Scottish Soldier*, pp. 182 and 197n4.
53 Maurice and Grant, *Official History*, vol. 3, p. 144.
54 'Mafeking and Its Lesson', *South Wales Daily News*, 21 May 1900, p. 4.

and its lack of regular soldiers. Dr Rutherfoord Harris knew Mafeking and its surrounding countryside, having practised medicine in pre-war Kimberley. A friend of Rhodes, he had been implicated in the organization of the Jameson Raid and had represented Kimberley within the Cape Colony Assembly. Now back in Wales, where he aspired to become the Unionist MP for Monmouth Boroughs, he declared that

> Other sieges have displayed British valour and heroism, but the sieges of Lucknow, Gibraltar, and even of Ladysmith were unlike the siege of Mafeking, because Mafeking was only an open, unfortified village, inadequately provisioned [*sic*], slightly armed, and garrisoned with only a few hundred volunteers, who were not trained to war.[55]

In fact the reputation of the Victorian volunteering movement was such that many commentators saw positive virtues in relying upon volunteers to defend Mafeking. These were 'adventurous men', claimed the *Edinburgh Evening News*, who 'had little knowledge of the barrack-room, and knew nothing of the mysteries of pipe clay, but they were pre-eminently handy men – the type which gave us our great empire'.[56] Nevertheless, the challenge facing Baden-Powell and his small garrison of volunteers seemed so much greater by virtue of Mafeking's location and its sheer isolation 'on the outposts of the Empire, and close to the enemy's gates'.[57] Ironically, too, at least in the mind of some commentators, Mafeking was a place 'of no strategic importance',[58] and 'its situation possessed no real strategic value'.[59] This critique, though contested fiercely by many imperialist writers, Conservative politicians, and not least by Baden-Powell himself,[60] had an importance beyond anticipating the revisionist writing of the late twentieth century. It was often coupled

---

55 'Dr Rutherfoord Harris at Usk', *Western Mail*, 19 June 1900, p. 6; see also Robert I. Rotberg, 'Who Was Responsible? Rhodes, Jameson, and the Raid' in Jane Carruthers et al (eds), *The Jameson Raid: A Centennial Retrospective* (Johannesburg: Brenthurst Press, 1996), pp. 131–51, at pp. 139–40, 143 and 147–8.

56 *Edinburgh Evening News*, 19 May 1900, p. 2, see also 'Mafeking', *Kilmarnock Standard*, 26 May 1900, p. 4.

57 'Mafeking', *Hampshire Advertiser*, 23 May 1900, p. 2, see also 'The Siege of Mafeking', *Standard*, 21 May 1900, p. 8 and 'The Relief of Mafeking', *Nuneaton Chronicle*, 25 May 1900, p. 6.

58 *Wigan Observer*, 25 May 1900, p. 5.

59 'The Last "Relief"', *Shrewsbury Chronicle*, 25 May 1900, p. 5; see also 'Mafeking and After', *Northern Echo*, 21 May 1900, p. 2.

60 'War Letter from Major F. D. Baillie, Our Special Correspondent', *Morning Post*, 19 June 1900, p. 7; 'Mafeking', *Dumfries and Galloway Courier and Herald*, 23 May 1900, p. 4; Baden-Powell, 'Narrative of Organization of Frontier Force', in evidence before the *RCWSA*, vol. 2, p. 424.

with an understanding, based on the precedent of Potchefstroom, that 'the defenders [of Mafeking] had little to loose [*sic*: lose]', and that 'surrender did not mean murder in cold blood' but simply 'removal from the horrors of Mafeking to the comparative comforts of a Pretorian prison'. Despite all these temptations, argued the *Wigan Observer*, 'this brave little garrison never for a moment entertained the thought of surrender'.[61]

John Morley MP, a Gladstonian Liberal and prominent critic of the war, sought to explain this apparent conundrum, and in so doing helped to explain how the memories of sieges had left a legacy that would spread across political and class divisions at home (apart from Nationalist sentiment in Ireland). Speaking at a banquet in Cambridge on the night when news arrived of Mafeking's relief, he declared that 'the public imagination today is excited to a degree almost, I think, without parallel'. He continued:

> Differ about the policy of the war and the results of the war as we will, every one of us recognized with admiration, and even something more than admiration, the heroic sense of personal and public duty, the manful regard for military honour, which has animated and inspired the fortitude and endurance, the patience and cheerful courage of the men of whom we were all thinking that day. So long as Englishmen were Englishmen – and he included in the idea of Englishmen Australians – they would admire pluck – physical pluck and moral pluck, especially when the two, as in this case, were so admirably combined.[62]

Setting aside Morley's rhetorical flourishes, and his oblique reference to the Australian Commonwealth Bill then passing through Parliament, he was quite right to focus upon the 'public imagination'. Siege histories had aroused and stimulated Victorian imaginations: as the pro-Boer *Manchester Guardian* observed, 'There is no story that so engrosses the imagination as the story of a great siege.' In the previous year, it claimed, 'the most fascinating military book' had been 'Sir G. Robertson's account of the siege of Chitral'; now Mafeking had been 'a great siege', not in the numbers of men engaged nor in the military issues involved 'but in the qualities of endurance, courage, and devotion' demonstrated by the defenders. 'The story', argued the *Manchester Guardian*, was 'all the more moving' because it involved not professional soldiers, so much as 'average Englishmen in the colonies' challenged in an exceptional way, and compelled to display a range of qualities if they were

61 *Wigan Observer*, 25 May 1900, p. 5.
62 'John Morley, M. P., at Cambridge', *Cambridge Independent Press*, 25 May 1900, p. 6 and 'Echoes of Mafeking', *Western Mail*, 21 May 1900, p. 4.

going to prevail.[63] Surviving sieges, in short, involved a test of character and of all the qualities required during a siege was, in Morley's words, the peculiarly English virtue of 'pluck'. This came from the innermost being, the heart as the seat of courage, and could manifest itself morally and/or physically in defiance of great danger or overwhelming odds.

On the Sunday after the relief of Mafeking, the Reverend John Watson delivered a sermon on pluck in his church at Sefton Park, Liverpool. Pluck, he described, as the 'spirit of manhood, which is the glory of a nation', and it was as evident in the Charge of the Light Brigade, the siege of Lucknow and the defence of Rorke's Drift as it had been at Mafeking. The defenders had not only fought and toiled but they had also kept watch, and suffered hunger, and they had done it 'all with a high heart, without grumbling or complaining, with unaffected cheerfulness and pleasant jesting, as if this were rather a comedy than a tragedy. No whining message beseeching for relief came for them any more than from Ladysmith' [the implicit contrast here is with Kimberley from which Rhodes made several pleas for relief].[64] The defenders, added Watson, had 'carried themselves like Britons of the old breed, who neither boast nor whine, and because they played the game and played up well, and played to the end, and by the will of God have won . . .'. It was a lesson in 'pluck', a 'homely word' that 'is a synonym for heart':

> It means doing your work and facing your danger, and bearing your pain and accepting your defeats, but fighting your battles and standing by your comrades, without grudging and without squealing. When a man has pluck he doesn't know when he is defeated, he speaks as if he were always winning . . . Pluck takes no account of itself, or of circumstances, or of hardships, or of enemies; it is modest in triumph, and honourable in conflict, and dies smiling.[65]

If this was a highly romanticized view of how men and women[66] comported themselves in the face of imminent danger, it underscored the Victorian fascination with sieges and their belief that overwhelming odds could only be overcome by the beleaguered communities displaying certain moral qualities,

---

63 *Manchester Guardian*, 19 May 1900, p. 9.
64 Spiers (ed.), *Letters from Kimberley*, p. 7.
65 'The Virtue of Pluck', *Lurgan Times*, 2 June 1900, p. 4.
66 Although women did not receive much recognition in the Mafeking speeches and editorials, their role has been analyzed admirably in recent scholarship, see Elizabeth van Heyningen, 'Women under Siege', in Smith (ed.), *Siege of Mafeking*, vol. 2, pp. 241–83.

or as the *Daily Chronicle* averred, 'by sheer superiority of pluck'.[67] It did not mean that defenders exhibiting pluck were bound to prevail, as Victorians had bitter memories of sieges failing through treachery, famine and disease, or through desperate and determined assault. Yet if defenders were going to prevail during a prolonged siege, they would have to display a range of moral qualities in a battle of wills as much as a battle of arms. Within this historical and cultural context, sieges conjured a traditional image of conflict in what had become a very different kind of war in South Africa.

In the early months of this war, press reports had described seemingly empty battlefields swept by fire from smokeless, flat trajectory and high-velocity magazine rifles. As the British army suffered a series of early reverses, including several surrenders by bodies of regular soldiers, and struggled to combat a highly mobile foe that was adept at fighting from entrenched positions, Victorians found reports of siege environments much more comprehensible. Whether at Ladysmith, Kimberley or Mafeking, the onset of siege warfare resonated as a more traditional form of military combat. Imaginations may have run riot at times but Victorians thought that they knew how sieges were contested, how leaders in these challenging circumstances had to behave, and how stoical and successful resistance redounded to the national honour.

67　*Daily Chronicle*, 19 May 1900, p. 4.

Chapter 3

Siege Preparations at Mafeking

If the chequered history of Mafeking exacerbated relations between Britain and the Boer republics during the mid- to late 1890s, Mafeking also suffered from an international relationship that became increasingly fraught. For several years prior to the outbreak of war, the Boer republics had struggled to resist the ambitions of Britain's colonial authorities and had sought to preserve their political autonomy and cultural identity. After the Jameson Raid they had rearmed their artillery with quick-firing and long-range guns, including four 155mm Creusot guns, later known as 'Long Toms', with a range of about 10,000 m, and acquired some 102,500 rifles, including 49,800 Mausers and 43,750 Martini-Henrys.[1] Diplomatically, they had been confronted by Joseph Chamberlain, the British colonial secretary, with his long-term ambition of forging a South African federation, and by Sir Alfred Milner, the British high commissioner in South Africa, who had championed the political ambitions of the *Uitlanders* in the Transvaal. Following the shooting of Tom Edgar, a mining engineer, by the Transvaal police on 23 December 1898, Milner exerted further pressure on the Boers, culminating in the Bloemfontein conference (31 May–5 June 1899). This proved abortive, as Milner refused to compromise on his demands for the enfranchisement of the *Uitlanders*, while President Kruger was only willing to halve the fourteen-year residency period.

Amidst the deteriorating circumstances, refugees began moving out of the Rand mainly towards the coast[2] but also across the Transvaal, both into and out of Mafeking itself. Although the railway line functioned on a north-south axis from Cape Town to Bulawayo, and so spared Mafeking from an even greater influx of refugees, the displacement of peoples began several months before the outbreak of war. As early as July 1899 Charles Payne, the assistant water engineer at the Pretoria waterworks, sent his wife and two children west to Mafeking, where he thought they would be safe or at least protected by his

---

1   Pretorius, *A to Z of the Anglo-Boer War*, pp. 17–18 and 384–6; Louis Changuin, *The Silence of the Guns: The History of the Long Toms of the Anglo-Boer War* (Pretoria: Protea Book House, 2001), p. 39.

2   Diana Cammack, *The Rand At War 1899-1902: The Witwatersrand & the Anglo-Boer War* (London: James Currey, 1990), p. 117.

brother James, an employee with the Cape Government Railway.[3] Meanwhile Isaac Cohen, who was involved in a tobacco business in Johannesburg, sent his family by railway to Cape Town, while fleeing to Mafeking at the outbreak of war. He later assisted in organizing the soup kitchens but initially was merely one of many late arrivals.[4] These included Samuel Cawood, who would serve in the Town Guard, several hundred black mine-labourers, and the last trainload of refugees from Mafeking, mainly women and children that had to return to the town on 12 October 1899.[5] Some were only in the town by accident, including William Sim, an engine driver, formerly of Lochee, near Dundee, who brought the last trainload of provisions into Mafeking. He later created the celebrated Sowens porridge, but had planned to leave the town only to be struck down ill two days before the war erupted and so witnessed 'that stupendous feature of war, a siege'.[6]

Mafeking, though, was not a prime target in the months before the war. The likelihood of war occurring still divided the British cabinet, with Sir Michael Hicks Beach, the Chancellor of the Exchequer, and Lord Lansdowne, the Secretary of State for War, among those hoping for a peaceful resolution of the crisis and opposed to precipitate and costly military commitments. This left Wolseley fuming: he was aware of the chronic lack of military forces in Cape Colony and Natal (only 10,289 men and 24 artillery pieces in June 1899), and despaired of a War Office 'system' that was 'unmilitary and opposed to all that tends to make an army efficient & to all the necessities of actual war'.[7] Experienced in South African affairs, he believed that a show of force was essential to demonstrate the resolve of the British government: otherwise 'if Kruger plays his hand well as he will do, we shall have no war & no real settlement of the S. African question now'.[8] Nevertheless, at this time the government only authorized Wolseley to send small additions of artillery and

---

3   'Shut Up In Mafeking: Arbroathians who have shared the horrors of the Siege', *(Dundee) Evening Telegraph*, 26 May 1900, p. 3.

4   Fuller, *Last of the Gentleman's Wars*, p. 68; see also 'Before The Siege. A Last Word From Mafeking', *Westminster Gazette*, 3 November 1899, pp. 1–2 at p. 2.

5   Davey (ed.), *Defence of Ladysmith and Mafeking*, p. 116.

6   'The Sowens-Maker of Mafeking', *(Aberdeen) Evening Express*, 11 July 1900, p. 4; see also 'Home From Mafeking. Lochee Man's Adventures', *(Dundee) Courier and Argus*, 20 July 1900, p. 5.

7   Brighton & Hove Libraries, Brighton & Hove City Council, Wolseley Collection, W/P, 28/30, Lord Wolseley to Lady Wolseley, 24 June 1899: on the forces in Cape Colony and Natal, see *RCWSA*, Cd. 1789, para. 22,189 and on cabinet divisions, Iain R. Smith, *The Origins of the South African War, 1899-1902* (London: Longman, 1996), pp. 337–41 and A. N. Porter, *The origins of the South African War: Joseph Chamberlain and the Diplomacy of Imperialism* (Manchester: Manchester University Press, 1980), pp. 222–3 and 228–31.

8   Wolseley Collection, W/P, 28/38, Wolseley to Lady Wolseley, 11 July 1899.

engineers to the Cape garrison, and despatch twenty special service officers to organize supplies, transport and the defence of the frontiers. The latter included Baden-Powell, who was renowned for his 'successful' independent commands in Africa and was thought likely 'by his personal influence to put in the field a force of about 1,000 men'.[9]

Although Wolseley, in briefing Baden-Powell on 3 July, may have advised him to 'prepare Mafeking for being cut off',[10] the town was not mentioned in B-P's official orders, which were sent by Sir Evelyn Wood, the adjutant-general. These orders required Baden-Powell to raise a regiment of 590 irregulars (later increased to two regiments with establishments of 450 apiece), and 'to endeavour to demonstrate with the largest force at your disposal, in a southerly direction from Tuli, as if making towards Pretoria'. The aims were to detain 'a considerable number of Boers', and to protect Rhodesia, operating with 'full discretion as to your action on the lines above'.[11] Despite subsequent criticism for abandoning mobile operations and allowing his forces to become besieged in Mafeking,[12] Baden-Powell was perfectly aware, not least from his previous service in Matabeleland, of what mobile operations might require. *En route* to South Africa, he prepared a draft organization for a four-company regiment, one that would have to be fully self-sufficient, mobile and supported by at least 'nine mule waggons per company' with another one-months' supplies in 'my base at Tuli'. For the 16 officers and 400 non-commissioned officers and men, he envisaged the acquisition of at least 500 horses (to offset the 'prevalence of horse-sickness') and 17 Maxim machine-guns. Having calculated the costs of these requirements, he sent his letter to Lord Lansdowne.[13]

It was only after the *Dunottar Castle* docked at Cape Town (25 July 1899) that Baden-Powell began to appreciate that he would receive precious little assistance from the local authorities. At his disastrous meeting with Sir William Butler, Baden-Powell realized that this Irish general had a profound fear of a war between the white races and opposed any planning for a forward defence of Natal and Cape Colony lest it precipitate hostilities. Even worse,

9   TNA, WO 32/7852, Col. William Everett, Secret 'Memorandum on the project of a raid from Southern Rhodesia on the Northern districts of the Transvaal in the event of war with the South Africa Republic', 1 July 1899; see also Cecil Headlam (ed.), *The Milner Papers*, 2 vols (London: Cassell, 1933), vol. 1, p. 508.

10   Wolseley Collection, Major-General R. S. S. Baden-Powell to Viscount Wolseley, 1 July 1900.

11   TNA, WO 32/7852, Sir Evelyn Wood, 'Memorandum for Colonel Baden-Powell, 5th Dragoon Guards', 7 July 1899, especially enclosures B and D; see also 'B-P's report', p. 891.

12   Gardner, *Mafeking*, pp. 39 and 42.

13   TNA, WO 32/7849, Baden-Powell to Secretary of State for War, 12 July 1899.

Butler, who shared the popular view that Jewish business interests lay at the heart of the evolving political crisis, regarded B-P's mission, which had been much touted in the Rhodesian press, as provocative in its own right.[14] Surprisingly Baden-Powell found that his subsequent meeting with Sir Alfred Milner was not much better. Despite their desire to protect the frontier, and shared frustration at Butler's attitude, Baden-Powell encountered deep reservations on the part of Sir Alfred. The high commissioner had never been consulted about the mission in spite of it operating initially under the aegis of the Colonial Office. He worried about how the local military authorities would respond to Baden-Powell superseding Colonel John S. Nicholson, the commandant of police in Rhodesia, and about the use of imperial officers to raise and train regiments of colonial irregulars. He opposed any overt recruiting in Cape Colony lest it outrage the Cape government, headed by William P. Schreiner and the South Africa Party (the Afrikaner Bond and its allies). He feared, too, that the deployment of frontier forces could provoke the Boers before reinforcements reached the colonies (the government only authorized the first major reinforcements of 10,000 men in September). Above all, Milner dreaded that a premature military débâcle could occur, followed by a British accommodation (as after Majuba), so frustrating the prospects for war and the creation of a British South Africa.[15]

He confided in the Hon. Arthur Lawley, the administrator in Rhodesia, claiming that 'Matters are much complicated by the fact that the War Office are sending out special service officers – Baden-Powell etc., to "organize" a fighting force in the Protectorate [of Bechuanaland] & Rhodesia. I hate this, and would much rather leave it all to Nicholson.'[16] Lawley agreed that 'if Baden-Powell is sent up to "boss" them [Nicholson, the police and the Rhodesian volunteers] they will be very loath to lend a hand. He is very unpopular here.'[17] Accordingly, Milner imposed stringent restrictions upon B-P's activities, banning any recruiting in Johannesburg, requiring all the imperial officers to wear civilian clothes and to travel on to Bulawayo under false names. He also prohibited these officers from buying horses or stores in Cape Colony. Lord Lansdowne agreed; on 27 July, he had already advised

---

14　Sir William F. Butler, *An Autobiography* (London: Constable, 1911), pp. 436 and 452; and Keith Surridge, "'All you soldiers are what we call pro-Boer'; The Military Critique of the South African War, 1899-1902', *History*, vol. 82 (1997), pp. 582–600.

15　Oxford, Bodleian Library, Milner Mss., dep. 212, f. 177, Sir Alfred Milner to Joseph Chamberlain, 8 September 1899; Headlam (ed), *Milner Papers*, vol. 1, p. 521; Jeal, *Baden-Powell*, pp. 214–15 and 217; Pretorius, *A to Z of the Anglo-Boer War*, pp. 408–9.

16　Oxford, Bodleian Library, Milner Mss., dep. 219, f. 49, Sir A. Milner to Hon. A. Lawley, 10 July 1899.

17　Oxford, Bodleian Library, Milner Mss., dep. 211, f. 409, Lawley to Milner, 19 July 1899.

the Colonial Office that 'the Mafeking force' (another early assumption that this was its likely focus) 'should be raised across the border, and that its headquarters should be in the Bechuanaland Protectorate'.[18]

After these unfortunate meetings in Cape Town, Baden-Powell, holding the title, Commander-in-Chief North-West Forces, travelled north to Bulawayo virtually empty-handed. He now had to raise two units of mounted infantry, a Protectorate Regiment under Colonel C. O. Hore (South Staffordshire Regiment) to defend Bechuanaland and a Rhodesian regiment under Lieutenant-Colonel H. C. O. Plumer (York and Lancaster Regiment) to defend Rhodesia. The two regiments, supported by mounted police and volunteer units, would number about 2,000 trained men, and were supposedly responsible for a combined frontier of over 805 km. They were 'As far as possible, to keep forces of the enemy distracted in this direction away from their own main forces.'[19] Baden-Powell had left Lord Edward Cecil, DSO (Grenadier Guards) behind to arrange what assistance he could in Cape Town. After 'several frustrated days and after consulting Sir Alfred Milner', he concluded his famous deal with Ben Weil for stores worth £500,000. As Lady Violet Cecil recalled, the Weils 'must have known that he himself had not a tenth of this money. But they banked on Lord Edward's personality and on his father's position [prime minister], and the deal saved Mafeking.'[20] In fact, as Julius Weil later explained, this contract was only to supply 'Colonel Hore's forces, consisting of about 440 Europeans, 80 coloureds and 30 natives, also 440 horses and 73 mules' for a period of up to three months. The Weil company knew that vast consignments of food and provisions had already been pre-stocked in the sheds and railway sidings of Mafeking in anticipation of a new customs levy, which was due to be imposed on all goods entering Rhodesia in 1899. Under the threat of war the levy was not introduced but it meant that the extra supplies secured by Lord Edward buttressed those of a well-stocked town.[21]

Meanwhile Baden-Powell found most of his military supplies in Bulawayo, left over from the Matabele War of 1896–7. He acquired saddlery, equipment, ammunition, clothing and even old transport and stores, including a supply of tinned meat. He purchased additional supplies from the local traders, who had accumulated about eight months' stocks, on the advice of Nicholson, in anticipation of war. He found much more difficulty in securing officers,

18 TNA, CO 417/275, f. 473, R. H. Knox to the Under Secretary of State, Colonial Office, 27 July 1900; see also Godley, *Life*, p. 71 and Jeal, *Baden-Powell*, p. 215.
19 On the frontier, see Baden-Powell (19,871) evidence before *RCWSA*, p. 427 and B-P's orders in August, 'B-P's report', p. 891.
20 Viscountess Milner, *My Picture Gallery*, p. 126.
21 Julius Weil, telegram, *The Times*, 26 March 1900, p. 7 and Godley, *Life*, pp. 71–2.

as the twenty special service officers only accounted for one-third of his requirements. Among these officers were the two senior commanders, Hore and Plumer; Majors Lord Edward Cecil, B-P's chief staff officer, the Hon. Algernon Hanbury-Tracy (Royal Horse Guards), intelligence officer, Courtney B. Vyvyan (Buffs), base commandant Mafeking (later Commanding Engineer), and Alexander J. Godley (Royal Dublin Fusiliers), adjutant of the Protectorate Regiment; and notable squadron leaders, including Captains Lord Charles C. Bentinck (9th Lancers) and Charles FitzClarence (Royal Fusiliers), grandson of the 1st earl of Munster. Yet the recruiting of both officers and men proved fairly slow in August: 'a good percentage of loafers' were available in Bulawayo but 'good men' did not want to leave their jobs until the war appeared imminent. As a partial response Baden-Powell organized a squadron of 'young respectable fellows', who were still in employment but were willing to drill at weekends until he had all the horses, transport and other matters for their regiment, 'so that when war did come they came out as a squadron complete, and joined General [*sic*: Colonel] Plumer's force. They were first-rate.'[22]

By mid-August Baden-Powell was also recruiting discreetly in Cape Colony and Natal. Financed by the Colonial Office, his recruiters offered pay of five shillings a day, initially for a three months' engagement, with the option of retaining service in the war thereafter. They attracted men from the larger population centres like Grahamstown, King William's Town, East London, Port Elizabeth and Cape Town itself. In Cape Town Alfred Hellawell, formerly of the 13th Hussars and Cape Rifles, accepted a commission, and he would later serve not only in the Protectorate Regiment but also as a special correspondent for the *Cape Times* and *Daily Mail* before his capture by the Boers in mid-December.[23] Charles Rose, an Aberdonian, who had lived in Kimberley for two years before moving into farm management, also enlisted in August. Having received assurances that he could return to his job as soon as the hostilities ceased, he never imagined that he would take part in a prolonged struggle. He had good credentials, nonetheless, as he had served in the Diamond Fields Horse, where he won prizes in marksmanship, and had become a skilled horseman. Once he reached the enlistment and training area at Ramathlabama, 29 km from Mafeking, he was promoted lance corporal within a week and a full corporal before the end of the second week.[24]

---

22   Baden-Powell (Qs. 19,836-8 and 19,843) evidence before *RCWSA*, p. 426.
23   Ibid (Q. 19,840), p. 426 and 'A Keighley Officer with Baden-Powell', *Bradford Daily Telegraph*, 25 October 1899, p. 3.
24   'A Hero of Mafeking: Aberdeenshire Man on the Siege', *(Aberdeen) Evening Express*, 28 August 1900, p. 5.

A man with Rose's skills stood out because the recruits remained, in Baden-Powell's phrase, 'a very mixed lot'.[25] While some were veterans of previous South African campaigns, others, recalled Godley, 'were of all classes and of all trades – butchers, painters, farmers, printers, tailors, actors, jockeys, soldiers of fortune, etc., and of all nationalities'[26] (Appendix A). They were by no means all gifted in shooting and riding, and several were discharged for drunkenness or being unfit for duty.[27] Recruits arrived in piecemeal numbers (neither regiment was up to strength until about mid-September), and the Protectorate troopers congregated at Ramathlabama, a mere railway siding in Bechuanaland, because Baden-Powell was proscribed from enlisting, basing, or training an armed force in Cape Colony. He was also banned from buying horses from the Army Remount Department, but, as he started buying them from other sources, even Butler relented and allowed the department to start supplying him with South African horses, albeit largely unbroken remounts. Once Butler resigned from his post on 23 August, his successor, Lieutenant-General Sir F. W. Forestier-Walker began to let more military rations and stores flow north from Cape Town.[28]

Only stores could be concentrated in Mafeking, but the accumulation became all too conspicuous, filling a shed by early September and requiring the stacking of more goods under tarpaulins near the railway station. Fearing an arson attack, Colonel Hore sent fourteen men to guard the stockpile that was growing with every train that arrived in Mafeking. J. R. More, the acting superintendent of the railway who would later command the Railway Division, feared for the loyalty of some of his gangers (labourers) and for the safety of his railway stock. While transferring disloyal gangers north of Mochudi, he ordered all spare permanent way, bridging material, three bales of grain bags, and 20,000 lbs (9,072 kg) of meal to be brought into Mafeking from as far north as Palapye and from as far south as Vryburg. From 9 to 12 October his men built a defence railway, 2.4 km long, to protect the northern front with an armoured train. The Railway Division also supplied an enormous quantity of material for the town's defences, including over 200 tons of rails for the bomb-proof shelters. Baden-Powell perceived these valuable stores as additional bait for the Boers and another reason to secure the defence of Mafeking.[29]

---

25 Baden-Powell (Q. 19,844) evidence before *RCWSA*, p. 426.

26 Godley, *Life*, p. 71; see also Hickman, *Rhodesia Served the Queen*, vol. 1, p. 75 and 'Where Three Frontiers Meet', *Glasgow Herald*, 3 October 1899, p. 7.

27 Brent. L., Vyvyan Mss., MS. 147/3/6/1, 'Record of Service', 28 August – 16 September 1899.

28 Godley, *Life*, pp. 71–2; Baden-Powell (Qs. 19,845-51) evidence before *RCWSA*, p. 426; and Lord Baden-Powell of Gilwell, *Lessons From The 'Varsity of Life'* (London: C. Arthur Pearson, 1933), p. 202.

29 Brent. L., Vyvyan Mss., MS. 147/5/1/40, More, 'Railway Report', pp. 1–2; Baden-Powell, 'Narrative of Organization of Frontier Force', *RCWSA*, p. 424.

Meanwhile, the training of the Protectorate Regiment continued at Ramathlabama where, as Corporal Rose recollected, it involved 'drill about four hours a day' and training 'exclusively of field movements'.[30] Baden-Powell later rationalized this process as an attempt to inculcate the basics of drill and discipline in the limited time available, and to train the volunteers in small units under their junior officers. The field days were largely a form of 'practical training', and the 'sham fights against each other', a means of installing discipline and small-unit cohesion that would prove essential during the siege.[31] Rose interpreted the training quite differently; he doubted that this training was ever designed as a preparation for the investment of Mafeking, as no trenches were dug apart from 'one or two' by the 'Cape boys'. He believed that 'a march into the Transvaal' was still intended, and that it remained a primary aim during the first two months of the siege, when the horses never had their 'saddles off their backs except for a short time on Sundays'. At short notice the troopers could have pursued the Boers should they 'at any time give up the siege and "make a bolt"'.[32] However fanciful this surmise, it reflects two critical points: first, that the preparatory training hardly seemed obvious if the aim, which was not mentioned in the official orders, was to defend Mafeking, and secondly, that options had to be kept open. 'I kept mounted men there,' argued Baden-Powell, 'both as a threat and because if they [the Boers] did go away we could actually make a raid and dash in if necessary.'[33]

Defending Mafeking

In the debates over Baden-Powell's pre-war choices and conduct, the citizens of Mafeking tend to be overlooked. Once the prospects of a peaceful settlement began to ebb away, they became ever more concerned about their own defence, or at least the safety, of their own community. In recent accounts of the siege, it has become fashionable to dwell on the reticence of the 'Mafeking's white citizenry', their failure to display constantly 'the same steadfastness of spirit as the military', and their supposedly grudging enrolment in the Town Guard. Doubtless opinions varied within the town, with pro-British views being much less conspicuous among those of 'Dutch' extraction, or among traders with Transvaal connections, or among a few Irish nationalists, who refused to

---

30 'A Hero of Mafeking: Aberdeenshire Man on the Siege', *(Aberdeen) Evening Express*, 28 August 1900, p. 5.
31 Baden-Powell (Qs. 19,858-61) evidence before *RCWSA*, p. 427.
32 'A Hero of Mafeking: Aberdeenshire Man on the Siege', *(Aberdeen) Evening Express*, 28 August 1900, p. 5.
33 Baden-Powell (Q. 19,873) evidence before *RCWSA*, p. 427.

take an oath of allegiance.[34] Incoming journalists made snap judgments about local morale, with Angus Hamilton claiming that 'men are uncertain whether to face the music or to skip with their women and children'. As time wore on, and Boers began to mass on the borders, he observed that 'the number of men available for actual volunteer service grows beautifully less'.[35] W. H. Goodwin was one of those who fled Mafeking the day before war broke out, driving his cattle and sheep towards the Kalahari Desert, where he found that the 'Bechuanas were, with very rare exceptions, very loyal to the British' and had a 'great dislike' of the Boers. He eventually returned to his homestead near Mafeking, where he found his house and store wrecked and 'every moveable article of any value stolen'.[36]

Such pusillanimity was not all-pervasive. Leading town spokesmen, reflecting upon the siege in retrospect, may have exaggerated the degree of community cohesion and the extent of local patriotism, but loyalism was certainly evident among the English-speaking community. The Anglican Rector of Mafeking, the Reverend W. H. Weekes, spoke of the 'strategical position of Mafeking' as 'great', and feared that had Mafeking fallen at the outset of the war, the Boers 'would have swept through Cape Colony'. The town was sufficiently important for the enemy to fire 'the first shot of the war' in the Mafeking district, which was also the centre of 'a very large native population'. Those blacks were loyal, Weekes insisted, 'but if they had seen the Boers successful at first, they would have thrown in their lot with them'.[37] Frank Whiteley, the staunchly loyal Yorkshireman who was mayor of Mafeking, concurred: 'Had Mafeking fallen, as the Boers expected, Kimberley and even Rhodesia would have been in danger.'[38]

Bellicose sentiments were voiced, too, as the balance of local opinion began to shift. 'As the uitlanders came into town', noted Frederick Saunders, who was a bugler in the recently-formed Bechuanaland Rifles, 'the Boers [or at least some of them] went away. The lines were being sharply drawn. Angry men pointed accusing fingers at others who did not demonstrate the expected amount of patriotism.'[39] Thomas Morse was not alone in his fierce support of the *Uitlander* cause. A former apprentice with the *Stroud Journal*,

34 Bill Nasson, *The South African War 1899-1902* (London: Arnold, 1999), p. 97; M. Flower-Smith and E. J. Yorke, *Mafeking: The Story of a Siege* (Welrevredenpark; Covos Bay, 2000), pp. 20–1; and Crauford, 'A Nurse's Diary', p. 61.
35 Hamilton, *Siege of Mafeking*, p. 50.
36 'The Siege of Mafeking: Interesting Letters', *Leicester Chronicle and the Leicestershire Mercury*, 1 September 1900, p. 4.
37 'The Siege of Mafeking Described', *Cambridge Independent*, 2 November 1900, p. 2 and 'The Rev. H. J. [*sic*: W. H.] Weekes on Mafeking', *Bath Chronicle*, 20 December 1900, p. 6.
38 'Mafeking and its Mayor. Mr. Whiteley Interviewed', *Leeds Mercury*, 23 July 1900, p. 3.
39 'A Stroud Man Home From Mafeking', *Stroud Journal*, 10 August 1900, p. 3.

he had arrived in South Africa twenty-six years previously, and served with the Frontier Mounted Police, and later the Cape Mounted Rifles, in the Morosi Rebellion (1879) and the Basuto War (1880–1). Thereafter he moved into Johannesburg, where he worked as a printer and trained as a volunteer during the build-up to the ill-fated Jameson Raid. He moved subsequently onto Mafeking, finding employment on the railway, but still complained 'bitterly' about the treatment of the *Uitlanders* and shared 'the opinion that the struggle for supremacy in South Africa was inevitable'.[40] However fervent such feelings, the citizens were not inclined to be reckless or provocative: when Dr Jameson arrived in the town *en route* to Rhodesia, he was 'hustled away with more haste than courtesy', as Lady Sarah Wilson recalled. Baden-Powell, then in command, maintained that if Jameson 'meant to stay in the town a battery of artillery would be required to defend it'.[41]

Even more important was the contemporary perception of Mafeking's acute vulnerability. In a remarkably full account of the siege, an Eyemouth man, who worked as a clerk in Mafeking, and later served in the Town Guard, described the pre-war predicament of 'our little town'. In 'peaceful times', he observed, 'Mafeking's inhabitants number about six or seven hundred Europeans' but numbers had grown with 'the influx of refugees from the Transvaal and the farms, police from outstations and our Protectorate Regiment . . . . The town is situated on flat country. Signal Hill, which is about five miles [8 km] distant, being the only kopje near town.' Given the proximity of the Boers, and the continuing drift towards war, he feared that there was 'little time left' to defend the community.[42] A committee of the Town Council and other prominent townsmen had come to a similar conclusion. On 5 September it asked the Civil Commissioner, who was the local representative of the Cape government, how the government was planning to defend Mafeking in the event of hostilities erupting. Unimpressed by the 'evasive and unsatisfactory' reply, they wrote to Milner, stating that they had 'no confidence in the Colonial Government and asking him to see that local British interests were properly safeguarded'.[43] On 15 September Milner responded positively to the 'urgent' representations of Baden-Powell, and of the British settlers in Mafeking, who 'were in an intensely nervous condition', sandwiched between the Transvaal, the Orange Free State and 'a very disaffected & menacing Boer population'. He permitted the Protectorate Regiment to move into Mafeking to secure

40 Parenthesis added, Saunders, *Mafeking Memories*, p. 43.
41 Lady Sarah Wilson, *South African Memories*, p. 77.
42 'An Eyemouth Man in Mafeking. Diary of the Siege', *Berwickshire News*, 17 July 1900, p. 5.
43 Willan (ed.), *Edward Ross*, appendix, J. R. Algie, 'Comments on the Evidence Submitted by Major-General Baden-Powell', 8 December 1903, pp. 238–9.

their supplies, and, on 19 September, the regiment encamped near the railway depot and looked, in Nurse Crauford's words, 'very picturesque'.[44]

Although the Protectorate Regiment provided the core of Baden-Powell's 'trained men', it was only one of several armed units in Mafeking. The Bechuanaland Rifles already existed but was expanded quickly, as Corporal Oscar Hulse, formerly of Mexborough, South Yorkshire, explained, 'by the enlistment of British subjects from the Transvaal'.[45] Accordingly Bugler Saunders, who had enlisted in Mafeking, knew none of his squadron other than Corporal E. Ironside: 'They were wanderers from all parts of Africa, a hard-looking lot who were paired up or in small cliques.'[46] There were, in addition, two small contingents of British South Africa (BSA) Police and Cape Police as well as the untrained forces of the Town Guard, a railway division and the Cape Boy (coloured) contingent. Overall they numbered about 1,200 men:

	Officers	Men
Protectorate Regiment (Lt.-Col. C. O. Hore)	21	448
British South Africa Police (Lt-Col. J. A. H. Walford)	10	81
Cape Police (Inspectors C. S. Marsh and J. W. Browne)	4	99
Bechuanaland Rifles (Capt. B. W. Cowan)	5	77
Town Guard (Maj. C. B. Vyvyan later H. Goold Adams)		296
Railway and other employees (Capt. J. R. More)	1	115
Cape Boy contingent (Capt. C. Goodyear)	1	67
Total	48	1,183[47]

Baden-Powell, who assumed command of all the forces in Mafeking and of the town's defences on 4 October, also acknowledged that 300 blacks served as armed cattle guards but, as already stated, he probably armed over twice that number during the siege, including a Mfengu contingent, known as the 'Black Watch', under the command of Lieutenant H. T. Mackenzie of the Cape Police, and a Barolong contingent under Captain F. C. Marsh.[48] For armament, B-P's garrison forces possessed equal numbers of Lee-Metford magazine

---

44 Oxford, Bodleian Library, Milner Mss., dep. 212, f. 173, Milner to Chamberlain, 15 September 1899; Headlam, *Milner Papers*, vol. 1, p. 521; Crauford, 'A Nurse's Diary', p. 57; and Amery, *Times History*, vol. 4, p. 571. This spoils B-P's famous anecdote that he had moved his entire regiment into the town upon receiving permission to place an armed guard around his stores, Baden-Powell, *Lessons From The 'Varsity of Life'*, p. 202.
45 'The Siege of Mafeking', *Penistone, Stocksbridge Hoyland Chapeltown Express* (hereafter *Penistone Express*), 20 July 1900, p. 6.
46 Saunders, *Mafeking Memories*, p. 53.
47 *Official History*, vol. 3, p. 145 and 'B-P's report', p. 895.
48 Chapter 1, p. 1 and n.6.

rifles and Martini-Henry breech-loaders, with an allowance of 600 rounds per rifle, but artillery remained his greatest weakness. Mafeking had to rely upon four 7-pounder muzzle-loading guns (each with a range of 2,286 m), two 1-pounder Hotchkiss, one 2in Nordenfeldt and seven .303 Maxim machine guns. Baden-Powell had requested the despatch of two 5in howitzers but when the order arrived a few days before the war started, it was found that an error in the code word had produced another two 7-pounders (so comprising the four obsolete muzzle-loaders).[49] Replacement guns were then sent north but these were on the train intercepted by the Boers, and were added to the enemy's artillery.

The town, aided by the Base Commandant, Major (local rank, Lieutenant-Colonel) C. B. Vyvyan, had begun organizing its defences weeks before Baden-Powell arrived. As early as 13 September the town began enrolling citizens as special constables, and, on 21 September, constituted a local defence committee, including Vyvyan, which authorized the construction of local defences. On 28 September those who subsequently joined a Town Guard and Railway Division took an oath of allegiance to make themselves legal belligerents under the Geneva Convention. Townsmen and black labourers cleared brush and scrub to the north-east of Mafeking to deny the Boers any cover, dug wells in the town, and fortified Cannon Kopje, an old siege work about 2,280 m south of Mafeking. While tons of earth had to be dragged out to the fort to raise its ramparts, townsmen began constructing the inner defences of the town. They moved waggons across the ends of streets, protected key buildings like the Standard Bank with sandbags, placed thorn bush obstacles in front of the north and east sides, and erected barricades at the ends of streets open to the veld, loopholed for firing purposes. The Town Guard, wrote Saunders, 'seemed a happy gang. I'm not sure they caught the significance of what they were doing. It seemed more like a picnic, the women bringing tea and sandwiches and sometimes helping with the work.'[50]

Cannon Kopje was 61 m high and had a good all-round view as a signalling station, but it was only part of an outer defensive ring. The aim in this defensive perimeter was to extend trenches to the east and west of the old fort, coming closer to the town on the east, where they skirted the brickfields of ruined chimneys and kilns. Thereafter this defensive line enclosed the north-eastern side of the town, hospital, the two-storeyed convent, and the cemetery all to the east of the railway. More trenches, redoubts and forts were constructed west of the railway camp and women's laager (and later

---

49 Baden-Powell, 'Narrative of Organization of Frontier Force', evidence before *RCWSA*, pp. 423–4; 'B-P's report', p. 891; TNA, WO 108/284, Vyvyan, 'Defence of Mafeking', p. 2.
50 Saunders, *Mafeking Memories*, p. 47; see also 'Before the Siege', p. 2 and TNA, WO 108/284, Vyvyan, 'Defence of Mafeking', p. 3.

these would be extended as far as Fort Ayr, which was built in response to Boer activity during the siege, and used the rising ground about 3.2 km from the town). The defences then snaked back towards and around the stadt, ultimately linking up with Cannon Kopje. Within this outer set of defences were more trenches and redoubts, from which any enemy successfully penetrating the first line could be attacked in the flank. B-P later described this concept as 'a circle of independent earthworks round the town, giving a perimeter of 6 miles [9.7 km] (which was at first considered by some officers to be too large, but which eventually had to be extended to nearly 10 miles [16 km] before the town was out of the enemy's rifle fire)'.[51] Constructing this perimeter was arduous work, as the Eyemouth man stated,

> The little time left at our disposal previous to war being declared, was utilized in making defence works. Sandbag forts with earth thrown up in front, were quickly constructed at all the likely places around the town from which we were likely to be attacked. Trenches were dug, and filled with loose bush, and mines were also laid to hamper the advance of the enemy, in the event of a rush on their part. After a fortnight's hard work (native labour) we considered our little town fairly well fortified. This, however, did not prevent our officers from noticing weak spots, and gradually they have kept up the work of improvement . . . [52]

Vyvyan, an extremely conscientious and industrious officer, assumed responsibility for the defensive arrangements. He sought to make the town and stadt secure before constructing the outer perimeter but ultimately planned to drive back the enemy's advanced trenches. The aim was to

> establish a girdle of outlying forts covering grazing ground for the cattle. The scheme included the provision of bombproof and extensive covered approaches, gun emplacements, drainage etc. In all, some 60 works were constructed and about $6\frac{1}{2}$ miles [10.5 km] of trenches.[53]

Some of the outlying works were dummies, designed 'to draw the enemy's fire', but they were all generally semicircular redans, built with mud walls and sandbags on top, connected by telephone and kept very low. Later many of

51 Baden-Powell 'Preparations for Siege', evidence before *RCWSA*, p. 424; see also Godley, *Life*, p. 74.
52 'An Eyemouth Man in Mafeking', *Berwickshire News*, 17 July 1900, p. 5.
53 TNA, WO 108/284. Vyvyan, 'Defence of Mafeking', pp. 3–4.

them were raised in height, and head cover provided, to offset the difficulties of the long grass, drainage and the inaccuracy of the enemy's shellfire. In fact Vyvyan, who was later the Commanding Engineer, required labour gangs throughout the siege. They built trenches, forts, gun emplacements, and over 200 shelters, repairing many of these places, particularly after the heavy rains of November and December. They also dug wells, constructed saps and forts during the protracted Brickfields operations, and expanded the defences as Mafeking extended its perimeter outwards.[54]

The largest construction, located near the stadt, was the women's laager. It was 'about three-quarters of a mile [1.2 km] to the north west of the town . . . [and] thought to be well out of range of the enemy's fire. It was also well marked with Red Cross flags . . . '.[55] If the laager – 180 yards [164.6 m] long, six foot by four foot in dimension, protected by a roof of three-inch planks, corrugated iron and rammed earth, with entrances every 25 yards [23 m], protected ways and latrines – protected the women and children, it also served to reassure the husbands and fathers in the trenches about the safety of their families. On the eve of war, neither the construction of the women's laager nor the rest of the town's defences were finished. Even by 21 October, Baden-Powell could only describe the bombproofing of the laager and hospital, the two primary civilian requirements, as 'nearly completed'.[56]

Accordingly Mrs. Gustavus Simmonds expressed her fears in letters and fragments of her diary sent to her sister-in-law, Mrs. William L. de Normanville (née Simmonds), wife of the Borough Surveyor of Leamington Spa. After the Boer ultimatum expired on 11 October, she recorded in her diary for 13 October: 'For weeks past armed Boers have been massing on the borders of the Colony. The Bond Government hampered the military in every way. It would not sanction raising a Volunteer Defence Force.' Fortunately, 'One was raised . . . called the Border [*sic*] Protectorate Force, consisting mainly of men who had served in the Imperial and Colonial Forces. They are under experienced Special Service officers, Colonel Baden-Powell being in command.' While reassured by the readiness of 'the townspeople' to form another 'Defence Corps, and all the railway men enrolled as additional corps', she despaired of the enemy within, including 'the stationmaster' (Jimmy Quinlan) who 'refused to take the oath of allegiance; he is said to be a Fenian.

54 Ibid., p. 4; Brent. L., Vyvyan Mss., MS. 147/1/1/22, Vyvyan to his sister Mollie, 21 May 1900, MS. 147/2/2/1, Vyvyan, diary, 18 May 1900, and MS. 147/5/5/4/1, Vyvyan, 'Defence of Mafeking', 20 November 1899.
55 'An Eyemouth Man in Mafeking', *Berwickshire News*, 17 July 1900, p. 5.
56 National Army Museum (NAM), Acc. No. 1968-10-42, Baden-Powell, Staff Diary (hereafter NAM, 1968-10-42, B-P diary), 21 October 1899; see also Baillie, *Mafeking*, p. 10.

Martial law was then proclaimed, and the stationmaster arrested.' Finally, she dreaded an enemy that had seized the next station south of Mafeking, cut the railway line, and 'stopped communication north . . . so there we are cut off and surrounded by Boers'. Although occupational therapy helped, as she joined the five Sisters of Mercy and some ladies in making 'Red Cross armlets for the Ambulance Staff', she described the Boers as unlike 'any civilized nation. It is quite probable they will fire upon the laager; in fact, it is considered so likely that many women and children remain in the Railway Camp, considering it just as safe as the laager.'[57]

The large railway facilities of Mafeking, housing eighteen locomotives, provided their own form of reassurance. The construction of armoured trains, painted in camouflage colours, proved a conspicuous feature of the pre-war preparations. George Waine, who drove an armoured train, wrote home to Whitehaven on 8 October, describing himself as 'the safest man in Mafeking'. His engine with its 'steel plates all around and above' had been tested the previous day, when 40 shots were fired at it from 200 yards [183 m] without endangering the driver, fireman or the superintendent on the footplate. 'The other part of the armoured train', wrote Waine, 'consists of four trucks, fitted with all the latest machine guns.'[58] In fact, the armoured train was more often a two-truck version, as Nurse Crauford remembered one moving 'up and down all night' on the evening of 10 October. 'It is a great clumsy-looking thing', she noted in her diary, 'an engine and trucks, and, of course, very heavy and bulletproof, and painted light brown, so as not to show against the veldt. Captain More has named the trucks the *Firefly* and the *Wasp*. Each is armed with men and a Maxim.'[59]

The railway was also the site of the first shots in the war on 12 October at Kraaipan, 70 km south of Mafeking. A Boer commando under General Koos de la Rey intercepted the armoured train, which was bringing another two guns to Mafeking from Vryburg. Trooper Alexander Kennedy, formerly of Fochabers, Aberdeenshire, was one of the sixteen soldiers on the train. A veteran who had served with the Cameron Highlanders in the Nile campaign of 1884 before joining the Scots Guards, Kennedy now served in 'B' Squadron of the Protectorate Regiment. Under the command of Lieutenant R. H. Nesbitt, his unit had travelled south on H.M. *Mosquito*,

---

57 'Seven Months in Mafeking', *Leamington Spa Courier and Warwickshire Standard* (henceforth *Leamington Spa Courier*), 21 July 1900, p. 8; see also Thomas A. Young diary, 13–14 October 1899, Bottomley, 'A Scots "Salvationist Perspective', pp. 221–2.
58 'The "Safest Man In Mafeking"', *Western Mail*, 4 November 1899, p. 5. His Christian name is misspelt in the newspaper, see Brent. L., Vyvyan Mss., MS. 147/5/1/40, More, 'Railway Report', p. 13.
59 Crauford, 'A Nurse's Diary', p. 58.

successfully escorting the first train of refugees out of Mafeking on 11 October. However, they waited for 24 hours at Vryburg for two guns and ammunition to arrive from Kimberley. Fearful of rail damage, Nesbitt had taken a squad of railway workers with him for the return journey, and when the train neared Kraaipan, Kennedy described how the armoured engine went off the broken line:

> Every effort was made to repair the damage by the gangers in the squad, but after half an hour of hard work the Boers, 1500 [*sic*: 800] strong, opened a terrific fire from all sides, which they continued for $6^1/_2$ hours, during which time they must have fired thousands of rounds of ammunition. The 16 men replied from the armoured train with a brisk fire, which they gallantly kept up, although one after the other fell wounded until only four were left firing.[60]

At daybreak the Boers brought big guns into action, and 'after many misses' they managed to burst the boiler, prompting an immediate surrender. 'Of the 12 wounded', added Trooper Kennedy, 'one died and three were rendered useless for life'.[61]

John Dunphy, formerly of Glengarnock, Ayrshire, did not witness these events but, as the postmaster at Maritzani, the intervening station between Kraaipan and Mafeking, he learned that the rails and telegraph wires had been cut further south. He sent the second train, which was carrying women and children 'to Cape Colony for safety', back to Mafeking and warned Baden-Powell. The Colonel asked him to remain at his post and provide information about the Boer advance, promising the despatch of another armoured train for his 'relief'. Dunphy waited in the vicinity: 'About an hour afterwards 500 of the enemy came riding down to a farm close to the station . . . I waited till it was dark, then the Boers came riding down to the station, tore up the rails and cut the telegraph wires.' Having 'travelled for some hours along the line and found the train was not coming', Dunphy returned to the veld for safety but got lost and was arrested by Boers, who claimed him 'as their first Rooinek prisoner'. Interrogated by General Cronjé, Dunphy was exchanged for a prisoner in Mafeking on the promise that he did not take up a rifle or else would be shown 'no mercy when he [Cronjé] entered Mafeking on the following Monday, which he fully intended to do, as he had 7000 or 8000

60 'A Relieved Prisoner', *Elgin Courant*, 31 July 1900, p. 5.
61 Ibid. For a detailed account of the incident, see Hickman, *Rhodesia Served The Queen*, vol. 1, pp. 104–09.

men and Baden-Powell less than 1000'.[62] B-P was not alone in thinking that he was massively outnumbered at the start of the siege.

Defensive Arrangements

However vexing the loss of Nesbitt's armoured train and its valuable consignment of modern artillery, Baden-Powell and Vyvyan had laid the foundations for a successful defence. 'Trained men' occupied pivotal points along the outer perimeter. The Protectorate Regiment defended the western and south-western defences, with a squadron under Captain Marsh placed in the stadt to support the Barolongs and another squadron held in reserve at the old BSA Police fort, which served as Colonel Hore's headquarters. Walford's BSA Police held Cannon Kopje, with MacKenzie's 'Black Watch' and another group of blacks filling gaps to the left and right of the kopje. Inspector Marsh's division of Cape Police supported this part of the defensive line, while Inspector Browne's division occupied the south east corner of the town. The Bechuanaland Rifles under Captain Cowan held the north and north-west portion of the town, with a reserve in the Town Hall and 'B' squadron under Lieutenant H. B. Gemmell defending the cemetery, 'a gruesome spot' in his opinion, but 'a commanding position in the northern face', which 'had been sandbagged all round'.[63] The untrained men had specific responsibilities, too; the Railway Division under More defended the north and north-west front, including the railway camp, and operated the defence railway, while the Town Guard under Vyvyan held the trenches and defensive positions around the town itself.

Of critical importance was the engagement of the town in its own defence. As Mayor Whiteley maintained, Mafeking was willing to do its 'little best in the way of fortification', and by enrolling in the Town Guard, even before Baden-Powell arrived.[64] But B-P made every effort to sustain this enthusiasm and channel it productively. Once the news was confirmed on 12 October that the railway line and telegraph to the south had been cut, he assembled the Town Guard in the Market Square. Thereupon, as the Eyemouth man recalled, 'after a few words of advice and encouragement from our worthy

---

62 Dunphy later reneged on his promise by joining the Bechuanaland Rifles and serving in the cemetery where he took 'charge of the telephone station'. 'Letter From the Front', *Kilmarnock Standard*, 14 July 1900, p. 8.

63 'The Siege of Mafeking', *Ayr Advertiser*, 23 August 1900, p. 5. Although the author of this extensive letter is anonymous, it is clearly Lieutenant Gemmell as the sole officer in charge of this squadron, see Saunders, *Mafeking Memories*, p. 54. On force dispositions generally, Amery, *Times History*, vol. 4, pp. 575–6.

64 'Memories of Mafeking', *Bradford Daily Argus*, 27 July 1900, p. 4 and 'Mafeking and its Mayor', *Leeds Mercury*, 23 July 1900, p. 3.

commander, Col. Baden-Powell, the men under their respective commanders were marched to the different forts they were to occupy, and there await the approach of the enemy'.[65] Actually, as Neilly reported, the town guardsmen responded with much more enthusiasm than this dour Borderer recalled, especially to B-P's promise that 'if you act as I fully expect you will act, the Boers will never take Mafeking'. Their cheering for Queen and country, B-P and their officers, 'became epidemic and even the negroes who watched threw their ragged headdresses in the air and joined the shouts of the whites'.[66]

Nor did Baden-Powell neglect the importance of female support. On the same day, 12 October, he visited the convent, asking two of the nuns from the Irish Sisters of Mercy 'to go among the women [in the laager] and encourage them to bravery particularly during the firing', while another six should go to the temporary hospitals 'and assist in nursing the wounded'.[67] Baden-Powell also harnessed the willingness of civic and religious elites to support the impending siege: the mayor in managing the women's laager, Magistrate Bell in the welfare of the black community, and Father G. Ogle in urging the nuns to hold themselves 'in readiness to do anything the military officers might ask us'.[68] Baden-Powell understood from the outset that civilian engagement and morale could prove vital in the ensuing days and weeks.

Similarly, in approving the inclusion of the Tshidi-Barolong stadt and the other black refugee villages within the defensive perimeter, and in extending that perimeter to include areas of grazing land, Baden-Powell had taken another fundamental decision about the nature of the forthcoming siege. Black labour would be needed to dig trenches, build gun emplacements and redoubts, and serve as cattle guards, scouts and messengers. He paid for these services (3 shillings a day for men in the works and double for each 24-hours scouting)[69] but still depended upon the loyalty of the local black communities. At an emotional meeting between the Tshidi-Barolong leaders and Magistrate Bell, Chief Morshegare had stripped off his shirt to reveal an old bullet scar from a Boer-Barolong war prior to the British occupation of Bechuanaland, saying: 'I am going to defend my own wife and children. I have got my rifle at home and all I want is ammunition.'[70] Although Baden-Powell, like the magistrate, emphasized that this was to be a white-man's war, he had urged Chief Wessels and the headmen of the Barolong as early as

65 'An Eyemouth Man in Mafeking', *Berwickshire News*, 17 July 1900, p. 5.
66 Neilly, *Besieged with B.-P.*, pp. 27–8.
67 'A Nun's Diary in Mafeking', *Armagh Guardian*, 20 July 1900, pp. 2–3, at p. 2.
68 Ibid.
69 NAM, 1968-10-42, B-P diary, 7 November 1899.
70 Comaroff (ed.), *Diary of Sol T. Plaatje*, pp. 31–2.

2 October to be ready to defend their stadt, a task that could be presented as a defensive measure protecting their families and homes.[71]

Once the war had begun, Cronjé through Dr John E. Dyer, a Boer surgeon, protested on 29 October 1899 about the arming of 'bastards, Fingoes, and Baralongs [*sic*] against us. In this you have committed an enormous act, and one the wickedness of which is certain, and the end of which no man can foresee! You have created a new departure in South African history.'[72] As armed blacks from the Rapulana-Barolong were already serving on Boer sentry duty and blacks had torn up railways and spied for the Boers, the hypocrisy was all too evident. On 30 October, Baden-Powell coolly replied that the 'natives now taking part in the defence of Mafeking' had 'only taken up arms in defence of their homes and cattle, which you have already attempted to shell and to raid'.[73]

He insisted, too, upon the training of military units up to the eve of battle. The Town Guard, as George Green described, practised defending 'the town whilst the Protectorate regiment attacked it'.[74] Corporal Edward Illingworth, a Bradfordian who served in the BSA Police, recalled similar training after arriving in Mafeking on 30 September and moving up with an advanced party to the 'outlying post' of Cannon Kopje on 6 October. Thereafter 'We were all very busy up to the 12th October (the date that war was declared) with mounted parades and sham fights during the day and alarms at night, which necessitated saddling up in the dark and turning out ready for a skirmish.' The 'remainder of our corps', he added, 'came here on the 13th, with the exception of a few NCOs and men, who manned the armoured train'.[75]

Finally, Baden-Powell sought to reassure his troops and the townsfolk as far as possible. Having ostentatiously laid dummy mines to deter the enemy, he then had to deal with two trucks of dynamite that had been intended for Bulawayo but had been left outside the station. On 13 October, he had an engine push these trucks several kilometres outside of the town until the driver, W. Perry, saw Boers advancing whereupon he left the uncoupled trucks and returned to Mafeking. The Boers, thinking that the trucks were full of men, fired on them and detonated a massive explosion, which Goodwin heard

71   Richard H. Nicholson Collection, Hanbury-Tracy Mafeking papers [hereafter Hanbury-Tracy Mss.], record book, 2 October 1899; 'Why Baden-Powell Armed the Baralongs [*sic*]', *South Wales Daily Post*, 19 March 1900, p. 3 and Baden-Powell (Q. 19,875) evidence before *RCWSA*, p. 427.

72   Neilly, *Besieged with B.-P.*, pp. 96–8.

73   Ibid. pp. 99 and 102; see also Hanbury-Tracy Mss., Baden-Powell to Cronjé, 30 October 1899; NAM, 1968-10-42, B-P diary, 30 October 1899 and Jackson, *Boer War*, p. 39.

74   'A Penzance Man Home From Mafeking', *Cornishman*, 26 July 1900, p. 9.

75   'A Bradford Man in Mafeking', *Bradford Daily Telegraph*, 14 June 1900, p. 3.

about 19 km from Mafeking.[76] Baden-Powell also required Mayor Whiteley to reaffirm that martial law, as introduced on the previous day, was now in force, even if all the civilians did not appreciate what this would involve. The detention of the stationmaster, who had a code for messages among his papers, and several suspected spies, may have reassured loyalists but a much greater problem remained as 'more than half the families in the women's laager were Dutch, and of pro-Boer sympathies'.[77] Even some English-speaking colonials, as Thomas A. Young, a 'Salvationist' serving in the Town Guard, discovered, had family fighting with the Boers or, in the case of his bride-to-be, Eliza Maud Mathews, her mother and sister opposed the imperial cause and had to be placed under house arrest.[78] Given these divisions, Baden-Powell could hardly alleviate the anxiety that set in after the ultimatum expired. As Mrs. Simmonds noted in her diary for 13 October, 'The intense tension of the last two days has been terrible', a view echoed by Lieutenant Gemmell, who recalled that this 'was a time of anxiety, such as I hope never to have to pass through again'.[79] The waiting would soon end with the first skirmish on 14 October and the opening of the Boer bombardment two days later.

76 'The Siege of Mafeking. Interesting Letters', *Leicester Chronicle and Leicestershire Mercury*, 1 September 1900, p. 4; see also Crauford, 'A Nurse's Diary', pp. 60–1, Willan (ed.), *Edward Ross*, p. 17 and on mines, Hamilton, *Siege of Mafeking*, pp. 51–2.
77 'B-P's report', p. 897; see also Willan (ed.), *Edward Ross*, p. 16.
78 Bottomley, 'A Scots "Salvationist"', pp. 218 and 248–9.
79 'Seven Months in Mafeking', *Leamington Spa Courier*, 21 July 1900, p. 8 and 'The Siege of Mafeking', *Ayr Advertiser*, 23 August 1900, p. 5.

Chapter 4

Delivering 'Kicks' and Bluffing the Boers

In his accounts of the siege Baden-Powell repeatedly claimed that he tried to conduct an aggressive defence, delivering 'kicks' to the enemy whenever possible or his scarce resources allowed. In his post-siege report he listed these operations in succession, presenting an impression of sustained action, and later asserted that 'aggression is the soul of defence'.[1] However excellent an axiom in general and, if carefully calibrated, a means by which a much smaller force can deter, deflect or even demoralize a much larger, if poorly led, adversary, it was never the prime concern in Mafeking. Even when most of these 'kicks' occurred, that is, on seven occasions (14, 17, 20, 25, 27, 31 October and 7 November 1899)[2] during the 'Cronjé phase' of the siege (until he departed with the bulk of the burghers on 18 November), Baden-Powell had more immediate priorities. Given the acute vulnerability of Mafeking and the vast preponderance of firepower converging on the town, he had to bluff the enemy that his defences were much more formidable than they actually were. At the same time he had to ensure that the besieged, both military and civilian, were reasonably protected, fed and motivated to endure an investment of unknown intensity and uncertain duration. This involved not merely enduring the physical assault of the enemy, including an artillery bombardment, long-range rifle fire and periodic attacks or threatened attacks, but also the psychological pressure, which could be internally or externally generated. How Mafeking responded during the opening days of the siege, the remainder of the 'Cronjé phase', and its immediate aftermath would determine the viability of B-P's strategy and set the foundations for a successful defence.

Opening Days, 14–24 October 1899

The siege began with a 'kick' at Five-Mile Bank at 5.30 a.m. on 14 October, when a reconnaissance patrol led by Lord Charles Cavendish Bentinck encountered a strong party of Boers near the railway about 4.8 km north of

---

1   Major-General R. S. S. Baden-Powell, *Sketches in Mafeking & East Africa* (London: Smith Elder, 1907), p. 27; see also 'B-P report', pp. 891 and 897–900.
2   'B-P report', p. 891.

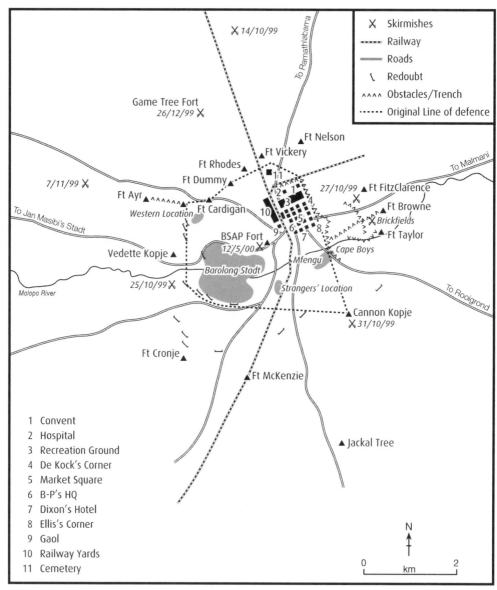

Map 2 Mafeking Besieged

Mafeking. After firing a couple of volleys, the patrol promptly retired and, in the process, passed the armoured train that Baden-Powell had ordered 'to rush the Boers and pour a heavy fire into them, as I wanted to make the first blow felt by them to be a really hard one'.[3] Commanded by Captain Ashley

3   Ibid., p. 898.

Williams, the train carried the 1-pounder Hotchkiss and a .303 Maxim and was manned by fifteen troopers from the BSA Police and some railway staff, with Waine driving the engine. By 6.30 a.m. the train engaged about 400 Boers, who had a Krupp gun and a Vickers-Maxim. As the fire sounded so heavy, Baden-Powell despatched 'D' Squadron of the Protectorate Regiment under Captain Charles FitzClarence to provide support. Finding the train hard pressed by vastly superior numbers, FitzClarence dismounted his men, and protected by the train on his left, manoeuvred to keep the enemy at bay and repulsed several attempts to encircle him. A Protectorate trooper, Bernard Short, formerly of Forest Hill, London, wrote that

> I was in the first fight. We found the enemy had crossed the border, and were advancing on Mafeking when they were surprised by us. The firing was very hot; we were within 500 yards [457 m] of them, and finally made them retire. I had some very narrow escapes, but was not wounded.[4]

In fact, Baden-Powell had had to send another troop led by Lord Charles Bentinck with a 7-pounder gun to cover the retirement of the train and FitzClarence's squadron after the four-hour engagement. For this operation, and two others, FitzClarence would be awarded the Victoria Cross, specifically for 'personal coolness and courage' that inspired confidence in his partially-trained men. He would be commended for a 'bold and efficient' handling of his men that not only relieved the armoured train but also inflicted a heavy defeat on the enemy, while suffering two fatalities and sixteen wounded (two of whom later died). B-P claimed that this 'smartly fought little engagement had a great and lasting moral effect on the enemy'.[5]

Privately Baden-Powell was less impressed. He worried about the risks that FitzClarence had run on this occasion, particularly in allowing himself 'to get too far out' without orders (and support).[6] Journalists confirmed that the Colonel had sent a cyclist and a despatch rider (Major Baillie himself) with orders for FitzClarence to retire at once, and Hamilton, who had joined 'D' squadron, criticized the advance in extended order, without supplies, artillery or even ambulances. As the Boers withdrew to a ridge from which they could cover every unit, Hamilton reckoned that they committed an 'extraordinary'

---

4   'A Forest Hill Man in Mafeking', *Kentish Mercury*, 11 May 1900, p. 3; see also 'An Edington Soldier on the Siege of Mafeking', *Somerset County Gazette*, 15 September 1900, p. 7.
5   'B-P report', p. 898; see also 'The Victoria Cross', *Morning Post*, 7 July 1900, p. 3 and *Official History*, vol. 3, pp. 147–8.
6   NAM, 1968-10-42, B-P diary, 15 October 1899; see also Jeal, *Baden-Powell*, p. 237.

blunder in ceasing fire. Had they not done so, he asserted, 'they might have wiped Squadron "D" out of existence', and he berated FitzClarence for his 'inopportune acts of gallantry'.[7] How far the Boers suffered from the skirmish was also disputed, as the notion of fifty-three killed came from a black spy in the Boer camp, while the Boers only acknowledged three casualties.[8] The latter was probably correct but the action had boosted morale within Mafeking, where the troops received 'a hearty cheer' on their return.[9] Four women heard the cheering and ran out to greet them: 'We waved to them', noted Nurse Crauford, 'and cheered them, and they looked so tired, but smiled and waved their caps when they saw us. It was sad to see the riderless horse.'[10]

With an eye for detail, Protectorate NCOs sought to learn lessons from the skirmish: as Corporal Thomas Dowson, formerly of Cockerton, a suburb of Darlington, observed, 'The fight lasted four hours. I was one of six corporals in the field that day, and strange to say, four were killed.'[11] 'The wily enemy', reckoned Corporal Rose, 'had noted the broad red stripes on the arms of these men, and had deliberately selected their victims. Thereafter the stripes were removed before going into action.'[12] Finally, as Major Godley shrewdly commented, 'the Boers held off' after this fight, 'and did not molest the town until eleven days later, during which valuable time the defences, which had hitherto been of the flimsiest description, were greatly strengthened'.[13]

The massing of at least 5,600 Boers initially in three large camps round the town provided a powerful incentive. The Marico Commando under General J. P. (Koos) Snyman and the Scandinavian Corps based themselves at McMullin's farm about 4 km east of Mafeking; the Rustenburg Commando split with some under Commandant P. S. Steenekamp encamped near Signal Hill and the remainder north-east of the reservoir; and Cronjé's Potchefstroom Commando encamped at Rietfontein, 5 km to the south of the town. Subsequently detachments of Boers established laagers to the west, south-west and north-west of Mafeking, including at Game Tree Fort (which they named as Platboomfort), 2.3 km north of the town and 800 m west of the railway. They also brought up their impressive artillery, which as *The Times* historian described was 'in every way superior to that of the defenders. At first

---

7   Hamilton, *Siege of Mafeking*, pp. 58–61 and Baillie, *Mafeking*, p. 18.
8   NAM, 1968-10-42, B-P diary, 15 October 1899 and Amery, *Times History*, vol. 3, p. 579.
9   'An Eyemouth Man in Mafeking', *Berwickshire News*, 17 July 1900, p. 5.
10   Crauford, 'A Nurse's Diary in Besieged Mafeking', *Crampton's Magazine*, vol. 16 (1900), p. 61.
11   'A Mafeking Hero', *North Star*, 6 July 1900, p. 3.
12   'A Hero of Mafeking: Aberdeenshire Man on the Siege', *(Aberdeen) Evening Express*, 28 August 1900, p. 5.
13   Godley, *Life*, p. 73.

they reportedly had 'two 7 pdrs, one 12 pdr, one 9 pdr, Krupp, two quick-firing 14 pdrs, and a pom pom, all fitted with a breech-loading action,'[14] but altered their ordnance throughout the siege. On 23 October they brought forward the formidable 155mm Creusot breech-loading siege gun, capable of firing a 94 lb (43 kg) shell over 10,000 m, and replaced the guns, which Cronjé withdrew in November, by others, including the two 7-pounder Mark IV rifled muzzle-loading guns captured at Kraaipan. Confirming the need for the Creusot was the outcome of first Boer bombardment from Signal Hill on 16 October, which was sustained over five hours without any reply from the garrison. After the barrage ceased at 1 p.m., the Boers sent an emissary to request the surrender of the town 'to avoid further bloodshed', Baden-Powell replied: 'But we haven't had any yet.'[15]

Given the widespread panic when the shelling began, B-P's coolness in the face of explosions, his confidence that 'Mafeking will not be taken' and his disdain for the Boer emissary, laughing, as the Eyemouth man surmised, 'at the Dutchman's audacity', boosted morale.[16] Even more important was the relatively mild impact of the five-hour cannonade. Shells fell either in the veld or if in town, as the observant Nun described, in the 'considerable' distances between buildings and the 'remarkably wide' streets, or passing straight through the 'soft' mud-brick buildings, and detonating, if at all, when they burrowed into the sandy ground.[17] Only in the two-storey convent was there any chance of people suffering from the collapse of an upper storey, and taking shelter could avoid the risk of injuries from shrapnel, if not from direct hits. Yet the 'very ineffective and amusing bombardment'[18] of the first day was important in other respects: it prompted Cronjé to tighten the siege by seizing the waterworks, and severing the town's principal water supply, while calling for the assistance of the Creusot siege gun. It also expanded the defensive requirements of the town, since the Boer gunners had not respected the Red-Cross flags over the convent, hospital, and women's laager.

Baden-Powell had anticipated the loss of the waterworks, urging people to conserve water before the siege, fill the tanks of railway engines, dig out wells, and rely on supplies from the Molopo River. He had the invaluable services of an Aberdonian plumber, W. C. Smith, and his team. They used the

---

14 Amery, *Times History*, vol. 4, pp. 579–80. The Boers only had 'five Krupp cannons and three Maxim machine-guns' initially, Pretorius, 'The Besiegers' in Smith (ed.), *Siege of Mafeking*, vol. 1, p. 71.

15 NAM, 1968-10-42, B-P diary, 16 October 1899.

16 'An Eyemouth Man in Mafeking', *Berwickshire News*, 17 July 1900, p. 5; see also Crauford, 'A Nurse's Diary', p. 64; Midgley, *Petticoat in Mafeking*, pp. 28 and 30; and Jeal, *Baden-Powell*, p. 239.

17 'A Nun's Diary in Mafeking', *Armagh Guardian*, 27 July 1900, p. 3.

18 Hamilton, *Siege of Mafeking*, p. 72.

railway steam pump to keep the railway overhead tank filled for the purpose of watering the horses, and also monitored and repaired, when necessary, the pumps at individual wells, including a new well dug during the siege. The task, as Smith admitted, required working 'all hours of the night and morning' as some of the pumps 'were outside our lines'.[19]

Responding to the attacks on buildings flying Red-Cross flags was more troublesome. As the Nun recorded in her diary for 16 October,

> it looked as if our lovely new building was the target at which most of the shells were aimed; a number fell in the garden and about the grounds. The boarders' refectory was laid out as a ward for the wounded, this was struck twice, two immense holes were made in the walls; another came through the roof, made holes in the wall and broke the windows in one of the sister's cells . . . . During this time the armoured train was stationed quite close to the convent; as soon as we appeared in the grounds the men cheered us again and again. They said their blood was boiling when they saw the shells coming down on us. They asked their Captain to let them fire on the enemy as they were in a position to reach them but the orders of the Colonel were 'No firing during the shelling.' . . . During the evening the house was crowded with visitors including the Colonel, Lord Cecil, Lord Bentinck and nearly all the officers to see the rooms that had been shelled and to congratulate us on our bravery and happy escape. [Two days later, 18 October] The rooms struck by shells [were] photographed by several of the correspondents.[20]

Baden-Powell both protested over the firing on buildings flying Red-Cross flags and authorized the excavation of shelters for the convent and hospital.[21] This work added to the bombproofing and ventilation of the women's laager, and the building of trenches, forts and other bombproof shelters. John Poole, formerly of Hungerford, who was the assistant foreman overseer for Vyvyan, described his duties as making 'gun emplacements, sand-bag forts, trenches, etc., etc., very risky work. Some of it had to be done in the night whilst the enemy were pulling off volleys in the direction of the noise made by pick

19 'Aberdeen Plumber in Mafeking', *(Aberdeen) Evening Express*, 4 July 1900, p. 2; NAM, 1968-10-42, B-P diary, 17 October 1899; Brent. L., Vyvyan Mss., MS. 147/5/1/40, More, 'Railway Report', p. 5 and MS. 147/2/3/1, Vyvyan diary, 9 and 12 March, 9 April 1900.
20 'A Nun's Diary in Mafeking', *Armagh Guardian*, 20 July 1900, p. 2.
21 Hanbury-Tracy Mss., Baden-Powell to Cronjé, 21 October 1899; see also Godley, *Life*, p. 74.

and shovel.'[22] The work also included the construction of a dummy fort to the north of town, with dummy guns, crew and two huge flagstaffs, which attracted a 'perfect hurricane of shells' on the following day until the Boer gunners realized their blunder.[23] Another 'bluff', as Sergeant J. W. S. Lowe recalled, was his posting with one other companion, armed with the town's only Nordenfeldt machine-gun in an isolated trench 2.4 km from town. As a former gunner in the Royal Navy, Lowe had 'to draw the Boer fire away from the town. The trench had to be rebuilt every morning for six weeks, so determined was the effort of the enemy to silence his fire.'[24]

Defensively Baden-Powell was delighted that his system of alarms, initially by bugle, had been taken to heart by the citizenry. As early as 17 October the alarm left the town, he claimed, 'entirely deserted within a few minutes', and the spectacle, as described by Thomas Morse, was akin to 'rabbits trying to escape from the sportsman's dog'.[25] The trenches were also taking shape: Mrs Simmonds had to abandon the pits in the railway shed as they were declared unsafe, but found new trenches near the engineer's office on 22 October, lined with 'tarpaulin and covered with sacks and bushes. We are all ready, food and drink packed, and at 4.30 a.m. we are to set forth.' She preferred this option to the women's laager where the 'ants are very troublesome' and the adults and children suffered from 'sore eyes'.[26] The Nun was simply fascinated by the 'natives' digging

> trenches in several parts of the town, they are about 5½ feet [1.67 m] deep, 6 foot [1.82 m] broad, and long enough to accommodate the number intended, the one prepared for the sisters being about 50 feet [15.2 m] in length, they are covered with corrugated iron, sand bags and clay, the air and light comes from openings in the sides; into these all will be obliged to retire while the shell is going off.[27]

---

22 'Inside Mafeking', *Newbury Weekly News*, 12 July 1900, p. 2.

23 Godley, *Life*, p. 74.

24 'With B.-P. in Mafeking', *Lloyd's Weekly Newspaper*, 21 October 1900, p. 2.

25 NAM, 1968-10-42, B-P diary, 17 October 1899 and 'A Stroud Man Home From Mafeking', *Stroud Journal*, 10 August 1900, p. 3.

26 'Seven Months in Mafeking', *Leamington Spa Courier*, 21 July 1900, p. 8. Sickness and ophthalmia became major concerns, especially among the children living in the laager, Crauford, 'A Nurse's Diary in Besieged Mafeking', *Crampton's Magazine*, vol. 17 (1901), pp. 37–42, at p. 42 and Dr Tom Hayes, diary, 18 October and 15 and 21 November 1899, in Bottomley (ed.), 'Siege of Mafeking and the Imperial Mindset', pp. 38, 65 and 68.

27 'A Nun's Diary in Mafeking', *Armagh Guardian*, 20 July 1900, p. 3.

Even when her trench was made bombproof, 'covered with railway sleepers, sandbags and gravel', and had entrances 'screened with sandbags', Mrs. Simmonds found it 'very damp and chilly. The doctor has sent us some quinine tabloids, with a message that all had better take some.'[28]

While this construction was underway, alarms tested the response of the defenders, whereupon, as George Green recalled, town guardsmen 'at once proceeded to the redoubts which had been previously erected all round the town'. These nightly alarms, sometimes in dreadful weather, often lasted for several hours.[29] At the same time Baden-Powell developed his style of command. He regularly visited the perimeter outposts at night, as well as the wounded, the nuns and the women's laager by day, exuding a cheerful optimism to sustain morale. He personally supervised the improvement of the ventilation system in the women's laager, and removed those Dutch women, who had been spreading defeatist talk in the laager, throwing them 'bag & baggage' into jail.[30] He was attentive, too, to the finer points of detail in the defence; discussing matters with his senior officers, ensuring the concealment of the camouflaged armoured train, and insisting that loopholes in the trenches be widened to 122 cm to expand the range of fire without compromising safety. Civilians and soldiers alike were soon appreciating his visits: Green, who lost a leg after handling an unexploded shell, affirmed that 'The gallant colonel, in spite of the onus on his shoulders, was a most diligent and kind inquirer after the progress of all those placed *hors de combat*',[31] while Corporal Rose recalled his inspections of the outlying forts, often accompanied by Lord Edward Cecil:

> These officers never passed a man, however humble his rank, without a pleasant 'Good morning" and Baden-Powell was always cheery and buoyant in manner. To see him, during his brief moments of leisure, leaning against the door of his private office, with hands in pockets generally whistling, one would have thought he had not a care in the world. But he would spend whole days on lookout on the top of Dixon's Hotel, when he had reason to believe that another Boer move was in prospect.[32]

---

28 'Seven Months in Mafeking', *Leamington Spa Courier*, 21 July 1900, p. 8.
29 'A Penzance Man Home From Mafeking', *Cornishman*, 26 July 1900, p. 5.
30 NAM, 1968-10-42, B-P diary, 19, 21 and 29 October 1899; Brent. L., Vyvyan Mss., MS. 147/2/2/1, Vyvyan, diary, 19 October 1899.
31 'A Penzance Man Home From Mafeking', *Cornishman*, 26 July 1900, p. 5; NAM, 1968-10-42, B-P diary, 16 October 1899; Amery, *Times History*, vol. 4, p. 581.
32 'A Hero of Mafeking: Aberdeenshire Man on the Siege', *(Aberdeen) Evening Express*, 28 August 1900, p. 5.

The 'Cronjé Phase' of Operations

Cronjé marked his investment of Mafeking by adding the powerful Creusot siege gun to his artillery and authorizing its first bombardment on 24 October. Known as 'Long Tom' in Natal, it had never been used on the western border and received various nicknames from the besieged, such as 'Big Ben', 'Grietje' or 'old Creechy'. Initially fired from the southern side of town, the gun emitted 'a tremendous cloud of smoke'[33] as it delivered the first of its 1,497 shells upon Mafeking, and the population scattered. Despite the massive size of these 94lb projectiles, there was no loss of life and 'everyone', wrote Corporal Hulse, 'began to gain confidence, and soon there was a brisk trade down in splinters of shells . . . to keep as curios'.[34] Yet three people were wounded, including Trooper Bernard Short, who was caught 'with terrific force' by a shell fragment 'as big as my fist . . . just below my knee, breaking my shin bone, splintering other bones in my leg, and making a very ugly wound'. He would be tied to a bed in splints for four weeks before the leg could be put into plaster of Paris, and always walked with a limp thereafter.[35] The Eyemouth man thought that they had been quite lucky as 'no strict lookout' was kept at first when so many of the shells from the first position 'landed in open ground'. Doubtless he spoke for many when he stated that 'the whistling sound of the shell in flight and the concussion of the explosion, if anywhere near, was a very unpleasant sensation'.[36] The physical damage could be considerable: as Mrs. Simmonds described when

> a 94-pounder came into our neighbour's house, smashed the front door to match-wood, knocked a hole about 8ft. [244 cm] square into the bedroom, demolished the door, and made short work of toilet crockery, ricocheted into the kitchen, smashed another door, blew out the window, and smothered the whole place in dust. Fortunately for us it didn't burst, but it gave us all a fearful fright.[37]

The Colonel could neither mitigate the psychological effects of 'Big Ben' nor prevent the physical damage but he improved the warning and alarm system. As the countryside was so flat, observed Lieutenant Gemmell, 'we could always see the big gun', so using lookout positions and powerful telescopes warning could be given using 'the Roman Catholic bell' . . . .

33   Hamilton, *Siege of Mafeking*, p. 80.
34   'The Siege of Mafeking', *Penistone Express*, 20 July 1899, p. 6.
35   'A Forest Hill Man in Mafeking', *Kentish Mercury*, 11 May 1900, p. 3.
36   'An Eyemouth Man in Mafeking', *Berwickshire News*, 17 July 1900, p. 5.
37   'War Letters. Lady's Letter from Mafeking. Downright Hungry', *Sheffield and Rotherham Independent*, 14 May 1900, p. 5.

First, when the look-out men saw the gunner loading the gun, 12 strokes were given on the bell; then when she was pointed, 6 strokes if directed at some of the outer defences and 3 strokes if at the town. Then when fired a handbell was rung, and this was taken up by a number of handbells all over the place . . . Altogether during the $6^{1}/_{2}$ months that the big gun was here she fired between 1400 and 1500 shells into Mafeking.[38]

If this alarm system and the bombproof facilities provided protection and reassurance against the effects of 'Big Ben', Baden-Powell could do little about the quick-firing weapons. He broadly agreed with Trooper Snook, who conceded that the 'big gun . . . did not do much damage, but that they had a $12^{1}/_{2}$ lb. quick-firing one. That was a beast . . . but worst of all was the 1lb. Maxim, called the Pom-pom.'[39] Just as galling was the long-range rifle fire: as Lieutenant Gemmell observed,

What we suffered most from in the early days of the siege was the continual rifle fire from the Boer trenches all round the town: when they were not volleying they were sniping at any living thing they could see, and to get about at all in the daytime was attended with great risk.[40]

Given these threats, it was imperative that the defenders responded to the Boer tactics of extending their entrenchments round the town and moving them inwards. Yet the four muzzle-loading guns under the command of Major F. W. Panzera were aptly described as 'miserable, both in quantity and quality'; they not only lacked the range of the enemy's guns but were also handicapped by 'worn rifling, dilapidated carriages, and rusty elevating gear'.[41] B-P had

---

38 'The Siege of Mafeking', *Ayr Advertiser*, 23 August 1900, p. 5. For a full account of the gun's impact, see Changuion, *Silence of the Guns*, pp. 36–43, 72–6, 96.
39 'An Edington Soldier on the Siege of Mafeking', *Somerset County Gazette*, 15 September 1900, p. 7; see also B-P, 'Use of Artillery', evidence before *RCWSA*, p. 424 and on the 'very little execution' of 'Big Ben', even when its gunners varied their tactics to defeat the warning system, NAM, 1968-10-42, B-P diary, 14 November 1899.
40 'The Siege of Mafeking', *Ayr Advertiser*, 23 August 1900, p. 5; and on the 'galling' rifle fire, see NAM, 1968-10-42, B-P diary, 9 November 1899 and the effects of the Mausers, T. Hayes, diary, 18 December 1899, in Bottomley (ed.), 'Siege of Mafeking and the Imperial Mindset', p. 87.
41 H. W. Wilson, *With The Flag to Pretoria: A History of the Boer War, 1899-1900*, 2 vols (London: Harmsworth, 1901), vol. 2, p. 599. B-P also worried about the fuses that had shrunk with age and had to be wedged in with paper, NAM, 1968-10-42, B-P diary, 31 October 1899.

to improvise, authorizing the manufacture of gunpowder, shells and fuses for the guns in the ordnance workshops, and moving the guns around at night. Seeking to maximize their surprise effects, he concealed their flash by firing them through blankets. Periodically he sent them out on nightly raids, and, on the eve of the arrival of 'Big Ben', sent a party, including Corporal Illingworth, 'to advance with one of our 7 pounders and stir up the enemy. We did stir them up with a vengeance. I was with the gun, and we put 15 shells into their earthworks at 2,000 yards [1,829 m] range.'[42]

Meanwhile Mafeking faced its first major assault on 25 October, an action preceded by the sustained bombardment of seven guns from south-west, east, and north-west from 6.30 a.m. to midday. Baden-Powell, who had received warning on the previous day that 'about 2000 to 3000 Boers' were massing opposite the 'native stadt' from 'SW 2 miles [3.2 km] distant', moved a troop from the reserve squadron of the Protectorate Regiment into the stadt, with orders 'not to allow firing until the enemy are close up'. So when the enemy, after several feinted attacks elsewhere, advanced on the stadt, and fired from long range at first, they only encountered periodic fire from Maxims. At closer range they encountered a fusillade of rifle fire from 'men under cover in their trenches', namely the Protectorate troops and the Barolongs using their Snider rifles.[43] Interestingly, in light of what Baden-Powell later said in his testimony before the royal commission, he admitted in his post-siege report that 'The Boers had expected the Baralongs not to fire on them, and so advanced more openly than they would otherwise have done; nor had they expected to find white men defending the stadt.' He surmised that their loss may have been 'pretty heavy'[44] but this was pure conjecture, as the enemy was moving through 'low bush'. 'Casualties on our side', he added in his diary, were '1 man wounded, 2 horses and 8 mules. Damage to buildings slight though it is estimated that about 250 to 300 shells were fired during the day.'[45]

This rebuff for Cronjé at the supposedly weak link in Mafeking's defences was followed by a bayonet attack, led by Captain FitzClarence, two nights later upon an advanced Marico trench that had come within 1,830 m of the eastern defences. It proved a night to remember: 'something I shall never forget to my dying day', wrote Trooper Dowson. The 57-man squadron 'got orders':

---

42 'A Bradford Man in Mafeking', *Bradford Daily Telegraph*, 14 June 1900, p. 3; see also Baillie, *Mafeking*, pp. 32–3; Baden-Powell (Q. 19,914) evidence before *RCWSA*, p. 429; and 'B-P report', p. 893.

43 NAM, 1968-10-42, B-P diary, 24 and 25 October 1899.

44 'B-P report', p. 898.

45 NAM, 1968-10-42, B-P diary, 25 October 1899.

to parade at 8 o'clock [*sic*: probably 9 p.m] to go take a Boer trench on the racecourse. When we formed up the captain [FitzClarence] told us we had the honour of being chosen to do the work 'something to be proud of'. Here we were served out with a badge something in the shape of a white rag tied round the left arm, so as to know each other in the dark. From thence we set out, three deep, distance being 1¹/₂ miles [2.4 km]. As we marched through Mafeking the people seemed to give us a look of sympathy, or as I might put it, poor devils; and Father Ogle walked along . . . and told us the hand of the Lord was with us in our work. After we marched about a mile [1.6 km] we came to a halt and fixed bayonets. Then on we went. The captain led us as straight as an arrow on an hour's march in the dark to the trench. Then the word came, left turn, charge, and then we cheered and the Boers yelled. Those who were there will never forget it.[46]

The surprise was less complete than Dowson recalled, as on the brink of the attack Boer guards heard a noise, and fired a volley, forcing the troopers to fall flat. FitzClarence shouted 'charge', whereupon they jumped up and plunged into the trench.[47] Trooper Snook remembered that 'the shower of lead was fearful', complicated by Boers firing into their own trench and the covering fire of two detachments of Cape Police from different angles. After a loud whistle, the squadron withdrew guided by two lights shining out from the town but, on returning, 'had to fall in again, as we thought they were going to rush the town, but they had not the pluck, so we went to our trenches and had a sleep'.[48]

'We didn't lose but six killed and two wounded', claimed Corporal Harry Kelland, formerly of the 17th Lancers, 'but the Boer loss must have been many more.'[49] Apart from the six killed, nine men, including FitzClarence, had been wounded and two taken prisoner, but the returning troops thought that the enemy had suffered heavier casualties from the bayoneting and friendly fire. Although Baden-Powell only observed three corpses being buried by the Boers on 29 October, he later claimed that Boer casualties may have been as

46 'A Cockerton Man's Mafeking Experiences', *Northern Echo*, 6 July 1900, p. 3.
47 'A Nun's Diary in Mafeking', *Armagh Guardian*, 27 July 1900, p. 3; see also Crauford, 'A Nurse's Diary', p. 38 and Jeal, *Baden-Powell*, p. 241 differ from the *Official History*, vol. 3, p. 152.
48 'An Edington Soldier on the Siege of Mafeking', *Somerset County Gazette*, 15 September 1900, p. 7.
49 'Corporal Kelland of Combwich and the Siege of Mafeking', *Somerset County Gazette*, 11 August 1900, p. 3.

high as 100 from a combination of bayonet and rifle fire.[50] This was certainly a gross exaggeration, despite the boasts of the Protectorate men, including FitzClarence who claimed several victims with his sword, and the screams of the Boers, which were heard in Mafeking. Three fatalities may be accurate but the Marico Boers were so unnerved by the assault that they abandoned the trench for many months.[51]

Meanwhile Cronjé planned his most formidable assault of the siege, aimed at storming Cannon Kopje and breaching Mafeking's southern defences. At daylight on 31 October the Boer artillery launched a heavy and accurate crossfire on the fort from the racecourse (east), the south-eastern heights, and Jackal Tree (south-west). The shelling smashed parts of the parapet, the supports of the lookout tower, and cut communications with headquarters. The fort lacked any shellproof cover and was only lightly held by the BSA Police colonel and one or two lookout men. Colonel Walford lived in a small hole within the fort, while the bulk of his 45-man garrison and machine-gun section remained in a slit trench about 36 m to the rear. Under cover of the bombardment, the burghers of the Potchefstroom Commando advanced in three converging parties, possibly about 700 men in all. They ran forward, then dropped into the long grass to pour rifle fire into the fort, and rose again. Only when they had reached about 360 m from the fort at nearly 6 a.m., with the foremost line digging a shallow trench, did Walford order his men to engage the enemy. Heavily outnumbered, the BSA Police officers and men were dreadfully exposed as they rushed forward and brought their two Maxims into action.

Corporal Illingworth described the three-hour engagement as 'the warmest corner during the siege. I have been under fire before, but never under a cross fire of shells and bullets such as this was. We lost heavily for so small a number of men – two captains, two sergeant-majors, and four men killed outright, and three wounded.' He didn't mention the 7-pounder gun under Lieutenant Kenneth Murchison, which Baden-Powell sent up in support, but expressed satisfaction in seeing the enemy retire 'beaten' by about 8.30 a.m. and gallop off on their horses. Apart from a minor injury, he had escaped 'scot free', despite fighting behind a 'low wall about four feet [1.2m] high topped with sand bags'. 'Captain the Hon. D. Marsham', he observed, 'was killed a few feet on my right, and a trooper was also shot dead next to me on the left'.

---

50   NAM, 1968-10-42, B-P diary, 29 October 1899 and 'B-P report', p. 898.

51   Hamilton, *Siege of Mafeking*, p. 90; Charles Bell, *The Mafeking Siege Diary of Charles Bell (Magistrate) 1899-1900*, 27 October 1899, p. 12; 'An Eyemouth Man in Mafeking', *Berwickshire News*, 17 July 1900, p. 5; Amery, *Times History*, vol. 4, p. 583; and T. Hayes, diary, 27 October 1899, in Bottomley (ed.), 'Siege of Mafeking and the Imperial Mindset', p. 47.

Illingworth was convinced that the enemy must have suffered heavily as 'their ambulance waggons were very busy for an hour or two'.[52] He was hugely proud of the victory: 'Ours is the most exposed post of all, likewise the post of honour, with no retreat. It was Cronje and his men who attacked us, and . . . it was an honour to have repulsed him, horse, foot, and artillery with our small body'. He appreciated, too, that Baden-Powell 'came up after the fight' and 'said it was one of the coolest and pluckiest bits of work under the hottest shell fire that he has ever seen'.[53]

Baden-Powell not only congratulated the survivors in person but also commended them in General Orders, lauding their 'gallant resistance' in the face of 'a very large force' that threatened the south-east portion of the town.[54] This only partially mollified those grieving over the heavy losses, including the highly-popular officers Captains Douglas Marsham and Charles Pechell, and men, such as Trooper F. R. Lloyd, who 'was a great favourite' in the hospital, where he had helped with the wounded while recovering from a bout of fever. In the battle he had been mortally wounded assisting a wounded man: 'all say', claimed the Nun, 'he was the most unselfish man they ever knew'.[55] Even more shocking was news of a drunken quarrel on the evening of 1 November between one of the heroes of the battle, Lieutenant Murchison, and Ernest Parslow of the *Daily Chronicle*, which ended with Murchison shooting Parslow dead. Murchison, whom Tom Hayes thought had gone insane, was later sentenced to death by court-martial before Milner commuted the sentence to penal servitude for life.[56]

Controversy erupted after the battle over the defences of Cannon Kopje, which Magistrate Bell described as 'a miserable place oddly constructed and quite inadequate for what is required of it'.[57] Trooper Arthur Williams, another BSA Policeman, explained that although the fort was 'the key to the

---

52　'A Bradford Man in Mafeking', *Bradford Daily Telegraph*, 14 June 1900, p. 3. Although he is supported by Amery, *Times History*, vol. 4, p. 585, which asserted that 'In this engagement the Boers lost more heavily than usual', Boer sources record only one killed and five wounded, Pretorius, 'The Besiegers', in Smith (ed.), *Siege of Mafeking*, vol. 1, p. 72.

53　'A Bradford Man in Mafeking', *Bradford Daily Telegraph*, 14 June 1900, p. 3; see also 'B-P report', p. 899 and *Official History*, vol. 3, pp. 153–4.

54　NAM, 1968-10-42, B-P diary, 1 November 1899; see also *Mafeking Mail*, 1 November 1899.

55　'A Nun's Diary in Mafeking', *Armagh Guardian*, 27 July 1900, p. 3; see also Crauford, 'A Nurse's Diary', p. 39.

56　'A Mafeking Tragedy', *Jackson's Oxford Journal*, 11 August 1900, p. 4; see also T. Hayes, diary, 2 November in Bottomley (ed.), 'The Siege of Mafeking and the Imperial Mindset', p. 55; Crauford, 'A Nurse's Diary', pp. 39–40; and 'A Nun's Diary in Mafeking', *Armagh Guardian*, 27 July 1900, p. 3.

57　Bell, 'Diary', 31 October 1899, p. 14; see also Hamilton, *Siege of Mafeking*, p. 97 and Gardner, *Mafeking*, p. 76.

town', it was 'not the best round here, there are too many rocks'. Accordingly, when attacked by 'Cronje's invincibles',

> We were terribly handicapped having to run a hundred yards [91 m] under hot fire from bomb-proof to fort. Both our Maxims were dismounted at the time, and we were not at all prepared. But we soon got 'under way', and poured volleys from our Lee Enfields into them. Our Maxims also found the range, and laid a few out.[58]

Conversely he reckoned that the enemy's concentrated shellfire, later calculated at 104 projectiles, the heaviest of the siege up to that date, and its 1lb. Maxim, accounted for most of the BSA Police's casualties. He believed, too, that the Boers may have used ambulance waggons to cover their retreat. As soon as they raised the Red-Cross flag, 'we had orders to cease fire. Had we not had this order we could have killed a lot more in their retreat, but they quickly took advantage of their ambulance waggons and cleared.'[59]

If Cronjé abandoned the option of a frontal assault after this battle, he resolved to tighten the cordon around Mafeking by extending the western defences and moving the Scandinavian Corps into the brickfields on the east, where they built a fort of railway tracks and sleepers. Weakening the enemy's resistance remained the objective of the daily bombardment (other than Sundays), and, on 6 November, the big gun was moved from Jackal Tree to a new work on the Rooigrond Road, 2,740 m east of Cannon Kopje from whence it resumed shelling. On 4 November the Boers sent a trolley loaded with fused dynamite down the railway track from the north towards the railway station, but it exploded about 2,415 m out of town, prompting the Nun to comment that 'God was watching over this place and its brave garrison.'[60]

Fearing that the Boers were planning a new attack from their small western laager, Baden-Powell despatched Godley with one dismounted squadron of sixty men of the Protectorate Regiment under Captain R. J. Vernon, supported by thirty mounted men of the Bechuanaland Rifles under Captain B. W. Cowan, two 7-pounders and the 1-pounder Hotchkiss under Major Panzera at 2.30 a.m. on 7 November. In describing how this 'nice little treat' was undertaken, Trooper Snook described how the two guns and the Hotchkiss were pushed forward on the left, while Captain Vernon and 'C' Squadron took up a position on the right, 'commanding the enemy's trenches':

58   'An Interesting Letter From Mafeking', *Bucks Herald*, 14 July 1900, p. 6.
59   Ibid; on the shelling of Cannon Kopje, see J. Emerson Neilly, 'Mafeking's Shell Record', *Pall Mall Gazette*, 11 August 1900, p. 2.
60   'A Nun's Diary in Mafeking', *Armagh Guardian*, 27 July 1900, p. 3.

Just before dawn the Boers' natives began preparing coffee, and
the light from their fires showed where the shells were wanted. A
7-pounder opened the ball, and fell short, but No. 2 gun immediately
planted a shell right on one of the enemy's waggons; several others
followed on the same spot, utterly demoralizing the Boers who were
seen scurrying around, apparently unable to find their guns . . . a
rush was made from their big laager to reinforce the entrenchments,
but this move was checked by the firing of about twenty men of C
Squadron, under Lieutenant Holden, who were to the left of the
guns, and some of Captain Cowan's Rifles on the extreme right.
The Hotchkiss got jammed after seven rounds were fired, and when
the Boers got to work with some three hundred Mausers, a 7-pound
Krupp, their 1lb. quick-firing Maxim, and another gun, a perfect
hurricane of bullets and shells peppered round our men. A retreat
was made, still keeping up the fire, and four or five men got slightly
wounded, but no broken bones.[61]

In fact Major Godley and four men were wounded, while the retreat was
covered by another 7-pounder west of the stadt, and a further one near Fort
Ayr operated by the Bechuanaland Rifles, which 'had a particularly hot time'
with thirteen horses shot.[62] Snook, nonetheless, witnessed the remarkable
extrication of the Hotchkiss gun, whose limber had broken, allowing the
horses to gallop away without the gun. Unwilling to leave this 'memento
of the occasion', Gunners R. Cowan and F. H. Godson, despite 'a hailstorm
of bullets and bursting shells . . . attached a rope and, assisted by Trooper
Arthur Day, they hauled the gun safely away, crossing the skyline where
every figure showed distinctly'. From the sight of two ambulance waggons,
and a couple of Scotch carts, working for an hour between the laager and
the trenches, Snook claimed that 'at least two or three dozen will not come
Mausering again just yet'.[63] Doubtless this estimate was exaggerated but,
like the extravagant claims from other skirmishes, it boosted the morale of
the defenders. Even more satisfying was the sight of Boers moving their
trenches further away on the following night: as Major Godley claimed, 'our
object had been attained'.[64]

61 'An Edington Soldier on the Siege of Mafeking', *Somerset County Gazette*, 15
September 1900, p. 7.
62 'The Siege of Mafeking', *Penistone Express*, 27 July 1900, p. 6.
63 'An Edington Soldier on the Siege of Mafeking', *Somerset County Gazette*, 15
September 1900, p. 6; see also 'B-P report', pp. 899–900.
64 Godley, *Life*, p. 76; see also Amery, *Times History*, vol. 4, p. 585.

An even greater boost for British morale followed on 18 November when Cronjé, acting on the orders of President Kruger, began moving south with the Potchefstroom and Wolmaransstad Commandos, the Scandinavians and six guns. 'Our spirits rose', Lieutenant Gemmell averred, 'when we saw the redoubtable Cronje's laager trek off about the middle of November, and we concluded that things must be getting pretty warm for the Boers elsewhere.'[65] Cronjé's reputation had suffered from his failure to storm Mafeking or to break its resistance. Yet Thomas Pakenham possibly exaggerates when he asserts that

> B-P had survived the first two months – the Cronje phase – partly owing to his own audacity, partly owing to the good fortune of having Cronje for an enemy. There can be no doubt that if any Boer commander worth his salt had commanded the six thousand besiegers, B-P's men would now have been enjoying a quiet game of cricket in the prisoner-of-war camp at Pretoria.[66]

In referring to B-P's good fortune, Pakenham is alluding to the costly nature of the 'kicks' delivered during this period. The seven 'kicks' during October and November included several minor raids and even these incurred casualties. On 17 October, when about 100 blacks, commanded by Cape Police (CP), fired a couple of volleys at the Boers guarding the waterworks, one injured black was captured and Trooper Sydney Webb of the CP was shot through his ankle.[67] Yet the seven 'kicks' were not as costly as Pakenham asserts; he reproduces B-P's claim in his post-siege report that '163 casualties' had been suffered in the Cronjé period but this looks as erroneous as B-P's initial claim that '2,000 rounds' landed in the town throughout the siege (corrected as '20,000' in his testimony before the royal commission). In his staff diary B-P recorded 118 casualties up to 8 December, composed of 81 whites and 37 'natives', so indicating a considerable error in the post-siege report.[68]

The aggressive posture paid off, inasmuch as it demonstrated just how costly any attempt to storm the town could prove. When Cronjé and his men withdrew, reducing the investing forces to about 1,400 men under General

65 'The Siege of Mafeking', *Ayr Advertiser*, 23 August 1900, p. 5; on Cronjé's departure, see Amery, *Times History*, vol. 4, p. 585.

66 Pakenham, *Boer War*, p. 401.

67 Willan (ed.), *Edward Ross*, p. 27; Pretorius, 'The Besiegers' in Smith (ed.), *Siege of Mafeking*, vol. 1, p. 95.

68 Pakenham, *Boer War*, p. 401; see also NAM, 1968-10-42, B-P diary, 8 December 1899; 'B-P report', pp. 891–2, 894; and Baden-Powell, 'Use of Artillery', evidence before *RCWSA*, p. 424.

Snyman, this more than compensated for the losses already suffered by the Mafeking garrison. In effect the besieged forces, particularly at Cannon Kopje, had displayed the defensive potential of the modern rifle and Maxim machine gun, and the value of interior lines of communication. Both the military and civilians understood the lessons. Sergeant K. Francis (Protectorate Regiment) wrote that 'One thing is clear in modern warfare owing to smokeless powder being used, unless you can get a surprise on, you have no definite object to fire on & a large amount of ammunition is expended with very little result, or perhaps I should say apparent result.'[69] This may explain both the time consumed by ambulance waggons in searching the more expansive battlefields for casualties and the exaggerated claims about the enemy's dead and wounded after each skirmish. By December Mayor Whiteley informed his wife, who was about to leave Cape Town and return to her home in Dewsbury, Yorkshire, that

> The Boers were much slacker, and that there was no fear of an assault. They got beans when they attacked Canon [*sic*] Kopje, but we lost heavily. The shells come crashing into the town, but somehow there are very few casualties. Their big gun is in position on the ridge in the Rooigrond Road, and others move about a good deal. Sniping is rather bothersome, and to have Mauser bullets, whizzing near you not at all pleasant. The people are in good heart, and the Boers know it is hopeless to try an assault, as they will lose half their men, and they are not prepared for anything like that. Baden-Powell is splendid, and he will pull us through.[70]

The Assault on Game Tree Fort

Boredom and shelling became the daily routine, with the Boer artillery reinforced by two 5-pounders and a pom-pom in November (to compensate for the guns withdrawn by Cronjé).[71] Sundays remained the only day of respite. Despite the grinding monotony, Hamilton of *The Times* wrote 'For almost seven weeks we have defied an enemy who encircle us upon every side . . . . They Mauser us, and shell us; they cut our water off, and raid our cattle; they can make life hell . . . but no one was ever so deluded if they

---

69 NAM, 1974-01-138, Sgt. K. Francis, diary, p. 4.
70 'Mayoress of Mafeking in England', *Scarborough Post*, 31 January 1900, p. 4; Boer numbers are inexact, as the burghers tended to come and go from the siege but 'about 1,400' is an informed estimate, Pretorius, *A to Z of the Anglo-Boer War*, p. 256.
71 Amery, *Times History*, vol. 4, p. 586.

think that by such means Mafeking surrenders.'[72] In her diary Mrs. Simmonds chronicled the ebb and flow of her emotions: on 9 November, she believed that 'everyone, from first to last, is tired and sick of the whole business. I wish to goodness the troops would come up; we are forever hearing of them, but they never come.' By 23 November her spirits were much more buoyant, learning that up to the previous night 'Big Ben' had fired 400 shells into Mafeking, and that as 'each shell is reckoned to cost £20 . . . at any rate, we have cost the Transvaal a good sum. On Sunday', she reflected, 'we had a very enjoyable concert. The Boers don't fight on that day, so we are able to move about, and do our shopping.'[73]

Adverse weather was now as much of an enemy as the Boers. On 27 November an afternoon thunderstorm flooded the nuns' trench, forcing the sisters to take shelter in the hospital. The 'natives' had to pump water out of the trench, leave the roof off to allow it to dry, and 'save any articles that had not been completely destroyed'.[74] An even worse thunderstorm struck on 5 December. 'Talk of rain!' exclaimed Mrs. Simmonds, 'I never saw anything to equal it. I believe eight inches fell in three hours. Our trench was full of water, full to the very top (five feet [1.52 m] deep). Everyone', she observed on 6 December, 'was in the same predicament. The Boers have been so busy drying their clothes to-day, so have not thrown many shells.' As rebuilding military trenches took priority, it would take until Sunday, 17 December, before a 'gang of natives, known locally as the "Black Watch"', were able to open and reconstruct her trench.[75]

Faced with the onset of a long-term blockade, Baden-Powell had to review food stocks, medical support and internal security. Soldiers like Corporal Rose were surprised that Baden-Powell had not commandeered all food stocks at the beginning of the siege, and instituted rationing. Instead when they tried to boost their half-rations by buying from local stores, they found themselves charged 'exorbitant prices' for basic items (three shillings for a tin of condensed milk, seven shillings for 1 lb of butter and four shillings for a 1 lb tin of bully beef).[76] By not imposing rationing initially, Baden-Powell had avoided a further strain on civil-military relations at a time when a divided civilian community was adjusting to the demands of

---

72   Hamilton, *Siege of Mafeking*, pp. 134–5.
73   'Extracts From Mafeking Diary', *Leamington Spa Courier*, 1 September 1900, p. 8.
74   'A Nun's Diary in Mafeking', *Armagh Guardian*, 27 July 1900, p. 3.
75   'Extracts From Mafeking Diary', *Leamington Spa Courier*, 1 September 1900, p. 8 and on the effects of the storm, 'Siege of Mafeking', *Penistone Express*, 10 August 1900, p. 7 and T. Hayes, diary, 5 December 1899, in Bottomley (ed.), 'Siege of Mafeking and the Imperial Mindset', p. 76.
76   'A Hero of Mafeking: Aberdeenshire Man on the Siege', *(Aberdeen) Evening Express*, 28 August 1900, p. 5.

siege warfare. He had already deflected protests from townspeople as early as 18 October, and suspected that hoarding and profiteering were rampant. Hence he began in November to commandeer the merchants' stocks of food and to re-sell items at a fixed price, a policy that prompted the gratitude of Chief Wessels.[77]

More vexing was the state of medical support, a specialist issue over which B-P had not been able to improvise in his pre-war preparations. He drew on the services of Surgeon-Major L. E. Anderson, who had supplied 'at his own expense, a large quantity of the medical stores'. The Principal Medical Officer (PMO), William (Willie) Hayes and his brother, Tom, were the main hospital doctors, as Surgeon-Major F. A. A. Holmden (BSA Police) was incapacitated with dysentery by late November, and another civilian, Dr S. Smyth, insisted upon the handsome payment of 30 shillings a day to work in the women's laager. He was 'in a moral funk', quipped Willie Hayes, and Smyth soon gave up, claiming that the work was too stressful for him.[78] At the Victoria Hospital, a thirty-bed civilian facility, the doctors had the assistance of the matron, Miss Kathy Hill, three nurses, four volunteer nurses, Mother Teresa and six nuns, and at least ten ladies, who volunteered their services. The shortage of space soon became acute; by 28 October, Willie Hayes described the hospital as 'full, many are dysentery cases caused by duty in the trenches, and a great many are wounds', and, by 11 December, Tom Hayes claimed that the hospital was 'full to overflowing, patients sleeping anywhere'.[79] Despite the creation of an extra ward on the verandah, the cramped conditions within the hospital fuelled tensions among the staff. Quite apart from his contempt for Dr Smyth, Willie Hayes discounted the services of all the volunteer nurses; despaired of the trade for Lady Sarah Wilson as 'we have enough women here to deal with without her'; and banned war correspondents from the hospital after Vere Stent of Reuters claimed that he was in the habit of operating on blacks without chloroform or ether.[80]

Compounding these tensions was the fact that the medical staff had to function under recurrent shelling and rifle fire. 'One man who was in hospital with a wound', commented Sister Gamble, 'was wounded a second time by a

77 NAM, 1968-10-42, B-P diary, 18 October and 19 November 1899.
78 Ibid., 2 and 4 November 1899; see also W. Hayes, diary, 28 and 31 October and 2 November 1899, in Bottomley (ed.), 'Siege of Mafeking and the Imperial Mindset', pp. 49, 52 and 56.
79 W. Hayes, diary, 28 October 1899 and T. Hayes, diary, 11 December 1899, in Bottomley (ed.), 'Siege of Mafeking and the Imperial Mindset', pp. 49 and 84.
80 W. Hayes, diary, 17 and 29 November and 3 December 1899 in ibid., pp. 66, 73 and 75; see also NAM, 1968-10-42, B-P diary, 30 November 1899 and on Nurse Crauford's 'disagreement at the big hospital and left of my own accord', 17 November 1899, Crauford, 'Nurse's Diary', p. 42.

bullet from outside. . . . We carried many of the men into passages, anywhere where we thought they would be safe; and we often had to pick the bullets out of the walls over the beds.'[81] Although Baden-Powell protested over the abuse of the Red-Cross flags whenever such incidents occurred, the Boers retorted that some buildings were being used for military purposes, and they had a case in respect of the convent. As the Nun explained, the Boer shelling of the convent was in retaliation to fire 'from a redoubt a few yards from us, and at a distance the Dutch imagined . . . came from the Convent'. By the end of November after the rains had flooded the trench of the Cape Police, she returned to the convent to find its 'floor . . . covered with ammunition which was left there to dry and a Maxim gun in the look-out room'.[82] The Maxim was still there at Christmas, prompting Mrs. Simmonds to exclaim, 'Fancy the Convent turned into a small fort.'[83]

Baden-Powell was even more concerned about the continuing seepage of information from the town and the spreading of misinformation within it. 'Nothing irritated and vexed Baden-Powell more deeply', claimed Corporal Rose, 'than the circulation of false rumours of relief being at hand. When the falsity of these rumours was demonstrated, the men were apt to become somewhat disheartened . . . . Again and again he set himself to trace the rumours.'[84] Mafeking, wrote Willie Hayes, 'is full of spies'; he was delighted that Mrs. Hammond, who had 'expressed herself so freely in favour of the Dutch', had been incarcerated, and noted, like many others, that the Boer women and children had all sheltered at the river bed on 30 October, before the shelling of the women's laager.[85] Baden-Powell was concerned not only about the direct leakage of information, imprisoning twenty-eight suspects without proof by 29 October, but also indirect leakage via the war correspondents, whenever they sought to evade censorship. All of them, he contended, had 'very incorrect views of the situation – some alarmist, others incautious', and they wanted to spread 'all the bar-gossip of the place in "interviews" on reaching Cape Town'. He famously had dreadful relations with Hamilton of *The Times*, recorded the drunkenness of Major Baillie, and temporarily

---

81 'Nursing at the Siege of Mafeking', *Poole, Parkstone and East Dorset Herald*, 26 July 1900, p. 8.
82 'A Nun's Diary in Mafeking', *Armagh Guardian*, 27 July 1900, p. 3. The Maxim gun was still there at the end of December, 'Extracts from Mafeking Diary', *Leamington Spa Courier*, 1 September 1900, p. 8.
83 'Extracts from Mafeking Diary', *Leamington Spa Courier*, 1 September 1900, p. 8.
84 'A Hero of Mafeking: Aberdeenshire Man on the Siege', *(Aberdeen) Evening Express*, 28 August 1900, p. 5.
85 W. Hayes, diary, 24 October and 1 November 1899, in Bottomley (ed.), 'Siege of Mafeking and the Imperial Mindset', pp. 43 and 54–5; NAM, 1968-10-42, B-P diary, 30 October 1899; Neilly, *Besieged with B.-P.*, p. 145.

withdrew the press pass of Neilly of the *Pall Mall Gazette* for trying to send an uncensored message.[86]

Baden-Powell was appalled, too, by the 'tissue of ingenious falsehoods' in the Boer press, and sought to retaliate by spreading dissension within enemy ranks. In his 'manifesto' of 11 December, which he distributed to each of the eight Boer camps, he threatened retribution 'in a few weeks' once the Transvaal was 'invaded by the English' for the shelling of women and children in Mafeking, and the destruction of 'native' farms. He urged the burghers to return to their homes, and, in act of further intimidation, required his orderlies to carry white flags on their lances 'to show that we had lancers among us'.[87] Neither counter-espionage nor propaganda availed him much in the planning of his next 'kick' at Game Tree Fort on 26 December.

Located some 2,286 m north of the town, and about 800 m west of the railway, Game Tree Fort commanded the northern line of communications. It was a site from which the Boers had bombarded Mafeking and had checked the grazing in the vicinity. Baden-Powell committed 260 men to the assault, which was meant to pound the right flank of the fort, while 'C' and 'D' Squadrons of the Protectorate Regiment, under their respective captains, Vernon and FitzClarence, attacked up the railway line on the left flank and towards the rear of the fort. An armoured train manned by twenty men of the BSA Police with a Maxim was to assist the assault, supported by seventy men of the Bechuanaland Rifles under Captain Cowan, the whole body being under the command of Major Godley. Lieutenant-Colonel Hore led the advance on the right flank of Game Tree Fort, with Major Panzera commanding a Maxim and three 7-pounder guns (one of which was left in support in Fort Ayr), escorted by a troop of the Protectorate Regiment. Panzera moved as far forward as possible, entrenched his guns under the cover of darkness, and opened fire at daybreak (4.15 a.m.) from about 1,190 m. While this bombardment alerted the Boers, who were in the process of changing guard and so had double the numbers of men available, it did little or no damage.[88]

The fort, as described by Sergeant Francis, was 'about 80 yards [73 m] square roofed in with iron and bags and earth, the walls being quite 9 feet high [2.74 m] & only one narrow entrance at the back'.[89] The main body

86   NAM, 1968-10-42, B-P diary, 29 October and 10 and 16 November 1899; 'B-P report', p. 897; Jeal, *Baden-Powell*, p. 250 and Willan (ed.), *Edward Ross*, pp. 44–5.
87   NAM, 1968-10-41, B-P diary, 7, 10 and 11 December 1899; Hanbury-Tracy Mss., 'Notice to the Burghers of the Z.A.R. At Present Under Arms Near Mafeking', 11 December 1899.
88   Saunders, *Mafeking Memories*, p. 95; see also *Official History*, vol. 3, pp. 161–3; 'B-P report', p. 900; and Amery, *Times History*, vol. 4, pp. 590–1.
89   NAM, Acc. 1974-01-138, Sgt. Francis diary, pp. 6–7.

of the attack had advanced undetected but were soon handicapped on the railway. 'The armoured train', as Corporal Hulse recalled,

> steamed up to get abreast of the fort, but alas, was prevented by the railway having been again broken during the night, so that it could not get within about 1,100 yards [1,006 m] of the work; then, to add to the dismay, the Maxim jammed after firing two or three shots, thus rendering the train practically useless.[90]

Unable to attack the rear of the fort, Vernon's men attacked the south and eastern faces in open order, and at about 450 m tried to storm the fort at the point of the bayonet. Officers and men reached the fort and fired revolvers and rifles through the loopholes but found the fort, as Corporal Kelland ('C' Squadron) described, 'impregnable, and we lost very heavily that morning'.[91] Captains Ronald J. Vernon and Henry C. Sandford and Lieutenant Harold P. Paton were among the fatalities as 'C' Squadron was 'completely cut up' by the Boer firepower at point-blank range. Many were killed against the wall of the fort, and others killed and injured in the retreat, leaving Kelland as only one of seven NCOs in his troop to return

> alive and sound. One sergeant lost an arm [H. R. Martineau, who won the Victoria Cross], and had it not been for his letters and papers in his breast-pocket he would have been killed . . . Most of them were wounded very badly. It was a terrible sight to see them all laid out in the cemetery. Some poor fellows were knocked completely out of recognition; some with half their heads blown away; others shot through the stomach . . . They were a jolly lot when turning out in the night, but those of us who managed to come back were not very jolly I can assure you.[92]

Under a Red-Cross flag Dr. Tom Hayes dressed some of the wounds and, working with Surgeon-Major Anderson, organized the removal of the dead and wounded on the train and ambulance waggons. 'Rough looking' Boers, who refused to let any Briton approach within about 70 m of the fort,

---

90 Exactly when the railway line was cut was a matter of conjecture but the overnight supposition suited the treachery theory of how the battle was lost, 'The Siege of Mafeking', *Penistone Express*, 17 August 1900, p. 6.
91 'Corporal Kelland of Combwich, and the Siege of Mafeking', *Somerset County Gazette*, 11 August 1900, p. 3; see also NAM, 1974-01-138, Sgt. Francis, diary, p. 6.
92 'Corporal Kelland of Combwich, and the Siege of Mafeking', *Somerset County Gazette*, 11 August 1900, p. 3.

brought down many of the dead and wounded. The dreadful wounds, Hayes attributed, to the effects of Martini-Henry bullets at 'close range', and not mutilations or the use of explosive bullets, as speculated by John R. Algie, the town clerk.[93] The Boers had looted the corpses, removing boots and leggings, and cutting off stars from officers' shoulders, but failed to remove the sword from an injured FitzClarence. As Rose, who had served as a galloper for Colonel Hore, recalled, 'the Boers would have taken his sword had he not shamed them into a more generous course by exclaiming – "Would you deprive a wounded soldier of his sword?"'[94]

However endearing, the story was scant consolation. The outcome, claimed Trooper Snook, 'knocks the pluck out of one. There was only one killed in our squad; the rest were in C Squadron.'[95] In fact, the assault cost the lives of three officers and twenty-one NCOs and men (several dying of their wounds), with Captain FitzClarence and another twenty-two men wounded, and three missing. Lieutenant Gemmell, who had served in the attack, struggled to describe 'the gloom which fell over everybody when it was known how many were lost. No officer in the garrison would have been more missed than poor Vernon, whose good fellowship and unvarying courtesy had endeared him to everyone.'[96] Corporal Hulse regarded the day as 'one of the saddest in my existence, and I was thoroughly overcome when night came, and I rolled myself in my blankets and lay down to sleep'.[97] Among the inhabitants, wrote Sol Plaatje, 'The consternation . . . was so deeply rooted that it is clearly visible amongst men and women and old and young of both whites and blacks.'[98]

Baden-Powell has borne the brunt of criticism for the lack of proper planning and reconnaissance.[99] Local citizens and soldiers, aghast at the carnage, suspected that treachery had cost them dear, and suspicions fell on E. J. Hayes, a Protectorate trooper, who later deserted to the enemy but only on 21 March 1900.[100] In his post-siege report B-P

---

93 Compare T. Hayes, diary, 26 December 1899, in Bottomley (ed.), 'Siege of Mafeking and the Imperial Mindset', pp. 94–5 with J. R. Algie, 'The Mafeking Siege Diary of John Ronald Algie (Town Clerk) 1899-1900', 26 December 1899, p. 83.
94 'A Hero of Mafeking: Aberdeenshire Man on the Siege', *(Aberdeen) Evening Express*, 28 August 1900, p. 5. p. 5; Hamilton, *Siege of Mafeking*, p. 182.
95 'An Edington Soldier on the Siege of Mafeking', *Somerset County Gazette*, 15 September 1900, p. 7.
96 'The Siege of Mafeking', *Ayr Advertiser*, 23 August 1900, p. 5.
97 'The Siege of Mafeking', *Penistone Express*, 17 August 1900, p. 6.
98 Comaroff (ed.), *Diary of Sol T. Plaatje*, p. 82.
99 Pretorius, 'The Besiegers' in Smith (ed.), *Siege of Mafeking*, vol. 1, p. 74; Gardner, *Mafeking*, p. 129; Flower-Smith and Yorke, *Mafeking*, p. 62.
100 Algie, 'Diary', 26 December 1899, p. 83; Saunders, *Mafeking Memories*, p. 100; and U. S. Scouting Service Project, Diary of William Robertson Fuller, 21 March 1900, www.usscouts.org/usscouts/history/siegediary.asp (accessed 3 September 2018).

accepted full responsibility for the débâcle, albeit without admitting the full extent of his culpability. He had actually wanted to attack not Game Tree Fort but the gunnery crew of 'Big Ben' (and was talked out of it by his senior officers only two days earlier, on Christmas Eve).[101] B-P knew that the Boers had begun to roof the trenches at Game Tree with corrugated iron as early as 16 November but lacked the time to mount a proper reconnaissance of the fort; he simply chose Sergeant Lionel Cooke (Bechuanaland Rifles) as a guide because he supposedly knew 'every inch of the ground'.[102] Nor had the Colonel maximized the element of surprise: knowledge of an imminent attack, as Algie confirmed, was known 'for days past', and Baden-Powell had informed Nurse Crauford on 16 December that 'we have been very quiet lately, and we should let them know we have plenty of "go" in us still'.[103] Having authorized a dress rehearsal for the 'Big Ben' raid, involving 150 volunteers under Captain FitzClarence and three officers on 23 December, he found himself under pressure to act. Coupled with previous successes, this pressure may have contributed to a reckless decision to switch targets and launch the impetuous attack.[104] The Boxing Day disaster cured him of any desire to deliver another 'kick'.

Assessment

The failure of the Game Tree Fort assault was complete. If Commandant J. D. L. Botha, as Angus Hamilton asserts, was correct, and the Boers had been 'expecting the attack for the past two weeks',[105] then the charge of treachery is irrelevant. Yet even if this was 'Baden-Powell's greatest blunder of the siege', it hardly warrants the additional charge that the 'kicks' had 'all ended in disaster'.[106] This gross distortion overlooks the fact that the opening 'kick' on 14 October, and 'the two or three subsequent knocks', as B-P informed Lord Roberts, 'had so good an effect that we gained sufficient time to arrange our defences': henceforth 'it would require a very large force to capture Mafeking and their losses would be necessarily very heavy'.[107] From the outset, the 'kicks' were part of a vital strategy of bluffing or 'hoodwinking' the Boer besiegers into

---

101 'B-P report', p. 900; see also Jeal, *Baden-Powell*, p. 256.
102 Brent. L., MS. 407/1/1, Sergeant Lionel Cooke Mss., 'Game Tree', 30 December 1899 and NAM, 1968-10-42, B-P diary, 16 November 1899.
103 Crauford, 'A Nurse's Diary', p. 116 and Algie, 'Diary', 26 December 1899, p. 80.
104 Jeal, *Baden-Powell*, pp. 256–7; Flower-Smith and Yorke, *Mafeking*, p. 61.
105 Hamilton, *Siege of Mafeking*, p. 183.
106 Hopkins and Dugmore, *The Boy*, p. 147.
107 NAM, Acc. 1971-01-23-6, Roberts Mss., Baden-Powell to Lord Roberts, 20 February 1900.

believing that the Mafeking garrison was much stronger than it actually was.[108] In so doing it detained some 5,600 Boers and about nine guns, including one of the four Creusot siege guns, in an investment far from the major theatres of the war. It damaged, too, the reputation of Cronjé, who had embarked on the war, as one of the more successful Boer commanders.

However exaggerated the claims of inflicting heavy casualties on the enemy, the strategy of 'kicks' had boosted the morale of a garrison and citizenry all too aware of their vulnerability within the small isolated town. It reflected B-P's style of command, one that had to be more energetic and challenging than the commands of Kimberley or Ladysmith, if only because he was relying upon such a small body of partially-trained troops. Adding to their firepower were the loyal Barolongs, as evident in the successful defence of the stadt, as well as the 'Black Watch', the Cape Boys and the resourceful fighting of the black cattle guards.[109] Even so this was a pitifully small garrison, and so a strategy of aggressive defence, or a projected capacity to do so, coupled with the resilience displayed at Cannon Kopje, demonstrated that mounting attacks upon Mafeking would prove costly. It had compensated for the town's abysmal artillery, and provided the enemy, particularly its risk-averse leadership, with pause for thought. Few imagined that this pause, apart from the sustained shelling of the town, would last for another four and a half months.

---

108 Pretorius, 'The Besiegers' in Smith (ed.), *Siege of Mafeking*, vol. 1, p. 70.
109 Young, diary, 12 December 1899, in Bottomley, 'A Scots "Salvationist" Perspective', p. 235.

'Colonel Baden-Powell and his Military and Civil Staff', H. W. Wilson, *With The Flag to Pretoria*, vol. 2 (London, 1900), p. 598.

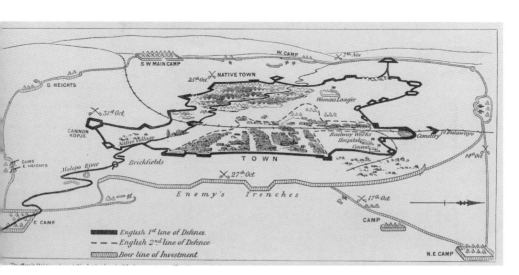

'Topographical Sketch showing British and Boer Positions', *Graphic*, 3 February 1900, p. 171.

'The Siege of Mafeking: In the Boer Trenches', *Graphic*, 31 March 1900, p. 451.

'The Siege of Mafeking: The Boers of Mafeking and their Long Tom "Creaky"', *Graphic*, 31 March 1900, p. 465.

'A Shell that took effect; a Store wrecked by a 96-Pounder [*sic*: 94-pounder] Shell', *Graphic*, 9 June 1900, p. 839.

'Armed Blacks' (photograph by J. Angus Hamilton), *Black & White Budget*, 21 April 1900, p. 78.

'Lady Sarah Wilson emerging from an Underground Shelter', Mafikeng Museum.

'Mafeking £1 note', H. W. Wilson, *With The Flag to Pretoria*, vol. 2 (London, 1900), p. 612.

'A common scene in Mafeking during the last few weeks of the siege: Killing horses for food' (photograph by J. Angus Hamilton), *Black & White Budget*, 2 June 1900, p. 266.

'The Eleventh Hour', *Punch*, vol. 118, 9 May 1900, p. 335.

'Mr. Frank Whitele Mayor of Mafeking *Supplement to Illustrat London News*, vol. 116, 2 May 1900, p. II.

'Colonel Plumer's Advance to the Relief of Mafeking: The Attack on a Boer Fort near Gaberones', *Graphic*, 7 April 1900, p. 484.

'Brigadier-General Bryan Thomas Mahon', H. W. Wilson, *With The Flag to Pretoria*, vol. 2 (London, 1900), p. 591.

"'Mafeking is Relieved'": 'Hampstead Rejoicing Over the Relief of Mafeking', *Graphic*, 26 May 1900, p. 759.

'The Relief of Mafeking: The March Past of the Relieving Forces before Lieut-General [*sic* Maj.-General] Baden-Powell', *Graphic*, 30 June 1900, p. 943.

'Major-General Baden-Powell' (drawn by R. Caton Woodville), *Illustrated London News*, vol. 116, 26 May 1900, p. 697.

Chapter 5

The Long Siege: Rationing, Shelling and Fighting in the Brickfields

As Angus Hamilton wrote, the coming of the New Year dashed any hopes of fulfilling 'the prophecy that relief would come by the end of December': on the contrary it ushered in a period that would define Mafeking as the 'long siege'.[1] The shelling and rifle fire persisted through the ending of 1899 and into the New Year, without the cessation of hostilities that graced Christmas Day (Mafeking had feared that the Boers would not cease fire on Monday, the 25th, which they did, and held many festivities on the previous Sunday as well as the Monday). Over those days Lady Sarah Wilson had excelled herself, sending a collection of sweets and toys for distribution among the children of the stadt; hosting a lunch with turkey and plum pudding for Baden-Powell and his staff; and sending a bottle of port to the Sisters of Mercy. Thereafter, aided by the officers' ladies, some Protectorate officers, including the obliging Captain Vernon, the nuns and English clergymen, Lady Sarah had organized a tea with a Christmas tree in the Masonic Hall for the English and Dutch children, ensuring that each child received two presents. Every effort had been made to observe the religious rituals, singing 'Adeste' in the midnight mass with the windows thickly muffled to avoid alerting the Boers, and enjoying some extraordinary meals, not least the famous multi-course menu at the Mafeking Hotel. However memorable these occasions, including the dinner held on Christmas Day by the Protectorate Regiment,[2] the Game Tree Fort disaster dwarfed their immediate impact. It compelled Baden-Powell to address the aftermath of the débâcle and the sustained shelling of the town. He also had to confront the implications of a long siege in respect

---

1   Hamilton, *Siege of Mafeking*, p. 190 and 'The Transvaal War. Relief of Mafeking. "*A Long Siege Ended*", *North Wilts Herald*, 25 May 1900, p. 7.
2   Extracts From Mafeking Diary', *Leamington Spa Courier*, 1 September 1900, p. 8; 'A Nun's Diary in Mafeking', *Armagh Guardian*, 27 July 1900, p. 3; Lady Sarah Wilson, *South African Memories*, p. 170; Comaroff (ed.), *Diary of Sol T. Plaatje*, p. 78; Crauford, 'Nurse's Diary', p. 117; Willan (ed.), *Edward Ross*, p. 77; Pakenham, *Boer War*, p. 404; and for copies of the menu, Rosenthal, *Character Factory*, p. 42 and title page, Neilly, *Besieged with B.-P.*

of rationing, and, until relief arrived, to engage the enemy especially in the hotly contested brickfields.

Aftermath of the Game Tree Defeat

Of all the defeats suffered by the British in December 1899, including those of Stormberg, Magersfontein and Colenso – the infamous 'Black Week' of 10–15 December – Game Tree Fort was the least significant. The defeat neither imperilled the operational mission of defending Mafeking nor eroded confidence in the defeated commanding officer. Within the confines of Mafeking, nonetheless, it was a shock, compelling Baden-Powell to move rapidly to mitigate the consequences. As the Protectorate Regiment had now suffered 110 casualties out of strength in excess of 400, he had to reorganize it into three squadrons.[3] He sought to boost morale among the remainder by parading the regiment on 31 December to announce gallantry awards for the Game Tree action, which were confirmed in General Orders. Among these awards was a commendation for Trooper David McLeish for acting 'with great coolness in leading Nos. 2 and 3 troops out of action, encouraging and steadying them, and exercising control over the retirement, all the officers and non-commissioned officers near having fallen. For this and other meritorious deeds', he received a double promotion and ended the siege with the rank of sergeant.[4]

The unprecedented number of casualties triggered the rearrangement of the hospital provisions. This involved the moving of about twenty-five convalescents out of the Victoria Hospital into a makeshift 'Railway Convalescent Home' under Surgeon-Major Holmden, with Lady Sarah Wilson and Nurse Crauford acting as matrons. Before the end of the year, B-P approved the creation of another hospital for women and children in the women's laager. Dr Tom Hayes was in charge and Nurse Crauford served as matron, supported by another two lady volunteers. As the Colonel explained to the Drs Hayes, these new arrangements also addressed the breakdown in relations between them and the volunteer nurses, and between the hospital and the railway community. In B-P's opinion, the doctors' lack of tact had 'caused much ill feeling and many patients declined to come into hospital where they were'.[5] While Baden-Powell remained above the squabbles between Willie

3   Baillie, *Mafeking*, p. 99; see also Wilson, *With The Flag*, vol. 2, p. 610.
4   'A Berwick Man Promoted at Mafeking', *Berwickshire News*, 31 July 1900, p. 5; see also NAM, 1968-10-42, B-P diary, 28 and 29 December 1899.
5   NAM, 1968-10-42, B-P diary, 29 December 1899; W. Hayes, diary, 27-29 December 1899 in Bottomley (ed.), 'Siege of Mafeking and the Imperial Mindset', p. 98; and Brent. L., Vyvyan Mss., MS. 147/5/1/40, More, 'Railway Report', p. 12.

Hayes and Captain More, and between Hayes and most of the nurses, he had to rely upon the medical skills and resilience of the Hayes' brothers, as the other medical personnel had succumbed to protracted illnesses and the strain of overwork.[6]

Baden-Powell was exasperated, nonetheless, by the continuing friction and administrative shortcomings within the hospital, where an investigation led by Captain C. M. Ryan (Army Service Corps, henceforth ASC), revealed an absence of any stock or issue book, stores kept in an unlocked pantry and the lack of diet sheets for the patients. Baden-Powell immediately directed Ryan to appoint a storekeeper, to keep ration returns in the hospital and to construct a room for reserve stores. Yet the discord and rows persisted despite an enquiry by the hospital board, and so, on 3 April, B-P appointed Surgeon-Major Anderson to be the new principal medical officer (PMO) while leaving Willie Hayes in charge of the hospital. Even so two more nurses, Miss Cramer and the highly respected Mrs. McCallum, resigned from the hospital five days later, exacerbating the shortage of medical care. When Willie Hayes succumbed to illness on 1 May, Baden-Powell appointed Major Anderson as the PMO of the hospital.[7]

The medical experience grew progressively dire. Victims of bullet and shell wounds received treatments without the benefit of X-rays, certain surgical appliances, dressings, and, like the amputees, often required weeks of convalescence. John Poole spent seven weeks in hospital after a Mauser bullet smashed his right arm just above the elbow, and E. J. Poole, from Fulflood, Winchester, suffered an even worse injury when a bullet passed through the right knee joint, flattening out inside the knee, and bursting out at the back, shredding his sinews and rendering the 'leg useless'.[8] The Nun described 'frightful' scenes in the hospital and the suffering of

> those poor fellows [who] have been wounded by shells, some have asked the doctors to give them something to end life. In some cases suffering is so excessive that they tear off the bandages and it is so

---

6   The Nun contracted typhoid fever on 1 January and required extensive nursing over several weeks, often while 94-pound shells bombarded the grounds of the convent, 'A Nun's Diary in Mafeking', *Armagh Guardian*, 3 August 1900, p. 3, and Nurse Crauford got malarial fever in March, requiring nursing attention from her sister, Mrs. Buchan, and Mrs. Hayes, Crauford, 'Nurse's Diary', p. 286.

7   NAM, 1968-10-42, B-P diary, 29 December 1899 and 13 January, 18 and 22 March, 3, 8 and 18 April and 1 May 1900; 'B-P report', p. 901; and Willan (ed.), *Edward Ross*, p. 146.

8   'Inside Mafeking', *Newbury Weekly News*, 12 July 1900, p. 2; 'Letters from the Seat of the War', *Hampshire Chronicle*, 14 July 1900, p. 6; and on the medical shortages, Hamilton, *Siege of Mafeking*, p. 145.

fearful to look at the serrated and maimed flesh, frequently gangrene sets in and the poor patient must be put in a ward by himself as the odour is unbearable, in this case death always followed.[9]

Like Nurse Crauford, she was particularly distressed by the injury on Majuba Day (27 February 1900), when a tall, good-looking Cape policeman, Frank Elkington, formerly a schoolteacher in Bedford, was hit in the face by a shell fragment from a 5-pounder. Blinded in both eyes, he was hideously disfigured across his nose, upper jaw and eyebrows. In Nurse Crauford's opinion, it 'was one of the saddest things in the siege'.[10]

Compounding the burden of injury was the spread of disease and malnutrition. Mayor Whiteley was probably correct in asserting that disease could have been far worse, and that the altitude of Mafeking – 'some 4,000 feet [1,284 m] above the sea – tended to preserve the health of our people'.[11] Nevertheless, the spending of long periods of time in underground shelters or in trench duty took its toll, and bouts of malarial and enteric fever proved recurrent. Corporal Rose suffered five malarial attacks, being hospitalised on three occasions, where he remembered Lady Sarah as 'an assiduous visitor', whose 'bright, cheery presence was always most welcome', and twice he received 'treatment in a kaffir hut'.[12] His fever was not too severe but others required isolation in areas defined by the presence of fever flags: one remote far out into the veld where a family coped with diphtheria; another between them and the stadt accommodating victims of smallpox; and then nearer the town a building housing cases of malaria, typhoid and enteric fever. Yet the strain on the hospital endured: by 25 April, the hospital had seen its number of patients grow within a week from seventy-one to eighty as it admitted fourteen casualties and thirty-one sick, but discharged only twenty-eight (six to the convalescent home) and suffered eight deaths.[13]

Unfortunately it became increasingly difficult to give these patients sufficient food to accelerate recovery. On 22 March Mrs. Simmonds recorded

9   'A Nun's Diary in Mafeking', *Armagh Guardian*, 3 August 1900, p. 3.

10   Ibid; Crauford, 'Nurse's Diary', p. 247; 'The War. A Mafeking Sufferer', *Luton News*, 6 September 1900, p. 4; T. Hayes, diary, 27 February 1900 in Bottomley (ed.), 'Siege of Mafeking and the Imperial Mindset', p. 130.

11   Mafeking is actually 1,284 m above sea level, 'Mafeking and Its Mayor', *Leeds Mercury*, 23 July 1900, p. 3.

12   'A Hero of Mafeking: Aberdeenshire Man on the Siege', *(Aberdeen) Evening Express*, 28 August 1900, p. 5.

13   NAM, 1968-10-42, B-P diary, 25 April 1900; on the isolation areas, Hamilton, *Siege of Mafeking*, p. 287; the strain on nursing in the 'isolation cottages', Crauford, 'Nurse's Diary', p. 288; and the experience of enteric (typhoid fever), Young, diary, 27 March 1900, in Bottomley, 'A Scots "Salvationist" Perspective', p. 244.

that a friend of hers had been 'very ill for 10 days, and the only comforts the doctor could order were two tins of milk and some lunch biscuits!'[14] 'What made us all so bad here', lamented E. J. Poole, 'was the shortness of nourishment.'[15] During the last few months of the siege, recalled Sister Gamble, dinner became acutely distressing as 'there was only a spoonful of porridge for some of the men, and nothing for the others', and 'a polony [sausage] made of horse or donkey' for those recovering from the effects of enteric.[16]

Rationing

As early as 3 December Baden-Powell had confided in his staff diary that 'The Boers do not intend to attack Mafeking, but mean to starve us out.'[17] In his post-siege report, he summarized how he had responded to this challenge, potentially the most serious for this small, isolated community of 1,708 whites (1,074 men, 229 women and 405 children) and about 7,500 blacks (as of the census of 14 November).[18] 'Early in the siege', he reported, 'I took over all merchant stocks and put everybody on rations. Beginning on the usual scale, I gradually reduced it to the lowest that would allow of the men being fit for duty. All lived strictly on the following scale:'

	At first	Latterly
Meat	1lb.	¾ to 1lb.
Bread	1lb.	5oz.
Vegetables	1lb.	6oz.
Coffee	½ oz.	$\frac{1}{3}$ oz.
Salt	½ oz.	½ oz.
Sugar	2 oz.	none
Tea	½ oz.	none
Sowens		1 quart.[19]

---

14 'Lady's Letter from Mafeking', *Mansfield Chronicle*, 18 May 1900, p. 3. There are several published versions of this letter but the references to husband, 'Gus', and daughter, 'Marjie', confirm that the writer is 'Mrs. de Normanville's sister-in-law', as described in her diary entries and letter, 'When Besieged in Mafeking', *Leamington Spa Courier*, 23 June 1900, p. 8.

15 'Letters from the Seat of War', *Hampshire Chronicle*, 14 July 1900, p. 6.

16 'Nursing at the Siege of Mafeking', *Poole, Parkstone and East Dorset Herald*, 26 July 1900, p. 8.

17 NAM, 1968-10-42, B-P diary, 3 December 1899.

18 Ibid. 14 November 1899.

19 'B-P report', p. 895.

In addition, B-P acknowledged that 'we had a large stock of meat, both live and tinned', and that the besieged 'had to open up wide extent of grazing ground' for the livestock. They ate fresh meat first, with tinned meat stored in bombproof shelters as a reserve, and during the last two months they lived on 'horseflesh three days a week'.[20] Although the stock of meal was comparatively small, they had a large supply of forage oats, which was ground into flour, with the residue fermented into Sowens (a form of porridge) and the remaining husks used as forage for the horses. The local citizens also grew vegetables within the defences, which formed a regular part of the ration for most of the siege. Soldiers paid 1s. and 3d. per ration or, with fresh vegetables, 1s. and 6d., civilians paid 2s., and women in the laager, 1s. and 2d.[21] 'For the natives', Baden-Powell reported, 'we established four soup kitchens at which horse stew was sold daily, and five Sowens kitchens. Natives were all registered, to prevent fraud, and bought rations at 1 quart per adult, and 1 pint per child, at 3d. per pint.' The 'defence watchmen, workmen, police, etc. and certificated destitute persons' received free rations, and the kitchens 'so managed paid their own expenses'.[22]

What this summary failed to explain was that Baden-Powell had had to devise a rationing policy for much of the siege upon uncertain and often inaccurate information. He suspected that hoarding had occurred within the town and stadt, illicit bread-making in certain premises, and rampant profiteering among the town's traders. Initial calculations of the available foodstuffs in the town and stadt (134 days for whites, 15 days for 'natives' from 14 November) proved massive underestimates. Recalculations of the stocks of meal and oats (once it became clear that bread could be made from horse's oats), coupled with plentiful supplies of meat and groceries, led to estimates of a 60-day supply for whites and blacks by 30 December. Confiscations of undeclared stocks followed, as Captain Ryan and his staff raided the premises of Indian traders and the stadt. The ASC distributed daily rations through official retail outlets in the town, stadt and Mfengu location, and private shops were closed for the sale of foodstuffs (if not luxuries periodically in lieu of meat) from 21 January. When Mr. J. W. De Kock, an attorney, led protests on behalf of the local traders, B-P had him arrested, tried and bound over, with bail of £50, to respect the dictates of martial law.[23] Similarly, on 12 February, the Colonel had Sergeant-Major Looney (ASC) arrested for operating a black market and distributing government stores to his friends. Looney would be dismissed from the service, forfeiting his pension

---

20 Ibid.
21 Ibid.
22 Ibid.
23 NAM, 1968-10-42, B-P diary, 6, 10 and 25 January and 1, 2 and 3 February 1900; see also Comaroff (ed.), *Diary of Sol T. Plaatje*, p. 97; *Mafeking Mail*, 21 January 1900, p. 1; and support for de Kock, Algie, 'Diary', 3 February 1900, p. 119.

rights, and sentenced to hard labour for five years. However, as some of his illicit recompense – special shirts, shoes, and cases of scented soap – came from the stocks of Benjamin Weil, this compounded the fraught relations between the military command and the main supplier in Mafeking.[24]

Baden-Powell was deeply suspicious of Weil's stocktaking, and of his desire to increase the price of rations above the contracted agreement. While Weil claimed that a price rise would merely offset his losses, B-P suspected that he was understating his stocks in the hope of raising prices later: 'Weil's unfortunate lapses from the truth and small inconsistencies make one suspect him of having more stuff in hand than he cares to declare.'[25] Weil emerged as an enigma throughout the siege, despite pre-stocking foodstuffs on such a scale as to help sustain the garrison and town over a seven-month period.[26] He wanted to be known as Mafeking's saviour (and gave six bottles of brandy to Vere Stent of Reuters for a report that extolled his accumulation of provisions prior to the siege),[27] but proved so difficult to deal with by the military authorities that B-P described his 'duplicity' as 'a constant annoyance if not a danger'.[28] What vexed the Colonel was that Weil was not simply a profiteer, who had raised many siege-prices by about 100 per cent,[29] but he was also keen that the siege should succeed and contributed generously towards this end. Weil supplied Christmas presents to the garrison units; tobacco and cigarettes to hospital patients after the Game Tree battle; offered £50 (ten times what B-P had awarded) to Foreman Conolly for inventing the 5in howitzer, which B-P refused to accept 'as not fair to the other workers'; and later free blankets for every officer and man of the garrison, accepted as 'most welcome and useful . . . in the thick of the wet weather, with bitterly cold nights'.[30]

So it was hugely frustrating when the report on Weil's belated stocktaking came through in late January, revealing over 36,500 lbs of goods. This included massive stocks of meats, including 10,488 lbs of roast and boiled

---

24   NAM, 1968-10-42, B-P diary, 12, 15 and 20 February 1900; see also 'The Siege of Mafeking. Diary of Recent Events', *Belfast News-Letter*, 15 March 1900, p. 5.

25   NAM, 1968-10-42, B-P diary, 3 and 25 January and 15 February 1900.

26   *Official History*, vol. 3, p. 174.

27   British Library (BL), Add. Mss. 46,848, ff. 257 and 259–60, Weil Mss., Vere Stent to Weil, 24 April 1900.

28   NAM, 1968-10-42, B-P diary, 15 February 1900.

29   Willan (ed.), *Edward Ross*, pp. 96–7; Lady Sarah Wilson, *South African Memories*, p. 193.

30   NAM, 1968-10-42, B-P diary, 18 April 1900; BL, Add. Mss. 46,848, ff. 41–2, 48, 45, 241, 244 and 250, Weil Mss., Christmas thanks from the Bechuanaland Rifles, 23 December 1899, 'B' Squadron, Protectorate Regiment and Cannon Kopje, 25 December 1899, Kathy Hill (matron), 31 December 1899, Baden-Powell to Weil, 19 April 1900, Lt.-Col. C. O. Hore to Weil 19 April 1900 and Capt. B. W. Cowan to Weil, 21 April 1900; and Add. Mss. 46,052, f. 128, Weil Mss., Baden-Powell, 'General Order', 1 March 1900.

mutton as well as many tinned meats and corned beef; 4,010 lbs of fish, including 144 lbs of tinned salmon and 2,450 lbs of sardines; and a copious array of vegetables, groceries and sundries, including 1,904 lbs of oatmeal and 1,360 lbs of corn flour.[31] Baden-Powell now anticipated that his supplies of meat, breadstuff, and oatmeal would last until 16 April, especially if bread were reduced to a ½lb. ration, with additional supplies of fancy meats, jams and fruits, and fresh vegetables on alternate days for the garrison, as well as groceries other than tea, which was getting low. He also cut the horse ration of composite forage from 10 lbs to 6 lbs and ordered horses to be grazed as much as possible. Even when Weil's separate stock of oats turned out to be 75,000 lbs and not 178,000 lbs, another recalculation on 1 March revealed an overall stock of 265,000 lbs, which allowed a weekly issue of 8,628 lbs oats to the stadt and 6,205 lbs of flour to the whites, enough to last 'easily' until the end of May. Characteristically, he ordered the headquarters mess to experiment with reduced rations before requiring others to do so.[32]

In fact, after a stocktaking error by the ASC, there were still 230,421 lbs of oats on 5 April, sufficient to feed the garrison, stadt and remaining refugees until 4 June. This was just as well, as B-P had to adjust his anticipated date of relief from mid-April to 18 May in response to a message from Lord Roberts, which arrived via Plumer on 24 January. Nearly three months later, on 20 April, a telegram from Lord Roberts, dated 9 April, required him to 'make supplies last longer . . . [as] there may be some delay in the despatch of relief expedition'.[33] This news only compounded the uncertainty after Plumer's defeat at Ramathlabama (30 March) about whether a relief column, if despatched, would actually get through.

Baden-Powell's other major uncertainty concerned livestock, most of which was owned privately by the Barolong and black refugees. The animals represented wealth, status and tribute (for wedding ceremonies) for the families owning the stock, and when the first census was taken (25 February), it recorded an astonishing 1,845 beasts within Mafeking, other than the 600 government horses and 200 government mules. Even more remarkably that tally increased to 1,858 by 1 April, a testament to the cattle-rustling and sheep-stealing skills of the Barolong, particularly Mathakgong, his band of cattle-thieves, and some Mfengu.[34]

31 BL Add Mss. 46,848, f. 112, Weil Mss, report on stock, 19 January 1900.
32 NAM, 1968-10-42, B-P diary, 30 and 31 January and 5 March 1900.
33 NAM, 1968-10-42, B-P diary, 11 February, 5 March, 6 April and 20 April 1900; *Official History*, vol. 3, p. 165.
34 Comaroff (ed.), *Diary of Sol T. Plaatje*, pp. 134–5, 142, 152–3; Willan 'The Siege of Mafeking' in Warwick (ed.), *South African War*, pp. 139–60, at p. 151; Jeal, *Baden-Powell*, p. 262; NAM, 1968-10-42, B-P diary, 25 February and 5 April 1900.

The military authorities bought most of the captured cattle, and by 15 April, Mafeking possessed a thirty-day supply of cattle, calves and sheep, and another thirty-day supply of tinned meat, enough to last until 15 June. This was quite apart from the horses and mules in government and private hands – animals suffering from limited forage and exhausted grazing land. Town Guardsman Bernard Baker, formerly of Scarborough, who would later serve in the remount depot of the 17th Lancers, described the 'poor beasts' as 'in a most shocking condition. We had nothing to feed them on, and on account of the shelling they could not get out any distance to graze.'[35] What alarmed Baden-Powell, however, was a sudden increase in animal consumption – 283 beasts during the first fortnight of April – thereupon he required that 'all animals should be registered and branded and owners would have to account for them when called upon'.[36]

Horsemeat and donkey became a staple of the diet latterly, and the first of four soup kitchens, which was in operation from 13 February, served a brawn based on horsehide, meal and oat husks. A sausage factory produced 1,000 lbs of horse or donkey sausages per day, and bakers produced new forms of biscuit and bread from inferior products. An even greater 'boon' to the entire community was Sowens porridge made from fermented oats after the flour had been removed, and one pound of damaged oats and spent oat bran made nearly a gallon of bitter porridge. William Sim, who had spent eight years working on the Kimberley to Bulawayo railway, prepared Sowens porridge for an initially sceptical Baden-Powell. Having found that Corporal Rose's unit relished the addition of Sowens to their daily ration, that the 'natives like it', especially the Mfengu who wouldn't eat horse,[37] and the townsfolk wanted to buy it, B-P authorized mass production. By 20 April he still had 132,940 lbs of oat bran and crushed oats in store, sufficient to make 212,704 quarts over 85 days, that is, up to the end of June. Jack Mackenzie, rightly proud of this Scottish contribution to the siege, wrote home that he was 'deeply indebted to Willie Sim', and that many inhabitants 'stated that he (W.S.) had kept the people alive'.[38]

No aspect of Baden-Powell's command proved more controversial than his rationing policy. He has been accused of overstating the hardships of the siege,

---

35 'Life in Mafeking', *Scarborough Post*, 7 August 1900, p. 5.

36 NAM, 1968-10-42, B-P diary, 16 April 1900.

37 Alfred Musson had negotiated with the Mfengu, see David Sinclair, *The White Tide* (Gweru, Zimbabwe: Modern Press, 2002), pp. 186–7; see also NAM, 1968-10-42, B-P diary, 13 March 1900; *Official History*, vol. 3, p. 174.

38 'The Sowens-Maker of Mafeking', *(Aberdeen) Evening Express*, 11 July 1900, p. 4; NAM, 1968-10-42, B-P diary, 24 March and 20 April 1900; Lady Sarah Wilson, *South African Memories*, pp. 192–3; 'Mafeking "Sowens". Letter from W. Sim', *Elgin Courant*, 10 July 1900, p. 5; 'Despatches From Mafeking', *Inverness Courier*, 27 April 1900, p. 3;

of starving the blacks to save the whites, and even of crimes against humanity. 'Seldom', wrote Rosenthal, 'has a siege been endured with less hardship – for those who weren't natives.'[39] There is no need to repeat the learned critique of such writings by Tim Jeal, especially where he exposed the misreading of primary and printed primary sources (both B-P's staff diary and Neilly's account), the failure to allow for B-P's early uncertainty about the longevity of known foodstuffs, and the continuing uncertainty about the timing of any relief.[40] Suffice to say racial prejudice did not determine the policy of reducing the number of mouths to feed: Baden-Powell actually discriminated in favour of the local Barolongs, whose stadt was part of Mafeking's defences, and the 'armed natives' who were vital to the defence, as distinct from the remainder of the 'refugee natives' driven into the town by the Boers (see Appendix B). He sought ways to induce the refugee group to escape through the Boer lines to food stored at Kanye by Plumer's column. This policy received the approval of Lekoko and the acting chiefs of the Barolong stadt (10 February), and of the leading members of the white community (14 March).[41]

Nor was maltreatment, still less starvation, the means by which B-P wished to drive surplus personnel out of Mafeking. When he first learned of blacks dying from starvation, Baden-Powell 'gladly' approved the creation of soup kitchens, as suggested by Major Goold-Adams, for the relief 'of old and indigent natives'. By 13 March 'five soup kitchens' were in operation, and when four days later, he learned that 'a large number of Fingoes', who would not touch horse, were sick with dysentery as a result of eating the husks of oats in the meal, he promptly approved a new soup composition. This was thickened with a jelly (made of starch, cows' feet and boiled-down hide) instead of oatmeal. Edward Ross duly observed that 'B.P. has done everything he could to alleviate distress amongst the natives, none of whom need now starve, if they are not too lazy to walk as far as the horsemeat soup kitchens.'[42] Nor was the commandeering of rationed foodstuffs and the initial closing of local grain stores, both white and black, any more than an attempt to curb

---

'A Hero of Mafeking: Aberdeenshire Man on the Siege', *(Aberdeen) Evening Express*, 28 August 1900, p. 5; and Weir, *Boer War*, p. 84.

39   Rosenthal, *Character Factory*, p. 43; see also Pakenham, *Boer War*, pp. 406–10 and Hopkins and Dugmore, *Boy*, p. 138.

40   Jeal, *Baden-Powell*, pp. 260–77.

41   NAM, 1968-10-42, B-P diary, 8 and 10 February and 14 March 1900. Sadly B-P is charged with 'undoubted racism' in this regard by Kenneth O. Morgan, 'The Boer War and the Media (1899-1902)', *Twentieth Century British History*, vol. 13 (2002), pp. 1–16, at p. 7.

42   Willan (ed.), *Edward Ross*, p. 194 and NAM, 1968-10-42, B-P diary, 31 January, 13 and 17 March 1900.

illicit trading and enforce a pricing policy. On 19 November Chief Wessels welcomed the policy as a means of regulating distribution within the stadt.[43]

Admittedly Baden-Powell's subsequent policy of discouraging refugees from staying in Mafeking, and encouraging them to walk the 120 km to Kanye, was more brutal. For this compulsory expulsion, B-P required the dismissal of servants, the sole employment of Barolong in labour gangs, and then the halving of rations for five days prior to closing the grain store, which was only used by refugees, on 20 February (the same day that a soup kitchen was opened). Small numbers of refugees escaped but attempts to convoy large numbers of refugees through the Boer lines were unsuccessful. On the night of 17 February a couple of abortive attempts were mounted to convoy 900 refugees through the Boer cordon, involving the assistance of Chief Magistrate Bell and Sol Plaatje, who regarded this 'matter of such a sweeping importance as puts all other questions in the dark'.[44]

By 13 March, after many Boers had gone north to confront Plumer, refugees began leaving of their own volition and passed through the depleted lines 'in better numbers', but, according to a census completed on 30 March, 7,019 'natives' remained in Mafeking.[45] An upsurge in departures only followed the arrival of Plumer's Intelligence Officer, Lieutenant Frank Smitheman on 4 April. He had demonstrated the ease of passing through the Boer lines, and before leaving three days later, he persuaded the Barolongs' Queen Mother, her family, and thereby most of the Barolong women and children, to leave for Kanye. Despite the failure of a mass breakout on 7 April when only ten escaped, and captured women were stripped, beaten and turned back by the Boers (and eight days later another nine were shot dead, possibly by mistake during an ambush of cattle rustlers), 60 women reached Plumer by 11 April, another 200 escaped on 13 April, and ultimately some 1,200 women and children reached Plumer.[46] 'We all know', wrote J. R. Algie, a persistent critic of B-P, 'that our ultimate success depends upon feeding the natives, and that every hundred natives we rid ourselves of increases the certainty of our triumph.'[47]

Baden-Powell was more vulnerable, both during the siege and subsequently, to the charge that he failed to relieve the suffering of 'hundreds'

43   NAM, 1968-10-42, B-P diary, 19 November 1899.

44   Comaroff (ed.), *Diary of Sol T. Plaatje*, pp. 124–6; NAM, 1968-10-42, B-P diary, 11 and 14 February 1900; BL Add Mss 46,848, Weil Mss., Baden-Powell, 'Notice', 11 February 1900; Jeal, *Baden-Powell*, pp. 266–8.

45   NAM, 1968-10-42, B-P diary, 13 and 30 March 1900.

46   Ibid., 8, 11, 13, 14 and 20 April 1900; *Official History*, vol. 3, p. 173.

47   'The Native Problem at Mafeking', *Liverpool Echo*, 5 May 1900, p. 4 and 'Letter From Mafeking. The Feeding of the Natives', *Daily News*, 12 May 1900, p. 3. Reports varied about the scale of the exodus: Plumer stated that 'over 1,200 natives' reached Kanye (Q. 17,950)

of blacks, as reported by Neilly, dying 'from starvation or the diseases that always accompany famine'.[48] The Shangaans, about one-quarter of the 2,000 refugees, were the probably the worst affected group; as Ada Cock observed on 27 March,

> There were a lot of Shangaans under the trees here and they have been stealing my fowls . . . They are dying of starvation. I don't know what they have been living on but the smell is something dreadful. They have been moved up to the empty Police Barracks and are killing and eating all the dogs they can get.[49]

An earlier report from Mafeking, dated 18 February, described 'natives' braving 'the dangers of the town' and wandering about 'with gaunt, hungry faces in search of work, which will entitle them to obtain an extra ration of meal'.[50] Yet the Shangaans were difficult to assist because, as Lady Sarah observed,

> They had done most of the trench work, and had been well paid . . . [but] they were strangers to the other natives, who had their own gardens to supplement their food allowance, and blacks are strangely unkind and hard to each other, and remain quite unmoved if a (to them) unknown man dies of starvation, although he be of their own colour.[51]

Free soup kitchens, later Sowens kitchens, and trying to corral the destitute for feeding in the Police Barracks all helped, but black deaths from starvation persisted, probably accounting for a substantial proportion of the 487 non-combatant deaths.[52] Neilly never blamed Baden-Powell for the distressing

---

evidence before *RCWSA*, p. 335; B-P claimed that 'nearly 2,000 native women and children' left, 'B-P's report', p. 892; while Bell estimated that nearly 3,000 left, mainly Barolong and not refugees, Bell, 'Diary', 21 April 1900, p. 116.

48 Neilly, *Besieged with B.-P.*, p. 228; for complaints of illiberality towards this group, see Hamilton, *Siege of Mafeking*, p. 249 and Weir, *Boer War*, pp. 58 and 60.

49 Midgley, *Petticoat in Mafeking*, p. 75; see also NAM, 1968-10-42, B-P diary, 19 February and 27 March 1900; Jeal, *Baden-Powell*, pp. 267–73.

50 'Mafeking Siege', *East Anglian Daily Times*, 9 March 1900, p. 5.

51 Lady Sarah Wilson, *South African Memories*, p. 191; for a similar observation, see Baillie, *Mafeking*, p. 210.

52 Estimates of the black deaths vary considerably. The Town Council claimed that 1,000 blacks had been killed or died of starvation and disease, Willan (ed), *Edward Ross*, p. 241 but this may have been exaggerated in a post-war letter to emphasize the role of local blacks in the siege. Jeal reckons that 700 may have starved to death, *Baden-Powell*, pp. 272–3 and for B-P's return, see 'B-P report', p. 893.

scenes he witnessed; he feared that sharing rations equally between blacks and whites would have exhausted the 'entire food supply in a few weeks, and we would either have died of starvation in the works or surrendered and been marched as prisoners of war to Pretoria'.[53] Similarly, the devout Charles Weir, who shared some of his meat ration with the 'starving natives', affirmed that '*One man we have faith in*, and that is COLONEL BADEN-POWELL. Everybody has the fullest confidence in him.'[54]

While Baden-Powell undoubtedly favoured his garrison and the white community in his rationing policy, it is a canard to state that the garrison, still less whites as a whole, enjoyed a 'comfortable' siege as a consequence.[55] B-P overstated the regularity of the rations and never dwelt on their quality, whereas these aspects dominated the correspondence of many survivors of the siege, both civilian and military. In her February diary Mrs. Simmonds despaired of the rations for children: 'Fancy a healthy child having only four ounces of bread and four ounces of meat, with no flour or oatmeal or anything to fall back upon. We keep Marjie going by supplementing plenty of cod liver oil.' She blamed not Baden-Powell, without whom 'we should have been taken long before this', but the Cape Ministry: 'It is entirely owing to them that we are in the plight we are.'[56] The quality of the food, particularly the bread, appalled many of the women, and, in her widely reported letter of 22 March, Mrs. Simmonds again complained that

> Everyone here feels the want of more, better, and varied food . . . . Sometimes the bread is awful black, and made from locally crushed oats, with all the husks on, simply split in long pieces. We are all downright hungry. . . . Last Sunday Weil's store was allowed to sell certain articles of food, e.g., pea flour and margarine; former 2s. 6d. a tin, latter 3s. per lb. The crush outside the store was so great that women fainted, and some were waiting for hours and then unable to get in. We were only able to buy ½ lb. of margarine, and 1 lb. pea flour which did not last long. My hens have given over laying, and eggs are 12s. and 6d. per dozen. Potatoes we haven't seen for weeks. Coal cannot be had. . . . Our meat is good but poor and tough. We almost entirely depend upon the natives looting enemy's cattle,

---

53 Neilly, *Besieged with B.-P.*, p. 231.
54 Weir, *Boer War*, p. 60.
55 Gardner, *Mafeking*, p. 157 and Rosenthal, *Character Factory*, p. 43.
56 'Extracts from Mafeking Diary', *Leamington Spa Courier*, 1 September 1900, p. 8. This contradicts the sweeping assertion of Hopkins and Dugmore that 'The white residents blamed Baden-Powell for all their woes', Hopkins and Dugmore, *Boy*, p. 153.

and sometimes we have horseflesh, but that I cannot manage, so on those days I am hungrier than ever.[57]

Soldiers shared the dismay. The Aberavon trooper, Edwin Davies (Protectorate Regiment), informed his mother that

We lived all right . . . until about Christmas, and from that time it started to get worse. The stuff I have eaten during the siege you would hardly believe . . . the bread . . . made out of oats and linseed meal. It was full of little husks . . . and also horse flesh. They started it by way of sausages. I didn't eat my share the first day, but next day hunger compelled me to, and I soon got used to it. . . . We used to fry our sausages in all kinds of stuff – salad oil, cocoa nut oil, and even fried them in dubbin and Vaseline.[58]

Eleven of his comrades delighted various newspapers by writing to the Colman company on 14 April to commend 'the exceptional purity and abilities of your No. 1 Pure Rice Starch. During the siege, while living upon short rations, we have used large quantities of it making puddings, blancmange, and also for thickening our soup.' Unfortunately they added, 'the supply has come to an end, not however, before the price reached 12s. 6d. per packet.'[59] In another example of how the rank-and-file coped, BSA Police trooper, Arthur Williams shared the recipe for 'siege brawn' with his mother:

Take a horse hide (needn't be fresh), chop into small pieces, boil the hoofs into a jelly (after removing the shoes), mix up the skin and jelly with a little glue, and boil down again; then pour in tin or pan and leave standing till cold, turn out ready for table. I don't think you would want two helpings of this, although we all ate it with a relish, as only half starved people could.[60]

Nevertheless soldiers, as Davies conceded, were privileged; they often had access to vegetables if they could afford them (cabbages at 2s.. 6d.. or 3s.

57 'Lady's Letter From Mafeking', *Mansfield Chronicle*, 18 May 1900, p. 3; see also Crauford, 'A Nurse's Diary', p. 287; 'A Nun's Diary in Mafeking', *Armagh Guardian*, 3 August 1900, p. 3; Lady Sarah Wilson, *South African Memories*, p. 194.
58 'In Besieged Mafeking', *Western Mail*, 18 July 1900, p. 6.
59 'Short Rations in Mafeking', *Essex County Standard*, 14 July 1900, p. 2; the letter also appears in *Grantham Journal*, 14 July 1900, p. 7; *Northern Echo*, 2 July 1900, p. 4; and *Essex Newsman*, 14 July 1900, p. 1.
60 'An Interesting Letter From Mafeking', *Bucks Herald*, 14 July 1900, p. 6.

each compared with pre-war prices of 3*d.* or 4*d.*),[61] and occasionally luxuries, which they could eat or trade. Baker informed his father, the vicar of All Saints, Scarborough, that 'For small tins of sardines, containing eight fish, I paid as much as 7*s.* 6*d.* a tin, and was offered a profit on my purchase to sell. For my six ounces of oat cake (made from condemned oats, the man's daily allowance), I have regularly been offered 10*s.*'[62] Far-sighted officers, like Lieutenant Gemmell, had anticipated the worst and bought in a stock of tinned goods early in the siege, 'or I don't know how my wife would have got on – she simply could not bear the sight of horse flesh'.[63] Even Protectorate troopers, like Corporal Hulse, on learning in advance of the proclamation to close all food shops, 'made the most of the opportunity and stored a good quantity of extras in the shape of jams, sugar, tinned fish, biscuits, etc'.[64] Most soldiers paid the excessive prices but, in explaining his reluctance to do so, Sergeant James Collins Taylor, formerly of Nottingham, claimed that 'the chances' were '10 to 1' that he would be killed,

> By my side men were gradually getting weaker and weaker, succumbing to the effects of exposure and starvation, so I concluded to look after my health and strength as long as I could. The consequence was that on the day the siege was raised, if not among the richest, I was one of the few healthy men remaining in Mafeking.[65]

However exaggerated these anecdotes, as the soldiers were hardly on the brink of starvation, Taylor was making a sensible point that short rations compounded the adverse effects of prolonged trench duty. Lack of exercise, argued the Eyemouth man, exacerbated these effects, despite the readiness of troops to use Sunday afternoons to play 'cricket, football and athletic sports'.[66] Again Corporal Kelland probably exaggerated, in writing home from the Imperial Yeomanry Hospital, Deelfontein, on 15 June, nearly a month after the siege ended, that 'it was the short and very bad rations that caused my illness' (a very severe attack of fever and dysentery). He was probably right, nonetheless, in suspecting that the quality of the food had hardly helped his recovery: 'The bread was worst of all; it was made of oats badly ground. You can't think how the husks used to stick in our throats.'[67]

61 'In Besieged Mafeking', *Western Mail*, 18 July 1900, p. 6.
62 'Life in Mafeking', *Scarborough Post*, 7 August 1900, p. 5.
63 'The Siege of Mafeking', *Ayr Advertiser*, 23 August 1900, p. 5.
64 'The Siege of Mafeking', *Penistone Express*, 31 August 1900, p. 7.
65 'Life in Mafeking under the Siege', *Nottingham Evening Post*, 25 June 1900, p. 4.
66 'An Eyemouth Man in Mafeking', *Berwickshire News*, 17 July 1900, p. 5.
67 'Lancer's Life at Mafeking', *Somerset County Gazette*, 14 July 1900, p. 3.

Complementing the concerns about rationing were fears about food security. At a time of scarcity and recurrent shellfire when soldiers were often manning redoubts or undertaking trench duty, and citizens left their homes to huddle in underground shelters, fear of theft was widespread. 'There were many acts of thieving', wrote Corporal Rose, 'with which Colonel Hore had to deal': the usual field punishment within the Protectorate Regiment was 'hard work with pick and shovel three hours a day' and tying up the delinquent for 'two hours at night'. Rose recalled that it felt 'rather painful' to have to tie up 'a chum – perhaps a thoroughly honest fellow under ordinary circumstances', who had been moved by hunger to steal 'a tin of potted meat'.[68] Local citizens were even more concerned about the looting of their property. When Edward Ross heard that the first black had been sentenced to be shot for housebreaking and theft, he noted in his diary: 'This sounds very severe, but as the whole town is left unprotected, and most places with openings made by enemy shells, something must be done to stop this.'[69] Ada Cock, who had to look after her four children while her husband, Willie, served with the Bechuanaland Rifles, found that she had to keep a loaded revolver with her to 'frighten' the thieves. By late April she encountered a rash of thefts, including those of 'a little Kaffir girl' who was a 'great help' in the house but 'stole a tin of road rations and a tin of corned beef which is a serious loss just now'. Much worse was the theft of a tethered cow on 28 April, which was found two days later 'half eaten'. The arrest of three culprits, and the padlocking of the remaining beasts, was scant consolation: Ada complained, 'how lonely it is with my babies asleep and never knowing when some thief won't be trying to thieve'.[70]

Of the 430 charges placed before the Court of Summary Jurisdiction in Mafeking, the 197 for theft comprised the largest number (followed by 184 minor offences, 35 for treason and 14 for house-breaking). The court imposed 291 punishments, predominantly corporal (115 sentences for a first offence involving theft), 91 imprisonments with hard labour, 57 fines, 23 detentions in gaol, and five death sentences (three for spying or spreading false information and two for theft, involving persistent offenders).[71] Baden-Powell, who never sat on the court, has been castigated for upholding the death sentences on the five blacks,[72] but the weight of evidence in two cases

68 'A Hero of Mafeking: Aberdeenshire Man on the Siege', *(Aberdeen) Evening Express*, 28 August 1900, p. 5.
69 Willan (ed.), *Edward Ross*, p. 74.
70 Midgley, *Petticoat in Mafeking*, pp. 87–8.
71 'B-P report', p. 897; see also Willan (ed.), *Edward Ross*, p. 223 and Cecil, *Imperial Marriage*, pp. 138–9.
72 Rosenthal, *Character Factory*, p. 43.

of spying so impressed the normally sceptical Hamilton that he concluded there was 'no alternative but that which implied immediate execution'.[73] In another case, tried by Bell and Lord Cecil, Baillie recorded that the 'native convicted as a spy . . . quite acknowledged the justice of his sentence, but only seemed to think that it was hard lines that he should be executed before he had time to procure any information at all'.[74] The sentences may have seemed draconian, or 'very severe' as Edward Ross observed,[75] but they were evidence-based and decided by a civil-military authority. Baden-Powell was not administering justice in a purely arbitrary manner: in upholding various sentences, he was confirming that security, including food security, was of paramount importance in the midst of a siege.

Shelling

Fortunately capital sentences were relatively rare: much more immediate was the threat to the garrison and citizens from shellfire and long-range rifle fire. Snyman had little option other than tightening the cordon, which was extremely difficult with so few men under his command. Sometimes he authorized a combined bombardment, as on 1 January, when five guns sustained their cannonade for six hours, and the 94-pounder apparently delivered twenty-one shells. Periodically the Boer gunners sought to outwit the Mafeking alarm system by varying the rate and intensity of their shelling, and Major Baillie reckoned that it was the firing of an odd shell, as distinct from sustained shellfire, which caused the occasional loss of life.[76] Magistrate Bell attributed the slight increase in shell casualties to an increasing carelessness within the community, and a failure of people to keep under cover 'while firing is going on'.[77] Greed contributed, too, as another seven men were killed or injured handling enemy shells by 4 May, since unexploded bombs or fragments of shell casings, particularly of the 94-pounders, were in great demand. 'Curio-buyers', as the Eyemouth man explained, paid handsomely 'for good specimens, consequently the Kaffirs used to be on the alert, and immediately a shell burst you could see them scampering all around for fragments'.[78]

---

73 Hamilton, *Siege of Mafeking*, pp. 215–17.
74 Baillie, *Mafeking*, p. 110; see also Bell, 'Diary', 17 January 1900, p. 75.
75 Willan (ed.), *Edward Ross*, p. 223.
76 Baillie, *Mafeking*, p. 105; on the New Year's Day bombardment, see the *Official History*, vol. 3, p. 164 and Neilly, 'Mafeking's Shell Record', *Pall Mall Gazette*, 11 August 1900, p. 2.
77 Bell, 'Diary', 2 January 1900, p. 64.
78 'An Eyemouth Man in Mafeking', *Berwickshire News*, 17 July 1900, p. 5; Hamilton, *Siege of Mafeking*, p. 144 and on the numbers of casualties, see T. Hayes, diary, 4 May 1900 in Bottomley (ed.), 'Siege of Mafeking and the Imperial Mindset', p. 150.

Luck played its part, as the Boer shrapnel did not burst in the air and the incendiary shells proved ineffective. During the artillery duel of 31 January, Edward Ross saw a 94-pound shell land about 14 m from a British 7-pounder gun but then 'ricocheted right over the heads of the gunners, and Major Panzera, who was there in command'.[79] On 27 March, when the Boers concentrated their fire all day from four different sides, using the 94-pounder, two 12-pounders, two 5-pounders and a 1-pounder Maxim to pour 400 shells into Mafeking, only four people were injured. They included Mrs Manthy and her maid, hit by a shell that penetrated the air hole of her bombproof shelter, and two soldiers, including Sergeant Abrahams (Cape Police), hit on the foot. Abrahams had to have his foot amputated.[80] The ingenious defenders devised new dummies as targets of distraction, including the one deployed at Fort Ayr on 6 February, which attracted valuable ammunition when it was first displayed. Other targets, like the Nordenfeldt gun position bombarded on 8 February, were simply too small. Here the high-velocity 12-pounder Krupp, 'a magnificent gun', as Ross observed, that 'shoots as straight as a die', pounded the earthworks 'time after time' but could not disable the little barrel, which emerged a 'couple of inches above ground out of the trench'.[81]

Assaulting larger targets like the hospital, the nearby convent and the women's laager, even without killing people, meant that the gunnery remained a powerful psychological threat, especially the shelling from the 94-pounder. The appalling damage it inflicted upon buildings, animals, and occasionally people, left Mrs. Simmonds bewailing on 13 February, 'If only that big gun could be stopped!'[82] Sometimes, as on 3 January, the gunnery proved counter-productive, when it pounded the women's laager with eight shells, killing a little girl and injuring the spine of a boy of eight, while the forewarned Boer women reportedly clapped and cheered from the safety of the river bank. 'This naturally caused an unusually strong burst of indignation against our cowardly foes', wrote Sergeant Francis,[83] while Corporal Illingworth reckoned that the enemy 'will have a lot to answer for'.[84] Even more demoralizing was the flaccid British response: rapid salvoes from the 7-pounder that fell short – 'our rotten little 7 pdrs,' wrote Willie Hayes, 'are worse than useless and

---

79 Willan (ed.), *Edward Ross*, pp. 115 and 124.
80 Bottomley (ed.), 'Siege of Mafeking and the Imperial Mindset', p. 141.
81 Willan (ed.), *Edward Ross*, pp. 134 and 137.
82 'Extracts from a Mafeking Diary', *Leamington Spa Courier*, 1 September 1900, p. 8; see also Changuion, *Silence of the Guns*, p. 43.
83 NAM, 1974-01-138, Sgt. Francis diary, 7 January 1900, p. 7.
84 'A Bradford Man in Mafeking', *Bradford Daily Telegraph*, 14 June 1900, p. 3; see also 'The Siege of Mafeking', *Newry Telegraph*, 24 February 1900, p. 3 and 'The Transvaal War', *Inverness Courier*, 16 February 1900, p. 5.

should be put in a museum'[85] – and a protest by Baden-Powell that elicited no response.

B-P, nonetheless, was cheered by the contribution of an old ship's cannon, dated 1770, which had been dug up on Rowland's Farm near the stadt. As the railway workshops had managed to mount it on a wooden carriage, and make round cannonballs for it, this weapon, known as 'Lord Nelson', was hauled into place by oxen. The Reverend Weekes described how it fired its shot like 'cricket balls', bounding over the veld into and beyond the Boer laagers. Although the shooting was wildly erratic, its range, at possibly 4,570 m, was longer than that of any other British gun.[86] In late February the railway workshops also produced a 4.5in howitzer, named 'The Wolf' after B-P's nickname. It added another dimension to the town's artillery by firing a 16-pound shell out to about 3,660 m, even if the fuses of the shells proved problematic at first and the ammunition supply a continuing concern. As ammunition for the 7-pounder and the Hotchkiss was running low by mid February, the railway factories proved invaluable in producing 7-pounder common shell, round shot and fuses as designed by Lieutenant R. M. Daniel (BSA Police).[87]

If the British guns drew the enemy's fire from the town or served in ambushes at night, and boosted morale on account of the range of the new ordnance, they hardly discomforted the enemy. On the contrary, it appears that the Boers were reduced to mirth and hilarity whenever they saw the gunpowder smoke or flashes from the British guns.[88] Unaware of this, Baden-Powell had to find other ways of coping with the enemy's shellfire, usually by extending his defences outwards, which required guns and detachments of sharpshooters to harass the Boer gunners. Such intimidation seemingly prompted some movements of the 94-pounder to various locations around Mafeking.[89] On other occasions B-P resorted to trickery; on 28 January, after another (possibly unintentional) shelling of the women's laager, he informed

85 Bottomley (ed.), 'Siege of Mafeking and the Imperial Mindset', p. 101.

86 'The Rector of Mafeking Speaks at Wickford', *Essex Newsman*, 8 December 1900, p. 1; NAM, 1968-10-42, B-P diary, 3 January 1900; Godley, *Life*, p. 77; Wilson, *With The Flag*, vol. 2, p. 610.

87 Brent. L., Vyvyan Mss., MS. 147/5/1/40, More, 'Railway Report', p. 5; MS. 147/5/5/4/1, Vyvyan, 'Defence of Mafeking', 13 January 1900; and NAM, 1968-10-42, B-P diary, 13, 26 and 28 February, 3 March 1900. Both More and B-P claimed that the 'Wolf' fired out to 4,000 yards [3657.6 m] 'B-P report', p. 896, but B-P insisted that the naval cannon 'was the best gun we had for distance', (Q 19,911) evidence before *RCWSA*, p. 429.

88 Pretorius, 'The Besiegers' in Smith (ed.), *Siege of Mafeking*, vol. 1, p. 76.

89 *Official History*, vol. 3, p. 164; Hamilton, *Siege of Mafeking*, p. 213; Changuion, *Silence of the Guns*, p. 43.

Snyman that he would erect a temporary gaol for his 'Dutch suspects' beside the laager, and, on 28 February, permitted the delivery of a letter from the 'Dutch women' to Snyman, urging him to stop shelling the women's laager.[90]

Nevertheless, famous near misses recurred, including the 94-pounder shell that entered the convent roof (26 January), demolishing a chapel and the wall of the room in which Lady Sarah, her husband and Major Goold-Adams were about to eat supper, and on 28 February, a shell wrecked the offices of the *Mafeking Mail*. Like Lady Sarah and her guests, the editor, Mr. G. N. H. Whales, escaped from the shell fragments landing within a few feet of him and emerged covered in dust. His escape, said Tom Morse, 'was little short of miraculous'.[91] Trooper Williams was lucky, too, avoiding a 94-pounder that fell a few feet away in Cannon Kopje; it devastated a card school, killing two men and wounding two others: 'the noise was awful', he recalled.[92]

Brickfields

In effect Baden-Powell could only try to limit the damage by pushing Mafeking's defences outwards, especially in the brickfields, where the enemy under Cronjé had established forward positions from which their 5-pounder gun, 1-pounder Maxim and sharpshooters with their Mausers harassed the townsfolk. Baden-Powell probed these defences in early November when he sent Mfengu and the Coloured Contingent (Cape Boys) under Captain Charles Goodyear into the brickfields, to draw the fire of the enemy and contest the space, including the brick kilns used by the enemy's marksmen. The Boers responded by pushing an advanced trench about 90 m forward, or until it was about 1,700 m from the town.[93] The ensuing conflict became a hazardous and labour-intensive form of warfare that continued over several months. In spite of their redoubt and use of snipers, the Boers found this form of warfare even more challenging after several thousand burghers trekked south with Cronjé. They sustained the siege by stretching their reduced manpower, employing the services of armed blacks, and calling upon the services of foreign volunteers.

So the imperial forces had the opportunity to consolidate their position in the brickfields; they exploited the undulating terrain and rocky ridges by building a series of miniature forts linked with trenches. Black labour

---

90 Hanbury-Tracy Mss., Baden-Powell to Snyman, 28 January and 28 February 1900; NAM, 1968-10-42, B-P diary, 28 January and 19 February 1900.
91 'A Stroud Man Home From Mafeking', *Stroud Journal*, 10 August 1900, p. 3; Lady Sarah Wilson, *South African Memories*, pp. 184–7.
92 'An Interesting Letter from Mafeking', *Bucks Herald*, 14 July 1900, p. 6.
93 Brent. L., Vyvyan Mss., MS. 147/5/5/4/1, Vyvyan, 'Defence of Mafeking', 3 November 1899; NAM, 1968-10-42, B-P diary, 3 and 9 November 1899.

gangs under Colonel Vyvyan, now the Commanding Engineer, worked systematically at night to extend the network of trenches along the northern bank of the Molopo River. They built forts and constructed, repaired and deepened parallel and communication trenches. Covering these working parties, and then occupying the trenches, were the Cape Police under Captain Marsh and the intrepid Coloured Contingent under Sergeant (later Lieutenant) H. M. B. Currie, who had replaced the mortally-wounded Captain Goodyear. The Boers contested these movements with shellfire, bursts of fire from their Maxims, and frenetic rifle fire, both volleys at night and sniping day after day, and sometimes on Sundays. As the two sides came closer during the New Year, they tried to cross each other's trenches or establish flanking and enfilading trenches. For about a fortnight the two sides were barely 55 m apart, with sniping parties active on both sides, and the 'Cape Boys' shouting insults and singing songs like 'Rule Britannia' and 'God Save The Queen' to annoy the enemy.

The Eyemouth man was by no means alone in commending 'these boys', who 'did splendid work, and accounted for several of the Dutch crack shots. They know not what fear is, and are ready to expose themselves when duty calls them.'[94] Corporal Hulse realized that the challenge of the Cape Boys was as much psychological as physical: 'These Cape Boys exasperate the Boers terribly. It is very amusing to hear them shouting to the Dutchmen calling them anything but gentlemen, and telling them they cannot shoot for nuts.'[95]

So important had the brickfields become that both sides, in spite of their depleted numbers, significantly increased their presence in the forts and trenches. Just after sundown on 11 February, upon learning that 'between 200 and 300 Boers' with another gun had joined the brickfields entrenchment, B-P moved 'the whole of the Col[onial] Contingent (45) into the advanced trenches', sent twenty-five Cape Police in support, and held three troops of the Protectorate Regiment and a Maxim 'ready to reinforce if necessary'.[96] Within two days he faced an acute dilemma, as the enemy had entrenched to the left of 'our adv. trench', and reopened a trench 'about 1400 yards [1,280 m] E of town', so putting the town within range of aimed rifle fire. On 16 February, Baden-Powell sent a Maxim up to fire from the most advanced trench but described this firing at night as 'more for moral effect than anything'.[97] In

---

94 'An Eyemouth Man in Mafeking', *Berwickshire News*, 17 July 1900, p. 5.
95 'The Siege of Mafeking', *Penistone Express*, 7 September 1900, p. 7; see also Weir, *Boer War*, pp. 59 and 64; Willan (ed.), *Edward Ross*, pp. 166–7; NAM, 1968-10-42, B-P diary, 9 January and 8 February 1900; T. Hayes, diary, 1 March 1900 in Bottomley (ed.), 'Siege of Mafeking and the Imperial Mindset', p. 131; Hamilton, *Siege of Mafeking*, p. 246.
96 NAM, 1968-10-42, B-P diary, 11 February 1900.
97 Ibid. 16 February 1900.

the ensuing exchanges as the two sides sapped and counter-sapped, snipers moved through the knee-length grass to shoot from '80 yards [73 m] and closer' at enemy gunners, while spies, such as Sergeant-Major William Ashton Taylor (a 'coloured' NCO of the Cape Boy contingent), crept to within 18 m of the enemy on several occasions, overhearing conversations and examining their forts and earthworks, before bringing back invaluable intelligence.[98]

On 28 February the Boers mounted a sapping operation to retake some of their former positions in the brickfields. Despite a counter sap begun on the same evening, Baden-Powell reckoned that the enemy had advanced to 'within 80 yards [73 m] of our Easternmost work (Taylor's post) by 1 March.[99] Hamilton, who had joined Marsh in his quarters within the brickfields, asserted that the enemy had filled their advanced trench with sharpshooters, who could fire through imperial loopholes 'at five hundred yards [473 m] range'. At daybreak, they had 'turned upon us a 9-lb. Krupp, a 5-lb. Creusot, a 3-lb. Maxim, and about 500 rifles', and 'for some hours afterwards . . . the air seemed to ring with the droning notes of the Martinis and the sharp crackle of the Mauser'. The besieged replied with volleys 'to impress upon the Boers the uselessness of their efforts', and the Cape Boys 'called them all the dirty names they could think of'.[100]

Even more formidable, though, was the assault launched on 3 March, which had the support of 'Big Ben' after its return to its Rooigrond location (following moves to and from McMullin's Farm and the Western laager). After enemy saps had come so close that three dynamite hand grenades could be thrown at the British trenches (all falling short), the Creusot pounded the British positions. Algie in his letter, published by the *Western Mail*, described how the gun directed its shells

> First at the more advanced trenches, then gradually working down, hitting and damaging one trench after another, until the whole of our position, right from the extreme front to base had suffered damage, her fire all the time being marvellously accurate and effective. These advanced trenches gave very little cover, being very shallow – in fact, when taking cover from the big gun our men were exposed to the

---

98 Ibid., 21 and 23 February, and 1 March 1900; T. Hayes, diary, 16 February 1900 in Bottomley (ed.), 'Siege of Mafeking and the Imperial Mindset', p. 123 and Willan (ed.), *Edward Ross*, p. 166.

99 Brent. L., Vyvyan, Mss., MS. 147/2/3/1, Vyvyan, diary, 28 February 1900 and NAM, Acc. 1968-10-42, B-P diary, 1 March 1900.

100 Hamilton, *Siege of Mafeking*, pp. 222–4; see also Amery, *Times History*, vol. 4, p. 593 and T. Hayes, diary 1 March 1900 in Bottomley (ed.), 'Siege of Mafeking and the Imperial Mindset', p. 131.

enemy's rifle fire. The onslaught was so severe and accurate that our men dared not show a finger even, and were able to reply only very slightly.

One of the shells mortally wounded Sergeant-major Taylor, who had done invaluable daring work with his Cape boys, and soon after four boys were severely wounded.[101]

Under the protective the fire of the 94-pounder, the Boers had dug across a British sap and built a loopholed work within it, from which they could rake the trench with rifle fire, at least as far as another loopholed wall held by the defenders. The 'Cape Boys' mistook an order from Vyvyan, and retired from this trench on 4 March, with Sergeant-Major Taylor and another 'Boy' mortally wounded. Retaliatory fire from a 7-pounder at De Kock's corner proved fruitless, as Algie observed, since only one of its twenty-six shells 'got anywhere near the Boer position, some of the shells rendering our own advanced positions dangerous'.[102] It then required extremely brave work by Hamilton and Corporal Rosenfield (Bechuanaland Rifles) to close the sap and ensure that the firing of thirty-four shells by the 94-pounder had availed the enemy nothing:

> Having succeeded in damaging to some extent our earthworks, the fire ceased, all we lost being a few yards of an incomplete, partially-made trench. The Cape boys deserve great praise for the plucky manner in which, despite the loss of their able officer, and several comrades, they stood up to the enemy's deadly effective fire. Later in the day one of our snipers killed the enemy's gunner.[103]

Informed of the loss of the trench to the Boers by telephone from Currie's post, Baden-Powell sent up reinforcements, whereupon Lieutenant J. A. P. Feltham (Protectorate Regiment) formed a new assault force composed of eight Bechuanaland riflemen and some Cape Boys. Throwing dynamite grenades as he ran, Feltham led the rush and scattered the enemy. Thereafter the Colonel reorganized the 100 men allotted to the brickfields operation, with FitzClarence in overall charge, Feltham commanding the advanced posts, now only 64 m from the enemy, and Inspector Browne (Cape Police) in command of the rear trench. Captain Marsh was hardly pleased, as Tom Hayes reported, since he had 'done all the hard work and was out there before

---

101 'Life At Mafeking', *Western Mail*, 30 April 1900, p. 6.
102 Ibid.; see also Brent. L., Vyvyan Mss., MS 147/2/3/1, Vyvyan, diary, 5 March 1900.
103 'Life At Mafeking', *Western Mail*, 30 April 1900, p. 6; see also *Official History*, vol. 3, p. 171 and Hamilton, *Siege of Mafeking*, p. 246.

any of the trenches were cut'.[104] Of the men allocated, about half were Cape Boys, another thirty-six Cape policemen, and twelve Bechuanaland riflemen.

Over another fortnight the brickfields remained a distinct and isolated theatre of operations, with heavy rifle firing recurring during daylight and darkness. There were supporting contributions from heavier ordnance, like the Nordenfeldt on behalf of the defenders, but not the Creusot, which had returned to its position at McMullin's Farm. Casualties continued to mount, including Trooper Webb (Cape Police), a highly popular son of a Port Elizabeth magistrate, who was shot through the head by an explosive bullet. His death warranted a large funeral at dusk on Saturday, 10 March, for a man who 'was well known in Mafeking and very much respected'.[105]

On 23 March, however, the Boers began dismantling the roofs from their huts, and abandoned both their advanced trenches and their redoubt in the brickfields. They left dynamite in an abandoned trench, which the defenders had to disable, before moving forward on 24 March to occupy all the former Boer positions. In the process they gleaned useful information about the fall of Bloemfontein from portions of newspapers abandoned in the trenches. Sergeant Francis and many others saw this as another triumph, maintaining that the Boers had withdrawn 'having been troubled a good deal in the Brickfields by our snipers'.[106] Without detracting in any way from the courage, resilience and determination of the fighters in the brickfields, another reason for the Boer withdrawal was probably the removal of detachments in mid-March to confront Plumer's column north of Mafeking and to serve in other theatres of the war. As the Boer forces, depleted since Cronjé's departure, were now even more diminished, and as brickfield fighting remained a labour-intensive mode of warfare, it was no longer worth continuing. The outcome, nonetheless, remained a significant victory for the defending forces, as the brickfields had been a key position for the enemy, 'one from which', as Vyvyan reflected, 'the town has suffered so much annoyance for months'.[107] 'The Boers', wrote Dr Tom Hayes, 'have now retired almost beyond rifle range of the town and the pressure is greatly relieved.'[108]

104 T. Hayes, diary, 5 March 1900 in Bottomley (ed.), 'Siege of Mafeking and the Imperial Mindset', p. 133.
105 'An Eyemouth Man in Mafeking', *Berwickshire News*, 17 July 1900, p. 5; see also T. Hayes, diary, 11 March 1900 in Bottomley (ed.), 'Siege of Mafeking and the Imperial Mindset', p. 135 and "Expectations of Relief', *Western Morning News*, 9 April 1900, p. 8.
106 NAM, 1974-01-138, Sgt. Francis diary, 23 March 1900; see also Willan (ed.), *Edward Ross*, pp. 194–5; and *Official History*, vol. 3, p. 172.
107 Brent. L., Vyvyan Mss., MS. 147/2/2/1, Vyvyan, diary, 24 March 1900.
108 Tom Hayes, diary, 24 March 1900 in Bottomley (ed.), 'Siege of Mafeking and the Imperial Mindset', p. 140.

Conclusion

In his official report on the siege, Baden-Powell said relatively little about the brickfields operation. In his description of 'Engagements during the Siege' he neither accorded it a separate section, as he did his various 'kicks' and the repulse of Commandant S. J. Eloff's attack on 12 May, nor listed the casualties incurred in those protracted actions. As a cavalry officer used to planning offensives that maximized the element of surprise and seized the offensive, often employing edged weapons (as in the form of bayonet attacks during the siege), he was not closely involved in the day-to-day fighting across the trenches. He had nonetheless intervened at key moments to invest extra manpower and alter the command arrangements: his summary of the fighting was pertinent,

> during January, February, and March, we pushed out counter-works, and gradually gained point after point of ground till we obtained grazing for our live stock, and finally, (after a hard tussle in the 'Brickfields,' in trenching and counter-trenching up to within 70 yards [64 m] of the enemy's works), we drove them back at all points out of range for rifle fire of the town.[109]

Baden-Powell greatly exaggerates in claiming that the other advantage of this 'tussle' was the scale of 'enemy losses', namely '40 per month killed', an estimate supposedly 'admitted by a Boer medical officer'.[110] Yet he is correct in emphasizing that the brickfields fighting, though crucial for the town, was only part of the overall operations. The latter would include consolidating positions in the most advanced redoubts, such as Fort Ayr, and sustained pressure by Barolong snipers against the more exposed Boer positions, such as Fort Cronjé in the south-west, until the enemy abandoned the position. In the east the Boers also evacuated their advanced trench near the Malmani road, which FitzClarence had charged on 27 October, and the new defensive position was renamed after that intrepid officer. Within the brickfields Baden-Powell had ordered the demolition of most of the former Boer positions, apart from one, renamed as Fort Browne, where emplacements were built for a 7-pounder, the new howitzer and even the old 16-pounder. The Boer artillery could still deliver a furious and sustained fusillade, as it did on 27 March, but the defenders could retaliate, firing upon the main Boer laager

---

109 'B-P report', p. 892.
110 Ibid. The Boers suffered casualties, including the odd fatality, in the brickfields fighting, but their records do not suggest anything like the losses claimed by B-P, see Pretorius, 'The Besiegers' in Smith (ed.), *Siege of Mafeking*, vol. 1, pp. 68 and 103.

and the big gun, both some 3,650 m distant.[111] Meanwhile Vyvyan continued consolidating the new positions in the brickfields, with four gangs of 120 labourers working there as late as 4 April.[112]

Baden-Powell's tactics had exposed the weakening capabilities of the investing forces as they deployed several hundred burghers to intercept Plumer's relief column. Plumer's defeat at Ramathlabama (30 March) enabled Snyman to bring back most of these burghers but Pretoria's demand for the return of the Creusot gun (12 April) significantly reduced the artillery threat to the town. As early as 22 March, Mrs. Simmonds expressed her confidence in 'Colonel Baden-Powell', who 'looks after us all, and we may be very thankful that the defence of Mafeking has been entrusted to such a capable man'. She hoped that 'we are getting in sight of the end now',[113] and once the garrison had pushed back the enemy's rifle fire, and 'Big Ben' had been withdrawn, a reduction in the intensity of Boer firepower would follow. Nearly a couple of months later Frank Firth, a trader who had left New Brighton fifteen years previously, wrote that

> with the exception of having eighteen bullets through the roof of the store, two 5-pound shells through, one 94-pound projectile, and one 5-pound bursting in the street four yards from the writer, and a bullet striking a box against which I was leaning, short rations, etc. I am happy to say I don't feel much the worse for the experience.[114]

Such insouciance was understandable towards the later stages of the siege, and in its immediate aftermath, but it hardly reflects the anxiety that was still evident in the early months of 1900. Had Baden-Powell not regarded the maintenance of civil-military relations throughout the seven months of the siege as of pivotal importance, and had he not preserved the vigilance of his military command, then events in the final days might have produced experiences much less reassuring than that those described by Mr Firth.

---

111 NAM, 1968-10-42, B-P diary, 27 March 1900; Amery, *Times History*, vol. 4, p. 592; *Official History*, vol. 3, p. 172.

112 Brent. L., Vyvyan Mss., MS. 147/5/2/50, Vyvyan to Colonel Commanding, 4 April 1900.

113 'Lady's Letter From Mafeking', *Mansfield Chronicle*, 18 May 1900, p. 3.

114 'The Siege of Mafeking. Experiences of a Late New Brighton Resident', *Wallasey and Wirral Chronicle*, 14 July 1900, p. 2.

Chapter 6

The Long Siege: Civil-Military Relations and the Defeat of Eloff

Although the municipal authorities and leaders of the English-speaking community had campaigned for the defence of Mafeking, and over 300 citizens had formed the Town Guard, the town was a deeply divided community. Not only did the war divide many colonial loyalists from their counterparts in the Dutch Reformed Church but it also divided both communities. Some Afrikaners remained loyal to the imperial cause while a minority of English speakers, not least among railway employees, expressed pro-Boer sympathies.[1] The pre-siege demographic movements in and out of Mafeking, particularly the ingress of English-speaking *Uitlanders*, probably bolstered the loyalist numbers but the bonds of commerce, inter-marriage and, in some cases, Freemasonry,[2] blurred divisions within the community. As loyalism co-existed with pro-Boer sentiments, Baden-Powell incarcerated over thirty people as suspected spies for the greater part of the siege. He also lost four soldiers through desertion to the enemy.[3] If these cases constituted the most extreme evidence of disaffection, he had to deal with lesser manifestations, sometimes expressed as grumbling or grousing. In effect, he had to attend to the security, morale and comforts of citizens throughout the long siege, and preserve a sense of vigilance among the dwindling numbers of troops under his command – a vigilance that would be tested as never before on 12 May 1900.

---

1 NAM, 1971-01-23-6/2, Roberts Mss., Baden-Powell to Lord Kitchener, 2 March 1900 and Brent. L., Vyvyan Mss., MS. 147/5/1/40, More, 'Railway Report', pp. 1 and 8.
2 Bill Nasson, *The South African War 1899-1902* (London: Arnold, 1999), p. 97. Lady Sarah claimed that Captain Kenneth McLaren received particularly attentive treatment for his wounds from 'brother masons among the Boers', 'Message From Mafeking', *Doncaster Gazette*, 20 April 1900, p. 8; see also Alan Amos Cooper, 'The Origins and Growth of Freemasonry in South Africa, 1772-1876' (University of Cape Town: unpublished MA thesis, 1980).
3 'B-P report', p. 897.

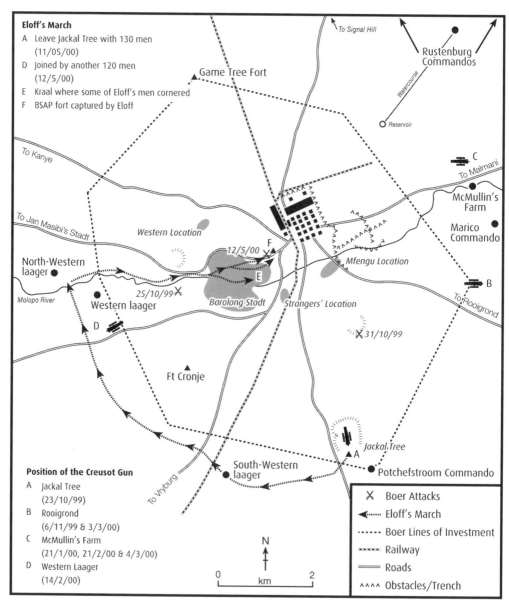

To Signal Hill

Game Tree Fort

Rustenburg Commandos

Watercourse

Reservoir

To Kanye

C To Malmani

McMullin's Farm

To Jan Masibi's Stadt

Western Location

Marico Commando

F 12/5/00

North-Western laager

Mfengu Location

E

B To Rooigrond

25/10/99

Molopo River

Western laager

Barolong Stadt

Strangers' Location

D

X 31/10/99

Ft Cronje

Jackal Tree

A

South-Western laager

Potchefstroom Commando

To Vryburg

N

0   km   2

X	Boer Attacks
◄‑‑‑‑	Eloff's March
‑‑‑‑‑	Boer Lines of Investment
═══	Railway
═══	Roads
^^^^	Obstacles/Trench

Map 3 Boer positions around Mafeking

Civil-Military Relations

Underpinning the tension that bedevilled citizens and soldiers in Mafeking was anxiety about relief. It was fuelled by rumours and speculation before and after the New Year, and persisted despite the warnings of lengthy delays by Baden-Powell on 11 February and 20 April. Just as Algie complained about 'numerous' rumours as early as 13 November, Mrs. Simmonds noted rumours of a 'flying column' from Kimberley on 6 December, and, in her diary for 13 January, wrote that 'we are continually hearing, through native runners, of the troops being on their way; yet they never come.'[4] The rumour mill was such that Lady Sarah wrote on 5 April that 'there is no news of relief, which seems further off than ever', while two days later, Corporal Illingworth claimed that 'we are expecting the relief force almost daily now'.[5] And in reflecting upon the 'monotonous life' in Mafeking, Neilly of the *Pall Mall Gazette*, queried 'Plumer! When would he be down? "In a few days", "in a week or so", "in a month". Such were the guesses hazarded . . . . It seemed incredible to the people that the tiny town could be left without relief.'[6] Despite B-P's efforts to share such information as he had, a lack of reliable information bedevilled civil-military relations throughout the siege.

Although Mafeking avoided a close blockade, with messages, despatches and letters passing in and out of the besieged town, the process was expensive and unreliable. Mayor Whiteley stated that each Barolong runner received about £6 per journey, and they 'usually set off on dark nights about eight o'clock . . . and we could generally tell by listening for the "sput", "sput" of the Mauser fire, whether the Boers forming the cordon had discovered them or not'. Sometimes the runners, organized by Sol Plaatje, left on moonlit nights when the danger was greater but they 'knew the country well . . . [and] were generally allowed to go their own way'.[7] As Boer numbers fell sharply after Cronjé's departure, the chances of getting through significantly improved but the movements remained costly and riddled with uncertainty. Baden-Powell and wealthy officers, town officials, war correspondents and merchants such as Weil, sent letters and messages, but this hardly warrants the gross exaggeration of Gardner that 'Ordinary individuals and officers alike found that communications with the outside world was [*sic*] scarcely interrupted.'[8]

Communication from Mafeking remained a fraught and frustrating process. Colonel Vyvyan and Magistrate Bell complained repeatedly that even

---

4   Algie, 'Diary', 13 November 1899, p. 42 and 'Extracts From Mafeking Diary', *Leamington Spa Courier*, 1 September 1900, p. 8.
5   'Message From Mafeking', , *Doncaster Gazette*, 20 April 1900, p. 8 and 'A Bradford Man in Mafeking', *Bradford Daily Telegraph*, 14 June 1900, p. 3.
6   Neilly, *Besieged with B.-P.*, pp. 94–5.
7   'Mafeking and its Mayor', *Leeds Mercury*, 23 July 1900, p. 3; on Sol Plaatje's role, see Comaroff (ed.), *Diary of Sol T. Plaatje*, pp. 68, 73–4, 80–1.
8   Gardner, *Mafeking*, p. 99. Short letters from B-P, including one hidden in a quill within a Black runner's pipe, got through, including 'Letter From Colonel Baden-Powell', *Sale and Stretford Guardian*, 14 February 1900, p. 3; 'Letters From The Front', *Huntingdonshire Post*, 17 February 1900, p. 7 and 'The Siege of Mafeking. Letters From Baden-Powell', *(Gloucester) Citizen*, 9 February 1900, p. 3.

if messengers got through, they rarely brought any news. By the end of the siege Vyvyan bemoaned the receipt of only one letter and three telegrams from home since 7 October, a couple of telegrams from Cape Town and a letter from Bulawayo.[9] Edward Ross would probably have welcomed this correspondence, having sent nine telegrams north and south of the town by 9 January without a reply, and likewise Lieutenant Gemmell, who realized after receiving a letter from home after the siege that at least one of his cables had never arrived.[10] In post-siege letters Troopers Dowson and Williams both explained that they had delayed writing home for fear of interception,[11] and several siege participants and their families admitted that they had not heard anything from each other throughout the siege.

Although mail from England arrived by runners from Plumer on 7 April, and more followed with the relief column on 17 May, John Poole probably spoke for many on 7 June, when he claimed that 'we have not yet received any mail from Europe since the siege began'.[12] Corporal Kelland only received letters from home on 11 June and a parcel, dated 4 December, on 20 June: 'being shut up so long', he wrote, 'without getting any news made one feel very dull'.[13] In these circumstances, Corporal B. Johnson ('D' Squadron, Protectorate Regiment) understood that his mother in Derbyshire must have been 'very anxious about me here',[14] and Frank Firth suspected that his old friend in New Brighton, Merseyside, 'knew more about Mafeking than we did'. As he explained, 'In a besieged town, taken so unawares as we were, we had a lot of Dutch amongst us, and had news been divulged to the townspeople, the enemy would soon have got to hear of it, consequently we heard nothing.'[15] Communications and the flow of information were by no means as reliable and straightforward as Gardner imagined.

9   Brent. L., Vyvyan Mss., MS. 147/1/1/21, Vyvyan to Aunt, 6 May 1900 and MS. 147/1/1/21, Vyvyan to Mollie, 21 May 1900; see complaints in MS. 147/2/2/1, Vyvyan, diary, 8 December 1899 and 26 February, 4, 23 and 27 March, 1 and 30 April, 1, 2 and 11 May 1900 and Bell, 'Diary', 23 November, 9 and 20 December 1899 and 9 February and 27 March 1900, pp. 35, 49, 57, 88 and 108.

10   Willan (ed.), *Edward Ross*, p. 93; 'The Siege of Mafeking', *Ayr Advertiser*, 23 August 1900, p. 5.

11   'A Mafeking Hero', *North Star*, 6 July 1900, p. 3 and 'An Interesting Letter From Mafeking', *Bucks Herald*, 14 July 1900, p. 6.

12   'Inside Mafeking', *Newbury Weekly News*, 12 July 1900, p. 2; see also 'Shut Up In Mafeking', *Stroud Journal*, 11 May 1900, p. 3. On the receipt of the first English mail, see NAM, 1968-10-42, B-P diary, 7 April 1900.

13   'Corporal Kelland of Combwich and the Siege of Mafeking', *Somerset County Gazette*, 11 August 1900, p. 3 and 'Lancer's Life in Mafeking', *Somerset County Gazette*, 14 July 1900, p. 3.

14   'Interesting Letter From Mafeking', *Derby Daily Telegraph*, 3 July 1900, p. 3.

15   'The Siege of Mafeking. Experiences of a Late New Brighton Resident', *Wallasey and Wirral Chronicle*, 14 July 1900, p. 2.

Information circulated around Mafeking through rumours and gossip, occasionally exchanges with the Boers on Sundays, but primarily through the columns of the *Mafeking Mail* in its special siege slip form. Baden-Powell, who had burnished his credentials as a military correspondent in previous campaigns, has been criticised for using the local newspaper to convert minor stories about the siege into 'major news events' to lift morale and promote his own qualities and prestige.[16] Undoubtedly B-P remained a major source of local information through his general orders, notices and eminently quotable and humorous remarks. He understood the importance of boosting morale and tried to do so throughout the siege. In commenting upon local military matters, he had to consider the possibility of leaks from people of a pro-Boer persuasion, and, on the course of the war, had to depend upon despatches from Plumer and the reports of spies and messengers, neither of which proved particularly reliable. There were at least six false reports of Kimberley's relief, several before Christmas, and another about the relief of Ladysmith in the *Mafeking Mail* of 6 January, all emanating from messengers. It wasn't until 26 February that accurate news of the relief of Kimberley and Ladysmith reached Mafeking.[17]

Disgruntled Mafekingites complained that Baden-Powell was holding back information, and Edward Ross alleged that G. N. H. Whales, the editor of the *Mafeking Mail*, was briefly arrested for remonstrating about this with B-P's staff.[18] The Colonel asserted that he distributed information whenever he had it (see Appendix C), including glum news from Lord Roberts about lengthy delays before relief.[19] Accordingly, the *Mafeking Mail* continued reporting in a cheerful and optimistic tone, albeit with an uncompromising hostility towards the enemy. When the *Stroud Journal*, a Liberal Gloucestershire newspaper, reviewed the siege reportage of the *Mafeking Mail*, it was impressed by the

> breezy spirit of hopefulness and certainty as to the ultimate ability of the plucky garrison to keep the old flag flying. We do not agree with everything that appears in the 'Mail'. We cannot bring ourselves to think and speak contemptuously of the Boers.[20]

---

16 Hopkins and Dugmore, *Boy*, p. 138 and Morgan, 'The Boer War and the Media', p. 7.
17 Comaroff (ed.), *Diary of Sol T. Plaatje*, pp. 59, 106 and 123; Neilly, *Besieged with B.-P.*, p. 179.
18 Willan (ed.), *Edward Ross*, pp. 64–5; despite the absence of corroboration from Whales or B-P, this charge is repeated by Jeal, *Baden-Powell*, p. 307 and Jacqueline Beaumont, 'Reporting the Siege' in Smith (ed.), *Siege of Mafeking*, vol. 1, p. 336.
19 'Latest News'. *Mafeking Mail*, 25 January 1900, p. 1; Jeal, *Baden-Powell*, p. 306; Comaroff (ed.), *Diary of Sol T. Plaatje*, p. 115; and Jacqueline Beaumont, 'The British Press during the South African War: The Sieges of Mafeking, Kimberley and Ladysmith' in Mark Connelly and David Welch (eds), *War and the Media: Reportage and Propaganda, 1900-2003* (London: I. B. Tauris, 2005), pp. 1–18.
20 'The "Mafeking Mail"', *Stroud Journal*, 17 August 1900, p. 3.

Frustrated by the lack of news, Ross and his ilk had to glean what they could from odd copies of Cape and Rhodesian newspapers, which were usually out-of-date by the time they reached Mafeking, or Boer newspapers, like Johannesburg's *Standard and Diggers' News*, which were either passed on at diplomatic meetings by Boer representatives or left behind in vacated trenches. English-speaking readers, though, regarded enemy sources as largely 'bombastic' propaganda,[21] which only compounded their lack of reliable information and so enhanced a sense of isolation and despondency. By late April, Angus Hamilton wrote that 'it is difficult to keep up one's spirit when from day to day there comes no news, only that curious, ironical instinct, that perhaps it may be that we are not to be relieved at all'.[22] Vere Stent agreed that the journalistic profession had become one of making 'bricks without straw in the shape of despatches without news'.[23] In these circumstances the public persona of Baden-Powell, 'always cheery and buoyant in manner', according to Corporal Rose,[24] and 'never seen to wear a frown', always warbling 'operatic airs and music-hall ditties', as Neilly recalled,[25] evoked mixed feelings.

At one level B-P's unremitting cheerfulness repelled the boredom of the long siege. Within a month of the siege beginning, Algie and Bell chafed at the monotony of the siege experience, and even revisionist writers agree that this monotony and boredom constituted 'the greatest hardship' of the siege.[26] The war correspondents, starved of major military engagements, complained about the weariness of the siege as early as November, and continued to do so until the end of the seventh month, when the *Mafeking Mail* regretted the 'awful monotony' that 'was sometimes irksome in the extreme'.[27] Yet boredom and B-P's good humour neither meant that the siege 'was almost totally uneventful'[28] nor that the garrison and townsfolk faced only a 'vague threat' from the enemy.[29] While the intensity of the Boer bombardments fluctuated

21 On unreliable local and Boer newspapers, Weir, *Boer War*, pp. 20, 35 and 49–50 and Willan (ed.), *Edward Ross*, p. 136; see also Fransjohan Pretorius, 'Boer Propaganda During the South African War of 1899-1902', *Journal of Imperial and Commonwealth History*, vol. 37, no. 3 (2009), pp. 399–419.
22 Hamilton, *Siege of Mafeking*, p. 286; see also Willan (ed.), *Edward Ross*, pp. 132, 136 and 194.
23 BL, Add Mss. 46,848, f. 257, Weil Mss, Vere Stent to Weil, 24 April 1900.
24 'A Hero of Mafeking: Aberdeenshire Man on the Siege', *(Aberdeen) Evening Express*, 28 August 1900, p. 5.
25 Neilly, *Besieged with B.-P.*, p. 166.
26 Gardner, *Mafeking*, p. 135 and Rosenthal, *Character Factory*, p. 38; see also Algie, 'Diary', 13 and 14 November 1899, p. 42 and Bell, 'Diary', 31 October 1899, p. 14.
27 Hamilton, *Siege of Mafeking*, pp. 134 and 208; Neilly, *Besieged with B.-P.*, p. 94; *Mafeking Mail*, 14 May 1900, p. 1.
28 Morgan, 'Boer War and the Media', p. 7.
29 Rosenthal, *Character Factory*, p. 39.

on a daily and weekly basis, the physical threat and psychological pressure endured. As Nurse Crauford observed perceptively at the end of February,

> There is little news to write – just the same old thing each day – shelling and sniping, grumbling sometimes, and working always. There is hardly a building in the town that has not been injured and a great many people have been killed – though few when one thinks of the number of shells.[30]

On Sundays, too, as long as the truce held, when Mafeking underwent a weekly transformation as 'gaily dressed ladies' gathered to watch various sports in the Recreation Ground, it 'could not have been believed', argued Corporal Rose, 'that the town was so nearly in the grip of a determined enemy'.[31]

External pressure remained but it is far from true that the 'white residents blamed Baden-Powell for all their woes'.[32] Admittedly Algie recorded malcontents in the Town Guard, berating B-P for not seeking external assistance in order to gain personal kudos after the siege.[33] Weil and De Kock famously clashed with B-P, and, on 18 March, the Colonel heard from three sources that townspeople were getting tired of the siege. This prompted the drafting of his timely 'grousing' memorandum, which was published in the *Mafeking Mail* of 29 March (see Appendix C).[34] Yet many citizens who were thoroughly fed up with the siege did not blame Baden-Powell. By late January Mrs. Simmonds, who had expressed her frustrations with the siege as early as 8 November, claimed that 'If members of the Cape Ministry were here, they would be treated to a taste of Lynch law. It is entirely owing to them that we are in the plight we are. If it were not for B.-P., we should have been taken long before this.'[35] Even Algie, an arch-critic of B-P, when writing on 6 March, insisted that the

> townspeople are getting sick of this tiresome monotony. They think it high time the authorities made some determined attempt to effect relief. They feel they have been the victims of culpably gross neglect, and sometimes think that the authorities are going to let them remain in a state of siege until the end of the war.[36]

---

30 Crauford, 'A Nurse's Diary', p. 245.
31 'A Hero of Mafeking: Aberdeenshire Man on the Siege', *(Aberdeen) Evening Express*, 28 August 1900, p. 5.
32 Hopkins and Dugmore, *Boy*, p. 153.
33 Algie, 'Diary', 18 October 1899, p. 14.
34 NAM, 1968-10-42, B-P diary, 18 and 20 March 1900, and *Mafeking Mail*, 29 March 1900, pp. 1–2.
35 'Extracts From Mafeking Diary', *Leamington Spa Courier*, 1 September 1900, p. 8.
36 'Life at Mafeking', *Western Mail*, 30 April 1900, p. 6.

Far from blaming Baden-Powell, many citizens and soldiers appreciated his contribution to the Sunday entertainments and the defence of the town. Although Sabbatarians had originally deplored the idea of using Sunday for recreation and entertainment, Mafeking Sundays boosted morale in many different ways. Church attendances rose, the soldiers and town guardsmen benefited from the cricket, football and athletics held on the Recreation Ground, and people flocked to the various entertainments. These included agricultural and horticultural exhibitions, a siege baby show, gymkhanas, dances, concerts and a major siege exhibition held by Mr De Kock with prizes for fancy work, model-making, shell collections, drawing, sketching and clock mounting (on 94-pounder shells). Baden-Powell proved a consummate showman, starring with his songs, piano playing, recitations, prize-winning sketches, his performing as 'Signor Paderewski', and acting as a ringmaster in the gymkhana. 'Our Colonel', wrote the Eyemouth man, 'was always to the fore with a comic rendering, which always went down well with a very appreciative audience.'[37] Corporal Rose remembered B-P keeping 'his audience laughing until the tears ran down their cheeks. His monologues were delightfully amusing . . . Baden-Powell', he claimed, was 'a great commander' but 'even greater as a comedian'.[38]

Nor did the soldiers and citizens of Mafeking assume that because B-P was a natural showman, and 'a good man at a party', he was thereby less gifted as a commanding officer.[39] They realized that the use of humour and sporting analogies were an intricate part of his leadership style. 'The Colonel is always so cheerful himself', wrote Nurse Crauford, 'so we feel we must be the same',[40] and her brother-in-law, James Buchan recalled B-P's 'dauntless and cheerful' manner, admitting on one occasion that 'the only bad news he had was that the Shamrock had lost to the Columbia'.[41] An even more memorable sporting analogy involved his reply to Eloff's challenge to a cricket match, when B-P declared, 'But just now we are having our innings and have so

---

37 'An Eyemouth Man in Mafeking', *Berwickshire News*, 17 July 1900, p. 5; see also 'The Transvaal War', *Inverness Courier*, 10 April 1900, p. 5; 'Mafeking Before Relief. How The Garrison Kept Up Their Spirits', *Manchester Courier*, 12 June 1900, p. 8; Lady Sarah Wilson, *South African Memories*, p. 200.

38 'A Hero of Mafeking: Aberdeenshire Man on the Siege', *(Aberdeen) Evening Express*, 28 August 1900, p. 5; see also Brent. L., Vyvyan Mss., MS. 147/2/3/1, Vyvyan, diary, 11 February 1900.

39 Gardner's canard that B-P was among the 'least "educated" in a military sense' of British officers is refuted by Jeal's evidence that out of 718 candidates for Sandhurst, B-P came 2nd in the cavalry list and 5th in the infantry, compare Gardner, *Mafeking*, p. 54 with Jeal, *Baden-Powell*, pp. 41–2.

40 Crauford, 'A Nurse's Diary', p. 288.

41 'A Portobello Man in Mafeking', *Edinburgh Evening News*, 15 August 1900, p. 2.

far scored 200 days not out, against the bowling of Cronje, Snijman [*sic*: Snyman], Botha, and Eloff; and we are having a very enjoyable game.'[42] As George Tighe queried, 'How could you fail to have faith in a leader like that?' and Theodore Mathias, a railwayman in Mafeking, agreed that the

> chief feature of the siege was the remarkable manner in which the people kept their spirits up, due of course, in large measure, to the encouragement and example of that great hero, Baden-Powell. . . . The successful defence was also due in large measure to the power of organization and the magnificent ability of Baden-Powell and the officers with him.[43]

Citizens appreciated that there was method behind B-P's merriment, and that his 'audacious humour', as Reverend Weekes described it, was intended to annoy and discomfort the Boers.[44] Bernard Short cherished memories of the Colonel's 'numerous good ruses' to fool the Boers, including a truck laden with bricks and carrying a stove pipe that resembled an armoured truck from a distance, which was sent down the railway line: 'They shelled it all day, and so took the fire off the town.' There was also a dummy fort rigged with half a lamppost on cartwheels that made 'an excellent gun' for a similar purpose.[45] The multiple talents of Baden-Powell, and the confidence inspired by him, resonated in Bernard Baker's letter of 16 April, written in the seventh month of a weary siege. 'In Baden-Powell', he wrote, 'we have a capital all round man. His abilities are great. He is not only a soldier, but an artist, author, elocutionist, and diplomat. He is undoubtedly the right man in the right place.'[46]

B-P coped with diverse challenges, including the suffering of Mafeking's 'wage-earning' inhabitants while business and work were suspended, and the plight of the European refugees. On the recommendation of Vyvyan, he approved the formation of a local relief committee, despite Vyvyan's perception that the refugees included 'undoubted wasters'.[47] The committee, as established on 15 November, relied on the energetic efforts of Alfred Musson, a local dairy businessman, to make 137 grants for 'clothing and

42 Hanbury-Tracy Mss., Baden-Powell to Eloff, 20 April 1900; see also NAM, Acc. 1968-10-42, B-P diary, 30 April 1900.
43 Tighe, 'How we defended Mafeking', p. 172 and 'Back From Mafeking', *Western Mail*, 24 July 1900, p. 5.
44 'Rector of Mafeking at Bristol', *South Wales Daily News*, 24 July 1900, p. 5.
45 'A Forest Hill Man In Mafeking', *Kentish Mercury*, 13 July 1900, p. 3.
46 'At The Siege of Mafeking', *Scarborough Post*, 15 June 1900, p. 5.
47 Brent. L., Vyvyan Mss., MS. 147/5/3/2, Vyvyan to Chief Staff Officer, 13 November 1899; see also Sinclair, *White Tide*, p. 185.

necessaries', worth £263.15.0, and grants of rations to 278 persons, amounting to £1,709.10.9.[48]

All this was done at a time when the town's money supply was steadily vanishing. During the siege the Standard Bank reckoned that there was £13,000 in circulation but so little of it came back to the bank that it struggled to pay the wages of the soldiers in January 1900.[49] While Lady Sarah thought that some of this was due to 'the natives . . . burying the money they received in wages', Baden-Powell suspected that the troops, who could neither afford to pay the wartime prices nor leave their money for fear of theft, simply carried cash on them.[50] At any rate he approached Edward Ross, an amateur photographer, and suggested turning his dugout into the 'Mafeking Mint' for the purpose of photographing £1 banknotes. B-P personally designed the notes with the famous 'Wolf' gun in the centre, a pile of homemade shells beside it, flanked by a loyal Dutch burgher on one side, a town guardsman on the other, and a woman kneeling with a child in her arms to symbolize 'the helpless inhabitants of the town'. Above the howitzer waved the Union Jack held by a trooper of the Protectorate Regiment. Printed on ordinary notepaper, and using a photograph brushed with a sanitising solution, the process enabled Ross and Captain Herbert Greener, the army paymaster, to produce about twenty £1 notes a day. Using the same wood block, they printed notes of various denominations from one shilling up to 10 shillings at an even faster rate. Despite a shell wrecking the 'Mint' on one occasion, production continued throughout the siege until 683 £1 notes and about 7,000 10-shilling notes were in circulation. They rapidly became souvenir items, as no-one presented a £1 note for repayment at the end of the siege, and only about fifty of the 10-shilling notes, so netting a profit of over £5,000 for the government. After the siege each note would be worth far more than its face value.[51]

More controversial was the decision to print postage stamps for issue within the town and defensive area with B-P's head upon them. Both at the time and subsequently, critics seized upon this act as proof of B-P's egotism and self-publicity, a charge that even his most authoritative biographer could not

48 Brent. L., Vyvyan Mss., MS. 147/5/3/2, 'Report on Local Relief Committee', 2 June 1900.
49 Weir, *Boer War*, pp. 43, 47 and 56.
50 Lady Sarah Wilson, *South African Memories*, p. 195 and NAM, Acc 1968-10-42, B-P diary, 31 January 1900.
51 Drooglever, "A Monument to British Pluck", pp. 65–6; for accounts of E. J. Ross's post-siege interview with *Photography*, see 'B.-P. as an Artist', *Elgin Courant*, 31 August 1900, p. 7 and 'How The Mafeking Pound Notes Were Made', *Belfast News-Letter*, 30 August 1900, p. 6.

deny.[52] Moreover, once it was clear that the stamps had caused offence, friends of Baden-Powell concocted a cover-up. In his autobiography Godley asserted that the idea of the stamp arose among various staff officers, and that the stamps were created 'as a surprise' for B-P. No-one, claimed Godley, suspected that stamps intended for local use would cause such offence.[53] In fact, Ross records in his diary that Baden-Powell sat twice for photographs for the 3d. stamp that was subsequently withdrawn when B-P realized that putting his image on the stamp was a case of lese-majesty. None of this inhibited soldiers, civilians and even chaplains from collecting sets of stamps, especially those surcharged with the words, 'Mafeking Besieged', confident that they, too, would appreciate rapidly in value. On 28 April Major Hanbury-Tracy assured Lieutenant Hoël Llewellyn (commanding the armoured train with Plumer's column) that the stamps were already 'fetching big prices now'.[54]

Relatively few Mafekingites expressed criticisms of Baden-Powell in print. The caustic assessment of Hamilton remains the most-quoted account; it testifies to B-P's purportedly 'keen appreciation of the possibilities of his career, swayed by ambition, indifferent to sentimental emotion'. Baden-Powell, wrote Hamilton, was 'eminently a man of determination, of great physical endurance and capacity, and of extraordinary reticence . . . . Outwardly, he maintains an impenetrable screen of self-control, observing with a cynical smile the foibles and caprices of those around him.' Less quoted by modern critics is Hamilton's subsequent assessment of B-P as a commanding officer: 'he has given to Mafeking a complete and assured security, to the construction of which he has brought a very practical knowledge of the conditions of Boer warfare, of the Boers themselves, and of the strategic worth of the adjacent areas'.[55] Mayor Whiteley, who worked more closely with Baden-Powell than most of the citizens, reckoned that B-P 'is a true soldier of the best modern type, destitute of all red tapeism [sic], and at all times prepared to adapt himself to circumstances. The people in Mafeking trusted him implicitly.'[56]

Ultimately soldiers, citizens and war correspondents judged Baden-Powell as their commanding officer. Some resented the restrictions of martial law or considered their services as town guardsmen insufficiently recognized, or deplored the length of the siege, scale of destruction, quality of the rations, and the tardiness of relief, but they all relied upon B-P and his staff for their

52 Jeal, *Baden-Powell*, p. 306.
53 Godley, *Life*, pp. 79–80.
54 NAM, Acc. 1997-02-13, Llewellyn Mss., Maj. Hanbury-Tracy to Lt. H. Llewellyn, 28 April 1900; 'An Interesting Letter from Mafeking', *Bucks Herald*, 14 July 1900, p. 6; 'Rector of Mafeking at Bristol', *South Wales Daily News*, 24 July 1900, p. 5; 'The Siege of Mafeking', *Penistone Express*, 12 October 1900, p. 7.
55 Hamilton, *Siege of Mafeking*, pp. 192–3.
56 'Mafeking and Its Mayor', *Leeds Mercury*, 23 July 1900, p. 3.

security. Baden-Powell exuded confidence that this security would endure. If he had any doubts about how his published reports, humorous asides, inventive tactics, and sheer resilience were being reported at home, his sister Agnes assured him in a letter that arrived on 10 April that 'Everybody is talking of you. You are the hero of the day. All the papers describe your many-sided talents . . . '.[57] Two days later came Queen Victoria's telegram: 'I continue watching with confidence and admiration the patient and resolute defence which is so gallantly maintained under your ever-resourceful command.'[58] Self-promotion had certainly worked; B-P had kept Mafeking firmly in the public eye, and had thereby enhanced the prospects of relief.

Some traders, like J. E. Jones, the chemist and manager of W. N. Cooper's pharmacy, were simply glad 'to come out alive'. Although he served in the Town Guard, Jones was surprised that the war had interrupted his weekly supplies from Kimberley. Forced to improvise and make what medications he could, he bemoaned his failure to profit from the siege and make the 'business one might have done'.[59] Many others had loftier feelings; they knew that they were making history. Writing in his diary of 9 January, Corporal Hulse noted:

> This is our 90th day of siege. We have now beaten a number of sieges during last century. Candahar was besieged for 34 days, Strasburg [*sic*: Strasbourg] 48 days, Metz 66 days, Potchefstroom 84 days, and Lucknow 84 days. We are getting quite proud of ourselves.

He knew, too, from newspaper accounts seen at the end of April that 'great festivals and celebrations' were being planned in Britain to commemorate 'the relief of Mafeking'.[60]

Writing on 10 February, Staff-Sergeant A. Elder assured his father in Pitlochry, Perthshire, that 'The Boers can never take this place while life's blood flows in the veins of the sons of Britain holding it. We are confident of success, and proud of our commanding officer, Colonel Baden-Powell.'[61] On 22 March Mrs Simmonds concluded her letter by giving thanks that 'the defence of Mafeking has been entrusted to such a capable man [as Baden-Powell] . . . . The siege of Mafeking', she anticipated, 'will be a memorable

57 Hillcourt, *Baden-Powell*, p. 195; on gripes about B-P, see Jeal, *Baden-Powell*, pp. 307–10.
58 NAM, Acc. 1968-10-42, B-P diary, 12 April 1900; see also *Mafeking Mail*, 12 April 1900, p. 1.
59 'Mafeking During The Siege', *Penistone Express*, 13 July 1900, p. 5.
60 'The Siege of Mafeking', *Penistone Express*, 24 August 1900, p. 6 and 28 September 1900, p. 7.
61 'A Letter From Perthshire Man in Mafeking', *Strathearn Herald*, 21 April 1900, p. 3.

episode in our lives.'[62] By the end of April, a Mafeking correspondent of the *Daily Chronicle* lauded the contributions of the besieged women and evoked the lineage of imperial siege histories: 'The spirit of the women of the garrison is beyond all praise. We know that Britain recognises that we are part of the same strain and blood as those who waited, trusted, and suffered at Delhi, Lucknow, and Cawnpore.'[63] Immediately after the relief, Bernard Baker assured his father that the thought of surrender had 'never entered our heads for a moment'. Englishmen, he insisted, 'can still fight as well as ever they could, and are willing to do so to uphold the country's traditions'.[64]

Eloff's Defeat

Such confidence was tested as never before by the daring assault on Mafeking led by Commandant Sarel Eloff of the Johannesburg Commando. A grandson of President Kruger, Eloff had stepped up when Snyman proved hesitant in mid-April about implementing an order from Pretoria to seek volunteers and make the long-delayed assault on Mafeking. Assembling the volunteers took nearly a month but Eloff was assured of covering fire from the east to mislead the defenders, the support of 500 mounted burghers, ready to follow at the predetermined signal, and, on the eve of the attack, the guidance of a deserter, 'Tottie' (E. J.) Hayes. Hayes reportedly revealed the location of the western outposts and offered to lead the advance along the banks of the River Molopo to the BSA Police fort. After the commando had marched from Jackal Tree to the Western laager in the early morning of 12 May, Eloff had some 250 volunteers under his command. He launched his assault at about 4 a.m. once he heard the artillery and rifle fire from Snyman's forces in the east.[65]

The timing of the attack could hardly have been more auspicious from a Boer point of view. After nearly seven months of siege, the garrison was suffering from mounting tolls of sickness, stress and sagging morale. The sickness rates had climbed steadily in March and April (with monthly hospital admissions of 82 and 103 respectively, or nearly double the 43 admissions in January and 52 in February). By 20 April Baden-Powell realized that 'the men are now much weakened by their continual work in the trenches on short rations',[66] and, on the following day, Lord Cecil, Goold-Adams and Godley agreed that 'the men are much reduced in strength by the long continuance of

---

62 'Lady's Letter From Mafeking', *Mansfield Chronicle*, 18 May 1900, p. 3.
63 'The Relief of Mafeking', *Hampshire Chronicle*, 12 May, 1900, p. 6.
64 'Life In Mafeking', *Scarborough Post*, 7 August 1900, p. 5.
65 For the best account in English of Boer planning and operations for this attack, see Pretorius, 'The Besiegers' in Smith (ed.), *Siege of Mafeking*, vol. 1, pp. 98–9.
66 NAM, Acc 1968-10-62, B-P diary, 20 April 1900.

low diet', with 'fever and dysentery becoming prevalent'.[67] Godley reckoned that the last month of the siege was 'on the whole the most strenuous of all'.[68]

Shrewd observers commented on the changing mood within the town and garrison. Lady Sarah described how the people, increasingly conscious of their extreme isolation, 'looked graver; a tired expression was to be noted on many hitherto jovial countenances; the children were paler and more pinched'. By 4 April, she was writing about 'the pinch of hunger . . . beginning to be felt'.[69] Similarly, on the eve of Eloff's attack, Corporal Rose wrote that 'The men stuck to their work doggedly, and there was no thought of surrender, but lightness of heart had disappeared.'[70] The stress of the protracted siege took its toll in differing ways: on 9 May, Baden-Powell sacked Lieutenant Ronald Moncrieffe, a heavy drinker, from his staff and 'put him in charge of forage supply' to give him something to do.[71]

If spirits were flagging, command, control and communications remained effective. Following the outburst of long-range rifle fire from the east, south-east and north-east on 12 May, which slackened after half an hour, Baden-Powell immediately telephoned McKenzie to put his forces on look out in the south-west. He quickly realized that the threat was from the west, as 'a strong force of Boers' had bypassed the pickets, entered the stadt and set fire to it.[72] Eloff's volunteers had filtered through the alleys of the stadt in three separate parties, and just before dawn one party under Eloff had rushed the BSA Police fort, where Colonel Hore, two officers and sixteen Protectorate troopers were quartered. Undetected in the darkness, the Boers surrounded Hore's men, who withdrew to the mess house at the eastern end, before surrendering. Angus Hamilton, who had ridden over to the fort and became a prisoner himself, described the fate of the prisoners in his siege memoir, but Corporal Rose retold the story of how 'Tottie' Hayes confronted his former commanding officer. Hayes 'pointed his revolver at Colonel Hore', and would have fired 'had not Eloff, to his credit be it said, promptly interposed, peremptorily ordered the ruffian to drop his weapon, and claimed the Colonel as his prisoner'.[73]

When Baden-Powell telephoned the fort and a burgher answered, he had the line disconnected. Having already ordered Godley to close up the western

---

67   Ibid., 21 April 1900.
68   Godley, *Life*, pp. 80–1.
69   Lady Sarah Wilson, *South African Memories*, p. 188 and 'Message From Mafeking', p. 8.
70   'A Hero of Mafeking: Aberdeenshire Man on the Siege', *(Aberdeen) Evening Express*, 28 August 1900, p. 5.
71   NAM Acc 1968-10-42, B-P diary, 9 May 1900.
72   Ibid., 12 May 1900.
73   'A Hero of Mafeking: Aberdeenshire Man on the Siege', *(Aberdeen) Evening Express*, 28 August 1900, p. 5; see also Hamilton, *Siege of Mafeking*, pp. 296–9. Gardner claims

posts, he formed an inner defence line between the stadt and the town, deploying the reserves of Bechuanaland Rifles, men of the Railway Division and the Town Guard to protect the south-west angle of the town. He called in Cape Police from the brickfields to act as a reserve in town, moved two of Panzera's guns to the western face of the town, and sent Protectorate reserves under Captains FitzClarence and Lord Charles Bentinck to assist Godley.[74] As a commanding officer, Baden-Powell had promptly deployed forces that would punish Eloff for his mistakes in setting fire to the stadt (and so alerting B-P to the point of attack), splitting his forces, and relying on Snyman's promise to supply mounted support when the stadt was burning.

The attack galvanised both town and garrison. Townsfolk turned out to watch, with the women, 'huddled in shawls' fearing, as Mrs Simmonds recalled, lest they be 'marched off to Pretoria'.[75] So desperate were the circumstances that prisoners in the nearby gaol were armed and ordered to fire on the Boers in the fort, while Barolong women and children scurried into the town. Corporal Hulse described how Lord Edward Cecil ran over to his barracks and ordered the Bechuanaland Rifles to fall in. As they ran across Market Square, Hulse saw that

> a magnificent spectacle presented itself, dozens of kaffir huts in the native stadt were blazing away like huge bonfires, the whole western portion seemed ablaze. Volumes of smoke rolled skywards from a line of burning mass half a mile in length, while the whole place seemed alive with cracking rifles, intermingled with the frequent boom of the enemy's cannon. I shall never forget the magnificent grandeur of the scene . . . . However, things looked lively, and we all knew in an instant that the Boers had broken through our outlying forts and were close upon the town itself, so it devolved upon every man to do his utmost to stop their further progress.[76]

As the riflemen took up positions behind a low earthwork opposite the BSA Police fort, about 450 m from the captured position, they realized the nature of the Boer predicament. Lieutenant Gemmell described the intervening terrain as 'quite flat and destitute of cover of any kind, so that any attempt at a rush

---

that B-P's communications with Godley were severed for a time, and that Godley was the real hero of the battle but Godley insists that he always remained in touch with B-P. Compare Gardner, *Mafeking*, p. 183 with Godley, *Life*, p. 81.

74 NAM Acc 1968-10-42, B-P diary, 12 May 1900; *Official History*, vol. 3, pp. 177–9; Amery, *Times History*, vol. 4, pp. 594–5.

75 'When Besieged in Mafeking', *Leamington Spa Courier*, 23 June 1900, p. 8.

76 'The Siege of Mafeking', *Penistone Express*, 12 October 1900, p. 7.

by the enemy must have meant great loss of life to them. We kept up a brisk rifle fire upon them whenever we saw signs of men moving about among the buildings round the fort.[77] After the Boers rejected a request to surrender at about 8 a.m., sniping continued all day (with Nurse Crauford, her sister, Mrs Helen Buchan, and Dr Willie Hayes treating the Boer wounded in the nearby 'Isolation Cottage'). Snyman, who had never favoured storming Mafeking, only provided firepower in support, with the 12-pounder gun delivering the heaviest daily shelling of the siege, some 179 shells.[78]

Several shells landed on the Bechuanaland trench, forcing Gemmell and his men to seek refuge in adjacent buildings but he still followed the course of events, especially after Godley had completed his cordon around the stadt:

> About 4 in the afternoon some of the Protectorate Regiment and Cape Police under Captain FitzClarence, went into the stadt to assist the Baralongs in rounding up some of the enemy, and soon after a party of 25 of them surrendered in a stone kraal and were brought prisoners into the town – the enthusiasm being tremendous.[79]

The Barolongs, as B-P commended in his General Order of 24 May 1900, now rendered invaluable services, a contribution that was illustrated subsequently in the *Graphic*.[80] Baden-Powell applauded the scouting prowess of Naderele and his willingness, despite being shot through the shoulder, to continue serving Captain Marsh; Josiah Motsherere and his comrades (four of whom were killed) for seizing a kopje before the enemy could occupy it in force; Joshua Molema and a small party of Barolongs for hemming the Boers within the kraal; and the efforts of several Barolong latterly to hold positions 'under a heavy fire'. Above all, as the day wore on, they prevented the Boers from obtaining water, especially after the water tank on which they depended was riddled and emptied. In this General Order, if not in his evidence before the royal commission, B-P recognized this crucial military contribution of the Barolongs as warriors, specifically

77 'The Siege of Mafeking', *Ayr Advertiser*, 23 August 1900, p. 5.
78 Neilly, 'Mafeking's Shell Record', *Pall Mall Gazette*, 11 August 1900, p. 2; see also Crauford, 'Nurse's Diary', pp. 290–2, and 396–7.
79 'The Siege of Mafeking', *Ayr Advertiser*, 23 August 1900, p. 5. B-P claims that twenty-seven surrendered at the kraal, NAM, Acc. 1968-10-42, B-P diary, 12 May 1900 but two of these may have died, Jeal, *Baden-Powell*, p. 295.
80 'The Last Attack on Mafeking: Good Service By The Baralongs', *Graphic*, 7 July 1900, p. 4.

'the pluck and loyalty of the Natives', who 'so materially assisted' in the 'eventual defeat of the enemy'.[81]

Supported by the Barolongs, a 'British force of 60 picked men', as described by Corporal Rose, 'fiercely attacked the enemy, hunting them from rock to rock and kopje to kopje'.[82] The second party of Boers was then surrounded but when a group of them, augmented by some who had escaped from the fort, retreated along the route by which they had come, they threatened Lord Bentinck's small party in their rear. Baden-Powell ordered Lord Bentinck by telephone to draw off his party, and let the Boers escape by one road, while Godley was to press the remaining Boers down this road 'under a very hot flanking fire'.[83] Among Lord Bentinck's party was Sergeant Taylor, who described how

> I never want to be in a tighter corner than I was that night of May 12th, when the Boers tried to get out the way they got in. It was a bright moonlight night, and we could see each other almost as if it were day. Before we got the word to retire we were firing at 20 yards' [18 m] distance. I killed two Boers who waded the river and were firing at me.[84]

Meanwhile Baden-Powell ordered the Cape Police to complete the encirclement of the fort before dusk. Within the fort the Boers had ransacked the stores, looting tinned food, liquor and clothing, leaving Trooper Edwin Davies, as he later found, with only one spare shirt, a pair of socks and his 'letters and photos'.[85] Eloff, as Hamilton memorably described, recurrently visited the prisoners, sitting on a case of Burgundy with his legs dangling and spurs tapping. He reflected upon the fortunes of war, issued instructions, and complained about the absence of reinforcements.[86] In the early evening, as Corporal Hulse recalled, 'a large party of the Boers made a rush to try and escape; we gave them a hot time, and killed several, but the majority managed to get away'.[87] The firing on the fort intensified, and within about half an

---

81 BL, Add. Mss. 46,852, ff. 278–9, Weil Mss., B-P, General Order, 24 May 1900. On B-P's recognition of the importance of the water tank, see 'Baden-Powell Interviewed', *Morning Post*, 29 June 1900, pp. 3 and 5, at p. 3.

82 'A Hero of Mafeking: Aberdeenshire Man on the Siege', *(Aberdeen) Evening Express*, 28 August 1900, p. 5.

83 NAM, Acc 1968-10-42, B-P diary, 12 May 1900.

84 'Life in Mafeking Under The Siege', *Nottingham Evening Post*, 25 June 1900, p. 4.

85 'In Besieged Mafeking. An Aberayron Man's Experiences', *Western Mail*, 18 July 1900, p. 6.

86 Hamilton, *Siege of Mafeking*, pp. 296–7.

87 'The Siege of Mafeking', *Penistone Express*, 12 October 1900, p. 7.

hour Eloff surrendered, as Hore persuaded the besieging forces to cease firing. Eloff, Captain Baron von Weiss, Captain Comte dé Tremont, Assistant Commandants Anderson and Jacobs and sixty-eight men were then marched off to the Masonic Hall and gaol.

Conclusion

Altogether 108 Boers surrendered, another 10 were killed and 19 wounded, with their ambulances collecting the casualties. The defence lost four killed (including the jailer, Mr C. Heale, who was killed by a shell) and ten wounded, with another eight killed and ten wounded 'amongst the natives'.[88] Lieutenant Gemmell and his Bechuanaland riflemen were in charge of the prisoners, whom Gemmell described as

> a motley crew – half pure Boer and half foreign mercenaries – the latter all sorts, comprising three officers of the French army, a Portuguese colonel, a German captain, and an Italian navel lieutenant. The fellows were of course recruited in Europe by Dr. Leyds,[89] and a number of them had only landed in Delagoa Bay a fortnight before.

Understandably, they 'heaped curses on the head of Snyman', who was supposed to have attacked from the east as soon as he saw the stadt burning. Had he done so, 'it must have gone hard with us', observed Gemmell, who concluded that 'General Luck has been a staunch ally of General [*sic*] B. P. all through'.[90]

Of Eloff, the British formed a largely positive impression. Lady Sarah's description of the commandant from the post-battle breakfast is well known, namely a somewhat dishevelled, dejected, and exasperated young man, who felt bitterly let down by Snyman[91] but Corporal Rose, who escorted all the

---

88 Hanbury-Tracy Mss., Baden-Powell to Snyman, 14 May 1900; *Official History*, vol. 3, p. 181; see also 'B-P report', p. 900.

89 Dr. Willem Johannes Leyds (1859–1940), Transvaal state secretary, diplomat and historian, he relinquished his post as state secretary for health reasons in 1898 and became an ambassador extraordinary and minister plenipotentiary for the Transvaal in Europe during the war. Fransjohan Pretorius, *A to Z of the Anglo-Boer War*, pp. 242–3.

90 'The Siege of Mafeking', *Ayr Advertiser*, 23 August 1900, p. 5; see also Fransjohan Pretorius, 'Welcome but Not That Welcome: The Relations between Foreign Volunteers and the Boers in the Anglo-Boer War of 1899-1902' in Christine G. Krüger and Sonja Levsen (eds), *War Volunteering in Modern Times* (London: Palgrave Macmillan, 2010), pp. 122–49.

91 Lady Sarah Wilson, *South African Memories*, pp. 212–13.

prisoners down to Cape Town after the siege, saw him in a different light. Kruger's grandson, he described, as

> a tall, handsome, broad-shouldered man, and he bore himself under trying circumstances with a dignity and composure that compelled the admiration of his enemies. His men seem to idolise him, and at various railway stations along the route where the prisoners were permitted to detrain, they saluted their leader and gave every indication of devotion and affection.[92]

Few soldiers saw Baden-Powell in action. Corporal Rose repeated the tale of his reported reply to an elderly lady, who asked if the Boers were in the stadt. B-P answered: 'Yes, my good woman, it is perfectly true. They are in, but God alone knows how they are to get out again.'[93] Edward Ross, who recognized that the Colonel was a complex character, sometimes 'egotistical and always aiming at being before the eyes of the British public', now appreciated another side to the man when he saw him tested in battle. 'He stood there at the corner of his offices, the coolest of cucumbers possible', wrote Ross, rattling out his orders 'like the rip of a Maxim'. The commands resonated on account of

> his tone, his self-possession, his command of self, his intimate knowledge of every detail of the defences, where everything at that moment was, and where it was to be brought and put to, shewed [*sic*] us the ideal soldier, and what the British officer can be and is in moments of extreme peril. It is something I would not have missed seeing for anything . . . there he stood with his hands behind his back, a living image of a being knowing himself and his own strength and fearing neither foe nor devil. Such was B.P. the soldier.[94]

Finally, the defending forces had proved themselves in the ultimate moment of peril. As the Eyemouth man recorded, they had 'bagged' in 'killed, wounded and prisoners, about 140', which was an 'excellent day's work for a town whose garrison had undergone the severe strain of eight months' besiegement'.[95] They had fought not from prepared positions but against an internal threat, harrying the enemy with the support of the enraged Barolong through the confines of the stadt, and then by sustained

---

92 'A Hero of Mafeking: Aberdeenshire Man on the Siege', *(Aberdeen) Evening Express*, 28 August 1900, p. 5.
93 Ibid.
94 Willan (ed.), *Edward Ross*, p. 229.
95 'An Eyemouth Man in Mafeking', *Berwickshire News*, 17 July 1900, p. 5.

firepower compelled the surrender of more than a third of the intruding force. Thereafter they enjoyed the spoils of war, both supplies abandoned by the retreating foe – jam, white bread and biscuits, which Sergeant Taylor promptly consumed[96] – and captured Mausers, which B-P distributed to the Town Guard, while issuing their extra Lee-Metfords and Martini-Henrys to 'the Colonial & other corps'.[97] Even more important was the information received from the prisoners of war – not the Boers, as Lieutenant Gemmell acknowledged, but the foreigners, who did not see 'any sense in silly lies'. They told their captors that relief from the south was only a few days away. This created 'lively sense of expectation in the town', especially as the news was confirmed by information from Colonel Plumer's column on the following day, 14 May.[98] The siege would soon be over.

96 'Life in Mafeking Under The Siege', *Nottingham Evening Post*, 25 June 1900, p. 4.
97 NAM, Acc 1968-10-42, B-P diary, 13 May 1900.
98 'The Siege of Mafeking', *Ayr Advertiser*, 23 August 1900, p. 5.

Chapter 7

Relief of Mafeking

Mafeking was relieved on 17 May 1900, an achievement secured by columns from the north under Lieutenant-Colonel Herbert Plumer and the south under Lieutenant-Colonel Bryan Mahon. Of the two columns, only Plumer's had existed since the start of the war, and surviving accounts of its orders, movements and actions benefit from his despatches and post-war testimony, the correspondence of senior officers, and the odd individual diary.[1] If relief was the final outcome, Plumer's original orders from Baden-Powell were

> (1) To defend the border as far as it can be carried out from the neighbourhood of Tuli, as a centre. (2) By display of strength to induce the Boers to detail a strong force to protect their northern district. (3) To create diversion in the north of the Transvaal, cooperating with the invasion of the south by our main force, if necessary advancing into the Transvaal for the purpose. No portion of your force to cross the frontier till you receive orders. Instructions will be sent to you as to the date for co-operation with the other column.[2]

Eyewitness testimony by soldiers, railwaymen and other civilians will shed light on the challenges encountered by this column at the outset, and later in advancing down the railway from Gaberones. These will include the problems presented by the terrain, distances covered and the resistance of local Boers. Similar testimony will reveal the difficulties that its southern counterpart had to overcome, and finally consider an assessment of the relief in its immediate aftermath.

---

1   Lt-Col. H. C. O. Plumer, testimony before *RCWSA*, vol. 2, pp. 334–7; Steve Lunderstedt, 'The Relief of Mafeking' in Smith (ed), *Siege of Mafeking*, vol. 2, pp. 359–97; Amery, *Times History*, vol. 4, pp. 202–22; Gardner, *Mafeking*, Chs. 6, 10 and 14; *Official History*, vol. 3, pp. 186–203; Lieutenant-Colonel R. S. Godley, *Khaki and Blue: Thirty-Five Years' Service in South Africa* (London: Lovat Dickson & Thompson Ltd., 1935); TNA, WO 108/185, Captain Hervey de Montmorency, diary.
2   Plumer (Q. 17,950), evidence before *RCWSA*, p. 334.

Plumer's Column

When Plumer reached Fort Tuli on 11 October 1899, he commanded five squadrons (or some 450 volunteers) in his Rhodesia regiment and had the assistance of another 100 BSA Police at the fort. He possessed only limited armaments, namely a Maxim-Nordenfeldt 12.5-pounder gun, two 2.5in rifled muzzle-loading screw guns, and two .450in Maxim machine guns on naval carriages. This small force, as Plumer explained, was responsible for the defence of a frontier of 'about 500 miles [about 804 km]', along the River Limpopo, which was passable 'almost anywhere' except for periods in flood. In fact, as the eastern portion of the frontier was never threatened, and a small body of BSA Police and Rhodesian volunteers held Gaberones until 24 October, before being forced to withdraw to Mahalapye, the Tuli force was only responsible for the defence of '200 miles [322 km] of frontier'. In this respect it found itself occupied from 11 October until 26 November by 'about 1,700' Boers from the Waterberg and Zoutpansberg Commandos.[3]

On arrival at Tuli Plumer despatched reconnaissance patrols to locate the whereabouts of the enemy and posted vedettes at the six most vulnerable crossing points, including the junction of the Maklutsi and Limpopo, Pont Drift and Rhodes Drift 32 km due south from Tuli, and the more distant drifts: Baines to the west and Masibi and Middle drifts to the east. One trooper recalled that these patrols began soon after their arrival at Tuli, following a march of about 280 km from Bulawayo, and in his case involved a patrol to Masibi's Drift, 40 km east of Rhodes Drift. After fruitlessly searching for the enemy, he was part of small flanking party of four men on the return journey. Unable to move through the thick bush close to the bank of the river, his group crossed the Limpopo and patrolled several kilometres inland, where they encountered about twenty Boers, 'who at once started potting at us. They have a great advantage', asserted the trooper, 'in that nearly all their horses are trained to stand firing from the saddle, saving the time and trouble of dismounting.' Forced to retire, the whole patrol returned to Tuli, 'having covered about 120 miles [193 km] in four days'.[4] By the time of his return (24 October), other outposts had encountered much larger bodies of Boers, notably at Pont Drift (21 October), where thirty men of 'E' Squadron, according to Trooper Bert Isaacs, 'had a hard skirmish . . . losing four men wounded'.[5] Plumer had pulled back his more exposed units but still despatched reconnaissance patrols and sought to reoccupy Rhodes Drift, trying to convince the enemy that he

---

3   Ibid., pp. 334–5 and Lunderstedt, 'Relief of Mafeking' in Smith (ed.), *Siege of Mafeking*, vol. 2, p. 360.
4   'Colonel Plumer's March. A Trooper's Experiences', *Standard*, 2 June 1900, p. 3.
5   'With Plumer's Force Towards Mafeking', *Berkshire Chronicle*, 6 January 1900, p. 6.

had a much larger force than he had. Under Colonel the Hon. Harry White[6] and Captain G. Carr Glyn, parties of 20 to 25 troopers were sent 'to "worry up" the Dutchmen', sometimes fighting from kopjes, where, as the trooper recalled, we 'were met with a heavy fire, which we returned, though it was useless, as we were only firing at stones; not a man could be seen'.[7]

Much more serious, though, were developments on 2 November when a Boer commando of 400 men and two guns under Eloff and the German artillerist, Captain Baron Alfred von Dalwig, crossed the river and bypassed Lieutenant-Colonel J. A. (Jack) Spreckley's 'E' Squadron at Rhodes Drift. Some 6 km to the north, at a location known as Bryce's Store, it intercepted a supply convoy of eight waggons and overwhelmed the 26-man escort. Trooper Charles Herriot feared that they 'must have had information that the waggons were on the road'.[8] The Boers then turned on Spreckley's force, which was manning two kopjes, and, as Trooper J. R. King described, 'poured a fire into us for a solid 6$\frac{1}{2}$ hours, killing about 100 of our horses . . . . Not one of us was hit, strange to say'. Under a 'friendly darkness',

> we made as fast as our legs could carry us through the bush . . . . After a march of five hours through the most awful bush you can think of, we found ourselves (by midnight) lost, and back into Crocodile River at Rhode's Drift, and in close proximity to the Boer camp! Fancy our dismay at this unfortunate waste of time, and which meant life or death to us. By the aid of a compass and the stars we struck out in a fresh direction and got here [Tuli] somehow by Friday.[9]

After 'E' Squadron's retreat, carrying only rifles and bandoliers, Trooper Isaacs reflected that they were 'nearly all of them old hands, and men used to veld life'. Though outgunned by the Boers, he maintained that

> Our way of fighting is precisely the same as the Dutch, and I can assure you they don't like it. We are just as good shots, as they are, and are quite as used to the veldt also. The only thing that no doubt saved us was the fact that they hadn't the pluck to rush us.[10]

6 Colonel the Hon. Henry White (1859–1903), son of the Anglo-Irish peer, the 2nd Baron Annaly, he served in the Sudan with the Grenadier Guards (1885) but was best known as a Rhodesian pioneer. He was a Jameson raider, Mayor of Bulawayo in 1899 and later received a DSO for his services in the South African War.
7 'Colonel Plumer's March. A Trooper's Experiences', *Standard*, 2 June 1900, p. 3.
8 'Berwickshire Man at the Front', *Berwickshire News*, 30 January 1900, p. 5.
9 'With Colonel Plumer', *Aberdeen Weekly Journal*, 17 January 1900, p. 7; see also *Official History*, vol. 3, pp. 192–3.
10 'A Reading Man with Baden Powell's Forces', *Berkshire Chronicle*, 6 January 1900, p. 11.

Altogether the Boers, having lost only three men, captured eight men, 70 horses, 100 mules and nine waggons, with the additional waggon from Major Wilkinson Dent Bird's detachment at the Maklutsi confluence. They now dug in at Bryce's Store, posing a direct threat to Fort Tuli. Apart from 'C' Squadron at Maklutsi village, all Plumer's men were brought back to mount guard, dig trenches, and fortify Tuli. The Venerable Archdeacon J. H. Upcher, resplendent with his massive beard, volunteered to serve in the chaplain's place, and acted under the PMO, 'bandaging, nursing, cooking, fetching water, fishing for African turbot, soles, etc., in the Tuli River for the mess, heartening everyone (and they often needed it in that sandy fever-sodden place), and ministering to all the necessities of body and soul'.[11] Why the Boers did not attack the fort mystified Plumer's troopers but Trooper Herriot was convinced that the 400 men at Tuli had 'saved Rhodesia'.[12]

Far from attacking Tuli, the Boers withdrew from this part of the frontier on 25 November. General Fredrik A. Grobler, the assistant-general for the Waterberg, Zoutpansberg and Rustenburg Commandos, who had overall responsibility for guarding the northern and north-western borders of the Transvaal, had wanted to capture Tuli and destroy the western railway line, but Pretoria vetoed the plan. Forced to split his force into three detachments of 400 men apiece, each with a gun, Grobler had had to monitor several potential crossings, and then steadily saw his forces depleted by redeployments to Pretoria and beyond. He himself was later sent to serve in the Colesberg region on the southern front.[13] Finding Bryce's Store and all the main drifts evacuated by the end of November, Plumer led a reconnaissance across the Limpopo and into the Transvaal. This 'big patrol', as described by a trooper, involved

> about 250 picked men and horses, with Colonel Plumer himself. We had a rough time – had to carry our own rations, no waggons, and only overcoats with us. We were once in the saddle 22 hours, without rest, food, or water for man or horse; got to Breakpan [*sic*] within 50 miles [80 km] of Pietersburg, but found no water, so had to come back at once.[14]

---

11 'A Former Bury Clergyman at the Front', *Bury and Norwich Post, and Suffolk Standard*, 7 August 1900, p. 8, see also *Official History*, vol. 3, p. 192.

12 'Berwickshire Man at the Front', *Berwickshire News*, 30 January 1900, p. 5; 'Colonel Plumer's March. A Trooper's Experiences', *Standard*, 2 June 1900, p. 3; and Godley, *Khaki and Blue*, p. 69.

13 For correspondence between Grobler and the State Secretary of the Transvaal, 13 November 1899, see *Official History*, vol. 3, p. 193 and, on Grobler, Pretorius, *A to Z of the Anglo-Boer War*, p. 168.

14 'Colonel Plumer's March. A Trooper's Experiences', *Standard*, 2 June 1900, p. 3.

After a second reconnaissance on 19 December, which failed to find any enemy near the Brack River, and with the Limpopo in flood covering the drifts, Plumer decided to join the operations along the western railway. Leaving a small force of 120 men with the 12.5-pounder gun at Tuli, and another 20 men at Maklutsi village, he departed on 27 December, marching his 400 troopers in small detachments, with their 2.5in gun and Maxim, over the 282 km towards Palapye. While the leading units reached Palapye by the end of December, the dismounted men required twelve days to do so, marching only in the early morning and late evening.[15] Thereupon an armoured train, followed by three trains of stores, ammunition and the dismounted men, conveyed the force to Mochudi siding, and thence onto Gaberones, occupying the fort and station over 13 to 15 January 1900. On 17 January, the train deployed an advanced party of 240 men under Major W. D. Bird so that it could occupy a line of kopjes about 10 km south of Gaberones, covering a demolished railway bridge.[16]

The railway had already been the scene of extensive skirmishing. Colonel J. S. Nicholson, commandant-general of the BSA Police, who acted as base commandant in Bulawayo, had maintained troops along this section of the line, supported by armoured trains. Private F. Funnell, formerly of Lewes, Sussex, and now the Bechuanaland Rifles, was part of a detachment sent out of Mafeking before the outbreak of war to defend the railway bridge at Ramathlabama. The Boers, however, blew up the bridge and drove the detachment north to Mahalapye in the territory of King Khama of the Nqwato people.[17] Fellow trooper F. W. Longbottom now found himself in a party of twenty-five men, south of Mahalapye, ensconced 'on a rock or kopje about 500 feet [152 m] high' with a 'most wonderful' view. Writing to his father in Sheffield on 13 November, Longbottom explained how the riflemen, even supported by about 275 BSA Police sent down from Bulawayo, were outnumbered and outgunned by the enemy. They had skirmished with them and had the support of Khama's tribesmen. 'Khama's son', wrote Longbottom, 'is here with a few of his men, who are acting as scouts for us. Khama's men are all very pious (or act so) . . . singing hymns and praying to God. But they seem to think that stealing everything they may get their hands on is in no way wrong.' Khama would reject Grobler's demand for a right of passage through his territory, and promised another '800 men to assist us', added Longbottom: these men assisted in patrolling

---

15   Ibid.
16   Ibid. and *Official History*, vol. 3, p. 197.
17   'Letters From Lewes Men At The Front', *East Sussex News*, 18 May 1900, p. 8.

the Bechauanaland-Transvaal border, guarding the railway line, and getting messages in and out of Mafeking.[18]

At least two armoured trains provided the principal firepower along the railway. In command of the advanced armoured train Lieutenant Hoël Llewellyn, late RN, operated out of the base at Mahalapye. In the heavily-protected No.1 train he had fifty riflemen, a .450in Maxim and a 7-pounder gun, and patrolled as far south as Lobatse, where the Boers had destroyed all the bridges and rails. On 30 October in the face of Krupp guns, he retreated from Crocodile Pools where ten bridges and culverts were destroyed. Thereafter the train fought running battles with Boer riflemen, demonstrating that the 0.5in steel plating round the engine and the steel rails round the bogie trucks[19] were impervious to rifle fire. As Llewellyn observed, the enemy

> hate and dread the train, which has repeatedly caught them napping; and the Boers rarely escape without losing one or two out of even a small number. These northern or bushveldt Boers have hardly ever seen or heard of an ordinary train, so that naturally this armoured train is somewhat weird to them.[20]

The train's immediate task, though, was guarding and repairing the line, and by 16 December, it was back at Gaberones, having repaired half of the damaged bridges and culverts at Crocodile Pools.

The massing of Boers on the Bechuanaland border had placed these operations in jeopardy (and so influenced Plumer's decision to move south). Colonel George L. Holdsworth, who had arrived in Mahalapye on 4 November to assume command of the local operations, triggered these events. Having received permission to cross the border and attack the Boer laager at Derdepoort, he enlisted the aid of three Bakgatla regiments, led by Segale, half-brother of Chief Lentshwe (formerly Linchwe), whose territory sprawled across the Bechuanaland-Transvaal border and whose people had been ancient enemies of the Boers. In the ensuing raid (25 November 1899) Holdsworth remained on the Bechuanaland side of the border, while letting the Bakgatlas attack the laager, killing several burghers, including two

---

18 'A Sheffield Trooper in Khama's Country', *Sheffield Daily Telegraph*, 12 January 1900, p. 6; see also NAM, Acc. 1971-01-23-6, f. 2, Roberts Mss., Baden-Powell to Lord Kitchener, 2 March 1900 and Jackson, *Boer War*, p. 43.

19 'Mexboro' Engine Driver In Rhodesia', *Penistone Express*, 20 April 1900, p. 7.

20 'Interesting Letter From Captain Llewellyn', *Somerset County Gazette*, 10 February 1900, p. 2. On the number of armoured trains, Plumer claimed he had three (Q. 17,950) before *RCSWA*, p. 335, the *Official History* states that he had two armoured trains, only one of which was fully armoured, *Official History*, vol. 3, p. 197.

women, and temporarily abduct seventeen Boer women and children and a hundred-head of cattle. In a reprisal, on 22 December, the entire Waterberg commando devastated the Bakgatla settlements at Sikwane, Malolwane and Mmathubudukwane along the Transvaal border, killing many Bakgatla. They also threatened Holdsworth's advanced position at Mochudi.[21]

By linking with Nicholson's detachment, and moving onto Gaberones and its fort, Plumer established an advanced camp near Crocodile Pools station and presented a more significant threat along the railway. He had a notional force of about 1,000 men (250 of whom were sick, wounded, on the line of communications, or manning the armoured trains). His armaments included one 2.5in gun, a 7-pounder, two Maxims and, by the end of February, the 12.5-pounder gun brought from Tuli and another 2.5in gun from Bulawayo. Hanbury-Tracy congratulated Llewellyn on his reinforcement 'by Plumer & his lot & only hope that we may be able to join hands before any relief comes from the South'.[22] Although the Boers had redeployed some burghers, including Grobler to other fronts, they retained several hundred men about 64 km to the east of the railway at Derdepoort and another two hundred from the Rustenburg commando, with a 12.5-pounder gun and machine guns on the kopjes astride the railway. This commanding position was 8 km north of Crocodile Pools station.

Facing them was an outpost, grandiloquently known as 'Fortress Kopje', held by an under-strength squadron of Bechuanaland riflemen, including Sergeant W. Dickinson, formerly of Oldham. Halfway between the base camp and the Boer position, Dickinson described how his force 'had a very difficult position', sometimes cut off by a river in flood round the bottom of the hill, and daily under attack by Boer shelling. They built bombproofs and stone walls along a frontage 'short of 400 yards [365 m]', fired the odd shell at the enemy, mounted small-scale raids to detect the positioning of the enemy's rifles, and marvelled at their avoidance of injury. By late January, they were reinforced by two squadrons from Plumer's column and so 'felt somewhat safe'.[23]

Eager to advance and repair the bridge before the Boers sent reinforcements from Mafeking, Plumer planned a night assault on the Boer position at

21 André Wessels (ed.), *Lord Kitchener and the War in South Africa 1899-1902* (Stroud, Glos.: Sutton Publishing for the Army Records Society, 2006), p. 258n14; NAM, Acc. 1971-01-23-6, f. 2, Roberts Mss. Baden-Powell to Lord Kitchener, 2 March 1900; Jackson, *Boer War*, pp. 43–5; Pretorius, *A to Z of the Anglo-Boer War*, p. 210; Plumer (Q. 17,950) evidence before *RCWSA*, p. 335.
22 NAM, Acc. 1997-02-13, f. 27, Llewellyn Mss., Hanbury-Tracy to Llewellyn, 6 January 1900 and Plumer (Q. 17,950) evidence before *RCWSA*, p. 335.
23 'Bound for Mafeking', *Oldham Standard*, 24 March 1900, p. 3.

Crocodile Pools. After reconnoitring the area, Major Bird deployed nearly 200 men (140 Rhodesia Regiment, 20 BSA Police and 30 South Rhodesia Volunteers). As Captain John Sampson, a South Rhodesia Volunteer, recalled, the attack followed two abortive assaults, each launched on successive evenings and ruined by torrential rain. While the men returned exhausted on each occasion, the Boers reinforced their position in the interim, and, by 11 February, 'had two big guns, some 7-pounder Maxim-Nordenfeldt guns, one-pounder Maxims and Hotchkiss guns in their strong position, entrenched and covered by rifle pits, barbed wire entanglements, walls . . . . In fact', wrote Sampson, 'I think we have not the least chance of taking the place by assault now.'[24] He was proved correct on the following night when, after a rough march through the bush, the assault was launched from the foot of the kopje at 3 a.m. under the order: '"Don't fire a shot, but take the position at the point of the bayonet."' The enemy, as Trooper Herriot remarked, 'allowed us to get up almost to the top when we began to tumble into trenches and over barbed wire entanglements, and then they opened fire on us'. For a quarter of an hour 'it was simply h--- let loose', as the Rhodesians suffered from volleys of Mauser fire, artillery shelling, and then explosions from dynamite mines.[25] Forced to retreat, the assault force, wrote Private Funnell, lost 'about 30 killed and wounded', as only darkness and their proximity to the fort saved them from further carnage.[26] Sergeant Dickinson was both appalled and mystified that Plumer had sanctioned the attack.[27]

Fortunately Plumer chose to manoeuvre and not rely exclusively on frontal assaults along the railway. He moved his mounted troops westwards, a march of four nights and three days to Kanye, and, as a trooper described, 'We stayed there while waggons kept bringing down stores intended for a dash into Mafeking.'[28] By 20 February three convoys had brought thirty-seven waggon-loads of supplies to Kanye, only 120 km from Mafeking. While Colonel Holdsworth with the dismounted men remained at Gaberones, patrolling and repairing the railway, the Kanye base served multiple purposes. It turned the Boer flank, prompting their withdrawal to Lobatse, 48 km further south, and served as a place of refuge for 1,200 blacks escaping from Mafeking, an 'enormous saving of food for the Mafeking garrison'.[29] It was also a base from

---

24 'Drenched to the Skin', *Alton Mail*, 7 April 1900, p. 3.
25 'Letters From The Front', *Berwickshire News*, 24 April 1900, p. 6.
26 'Letters From Lewes Men At The Front', *East Sussex News*, 18 May 1900, p. 8. Funnell is reasonably accurate on the disputed numbers of casualties, see Gardner, *Mafeking*, p. 143n3, *Official History*, vol. 3, p. 199 and *Times History*, vol. 4, pp. 205–6.
27 'With Plumer. Disastrous Night Attack', *Oldham Standard*, 21 April 1900, p. 2.
28 'Colonel Plumer's March. A Trooper's Experiences', *Standard*, 2 June 1900, p. 2.
29 Plumer (Q. 17,950) evidence before *RCWSA*, p. 335.

which reconnaissance patrols could probe Boer positions near Mafeking and, if possible, draw Boers away from the siege.

In an early foray Plumer moved approximately 500 men south to Lobatse (6 March), about 72 km from Mafeking. In finding two to three hundred Boers there, he pushed two columns forward, one mounted under Major Bird, advancing as far south as Ramathlabama, and another of mounted and dismounted men, advancing by road and rail under Colonel Bodle to Pitsane. As Snyman sent substantial forces north, they engaged Bodle's advance guard, inflicting casualties and bombarding his laager with shells from a 12.5-pounder gun and a pom-pom. Lieutenant George Tordiffe, with 100 mounted and 50 dismounted men, served in the so-called 'Cossack' post, 274 m in advance of Bodle's laager, utterly exposed in the 'flat with hills in front, an awful place for so few men'. Required by Plumer to remain in place, protecting the withdrawal of waggons from the rear, they spent nearly two days under periodic shellfire with Boers creeping round their flanks, until they were allowed to retreat. As all the stores and dismounted men had been withdrawn by rail, and the troopers had left for Kanye, Tordiffe regarded it as 'a miraculous retreat, and not enough praise can be given to Colonel Bodle and Captain Bowden[30] for the way they retired with their men without any loss, after keeping the Boers at bay while the waggons were retiring'. On the following day, 17 March, the armoured train observed the Boers still shelling the deserted positions at Lobatse.[31]

Plumer now established a forward camp at Sefikile, a desert location but only 48 km from Mafeking, and ideally situated if the rumoured southern relief column travelled by the safer western route. He brought supplies forward by waggon and communicated with Kanye and Gaberones by relays of cyclists. He also sent out reconnaissance patrols, one as far east as Zeerust, and on 30 March, moved with 270 mounted men onto Ramathlabama and beyond, reaching Oaklands farm, 9.6 km from Mafeking. In open country he encountered a large force of Boers from the Marico and Rustenburg Commandos under Snyman and Steenekamp. By ordering a frontal assault on the Boer position, he left Sergeant Pearson ('C' Squadron, Rhodesia Regiment) none too impressed:

I think the captain [probably Captain Frederick Harding Crewe] must have been fairly off his head, for he took us right up to within 200 yards [183 m] of the Boer fire; he did not dismount us for firing, and

---

30 Lieutenant-Colonel William Bodle (BSA Police) and Captain Frank L. Bowden (Mashonaland Mounted Police) were both Jameson raiders. Bowden subsequently received a DSO for his services at Ramathlabama.

31 'A Devizes Lad With Plumer's Column', *Wiltshire Telegraph*, 19 March 1900, p. 3.

they were sending shot after shot into us. I went and told him that they were on the right, but all I got was that I was to obey orders, and go back to my troop. Afterwards I had to lift him; he was shot and the lieutenant too . . . . We had to retreat for twelve miles [19 km].[32]

Troopers William Adams and Bert Isaacs, serving with the dismounted rearguard of fifty men, were equally disconcerted. The column, claimed Adams, was

trying to draw the Boers on this side [of Mafeking and] 'Christopher!' we did draw them. They came out like ants when they saw our little party . . . . About three o'clock in the afternoon we had word that the Boers were coming, so we got all the cattle away and the waggons, and then we marched out to cover the retreat of our fellows coming in.[33]

'One couldn't help admiring the way the Boers came on', wrote Isaacs, 'continually trying to outflank us; in this, luckily, they did not succeed. We got the Maxim into them when they got to where our troops were waiting for them, lying down.'[34] Plumer then ordered the rearguard to make sure that the Maxim was withdrawn safely, before Isaacs and his comrades, still on foot and in extended order, were allowed to retire across 'a bare piece of veldt, up a hill, a long rise for about three-quarters of a mile [1,207 m]'. We did so, noted Isaacs, 'by making short rushes about 15 to 20 yards [13.7 to 18.3 m] at a time, and then lying flat down and firing as hard as we could.'[35] Both mounted and dismounted men suffered heavy casualties, which were confirmed after a three-day search of the battlefield by Corporal A. Simms (Medical Staff), Archdeacon Upcher and a party from Mafeking, led by Hanbury-Tracy.[36] Among the eight killed were Captain F. H. Crewe and Lieutenant Frank W. Milligan; the twenty-nine wounded included Plumer, Major A. Weston-Jarvis and Captain S. P. Rolt, and the twelve prisoners, half of whom were wounded, included Captain Kenneth McLaren, known by Baden-Powell as 'The Boy". The 'heavy loss' and failure to relieve the town

---

32 'Exciting Experiences With Plumer's Column', *Mansfield Chronicle*, 1 June 1900, p. 6.

33 'Letter from Colonel Plumer's Column', *Ashton-under-Lyne Reporter*, 16 June 1900, p. 6.

34 'With Plumer's Force Towards Mafeking', *Berkshire Chronicle*, 6 January 1900, p. 6.

35 Ibid.

36 NAM Acc. 1997-02-13, f. 29, Llewellyn Mss., Hanbury-Tracy to Llewellyn, 4 April 1900 and 'To Mafeking's Relief. Scarborough Corporal with Col. Plumer', *Scarborough Post*, 30 May 1900, p. 3.

earned sympathy from Mafeking, and widespread publicity due to Milligan's former status as a Yorkshire and England cricketer, who died reportedly with the next season's fixture list in his pocket.[37]

Lord Roberts ordered Plumer to desist from making another attempt to relieve Mafeking before the arrival of a 'relieving force' from the south,[38] so Plumer contented himself with supporting Mafeking from afar. He tried, though usually without success, to drive herds of cattle into the town but sent Lieutenant Frank Smitheman through to Mafeking (4 April), where he encouraged Barolong women and children to leave for Kanye. Smitheman brought back reassurance, as Trooper Fletcher (BSA Police) recalled, that Mafeking had 'plenty of tobacco, cigars, whisky, and scoff. They can last till June. All they are short of is meal . . . they are alright [*sic*], in fact much better off than we are as we are still on bully and they can have fresh meat.'[39]

Despite all the plaudits subsequently heaped on Nicholson for sustaining Plumer's supplies from Bulawayo, troopers complained bitterly about the quality and quantity of their half rations: 'everybody hungry and dissatisfied', wrote Issacs.[40] Surviving troopers were dejected by the series of costly frontal assaults on the Boers, fighting from prepared positions with flat-trajectory magazine rifles. They believed, too, as Trooper Ernest Pratt observed, that the column had always been 'outnumbered by men or guns', and so needed reinforcements of both before it could 'have a good try to relieve Mafeking'.[41] On 1 May 100 BSA Policemen with a 2.5in gun arrived from Mashonaland, and, on 14 May, after an extraordinary journey from Beira, covering 1,263 km by rail and coach – at times dampening sparks from the engine lest they explode the ammunition[42] – 'C' Battery, Royal Canadian Field Artillery under

---

37 NAM Acc. 1997-02-13, f. 29, Llewellyn Mss., Hanbury-Tracy to Llewellyn, 4 April 1900; 'How Mr. Frank Milligan Met His Death', *Yorkshire Post*, 31 May 1900, p. 5; 'The Late Mr. Frank Milligan', *Bradford Daily Telegraph*, 31 May 1900, p. 3.

38 NAM, Acc. 1971-01-23-114, f. 104, Roberts Mss., Lord Roberts to Plumer, 11 April 1900.

39 'With Plumer's Column', *Scarborough Post*, 6 June 1900, p. 3; see also Plumer (Q. 17,950) evidence before *RCWSA*, p. 335; NAM, Acc. 1968-10-42, B-P diary, 9 April 1900.

40 Compare *Times History*, vol. 4, p. 209 and Gardner, *Mafeking*, p. 145 with 'With Plumer's Force Towards Mafeking', *Berkshire Chronicle*, 6 January 1900, p. 6; 'Letter from Colonel Plumer's Column', *Ashton-under-Lyne Reporter*, 16 June 1900, p. 6; 'With Plumer's Force', *Scarborough Post*, 23 March 1900, p. 5; 'With The Column To Mafeking', *(Dundee) Courier & Argus*, 2 May 1900, p. 6.

41 'One of Plumer's Column', *Middlesex Chronicle*,, 14 July 1900, pp. 6–7.

42 'Chester Men With The Queenslanders', *Cheshire Observer*, 30 June 1900, p. 8, see also Carman Miller, *Painting the Map Red: Canada and the South African War, 1899-1902* (Montreal & Kingston: Canadian War Museum and McGill-Queen's University Press, 1993), pp. 181–7, at p. 182.

Major Joseph A. G. Hudon with four guns and an escort of 100 Queenslanders arrived at Sefikile. Having heard from Lord Roberts that a southern column had left on 4 May, Plumer advanced on Jan Massibi's kraal with 800 men, of whom 450 were mounted, and eight guns either drawn or carried by mules, including his 12.5-pounder gun.[43] The two columns met on 15 May.

Southern Column

Lord Roberts had begun raising the relief column by sending B-P's brother, Major Baden Baden-Powell, over to Kimberley to inquire about the possibility of equipping such a column, and then, on 19 April, at a breakfast in Bloemfontein gave Lieutenant-General Sir Archibald Hunter a free hand to organize the force. By 21 April, Hunter arrived in Kimberley to raise the column and plan its route. Knowing Lieutenant-Colonel Bryan Mahon from the Sudan campaign, he entrusted him with command of a mixed force of 1,100 men. This included 900 mounted Imperial Light Horse (ILH) from Natal and a Kimberley Mounted Corps, comprising veterans of the Diamond Fields Horse, Cape Police and Kimberley Light Horse (KLH); 100 artillerymen with four 12-pounder guns of 'M' Battery, Royal Horse Artillery (RHA) and two pom-poms; and 100 infantry from Major-General Sir Geoffrey Barton's Sixth Fusilier Brigade, 25 each from England, Scotland, Wales and Ireland. These troops had the support of 52 supply waggons but no Royal Engineers, a shortcoming that would become more acute as the column crossed rough and often waterless terrain.[44]

Instead of using regiments or brigades available in Kimberley, the composition of the flying column sought to demonstrate that every nation of the United Kingdom, and most English-speaking parts of the empire, had a stake in the relief of Mafeking. The choice of contingents from the Imperial Light Horse and the Kimberley Light Horse ensured that those who had served in one siege would relieve another. 'It's rather good', remarked Trooper H. E. Smith (ILH), a Ladysmith veteran, 'to be in one siege and the relief of

---

43 Plumer, evidence (Q. 17,950) before *RCWSA*, p. 335; *Official History*, vol. 3, p. 203 and Lunderstedt, 'Relief of Mafeking' in Smith (ed.), *Siege of Mafeking*, vol. 2, p. 382. These sources discount the exaggerated claim of 650 mounted men by de Montmorency, who also dismissed the Canadian guns as 'very indifferent weapons', TNA, WO 105/185, de Montmorency, diary, p. 26.
44 NAM, Acc. 1971-01-23-110-2, f. 429, Roberts Mss., Lord Roberts to Lord Lansdowne, 6 May 1900; Lunderstedt, 'Relief of Mafeking' in Smith (ed.), *Siege of Mafeking*, vol. 2, pp. 370–2; and Archie Hunter, *Kitchener's Sword-Arm: The Life and Campaigns of General Sir Archibald Hunter* (Staplehurst, Kent: Spellmount, 1996), pp. 141–3.

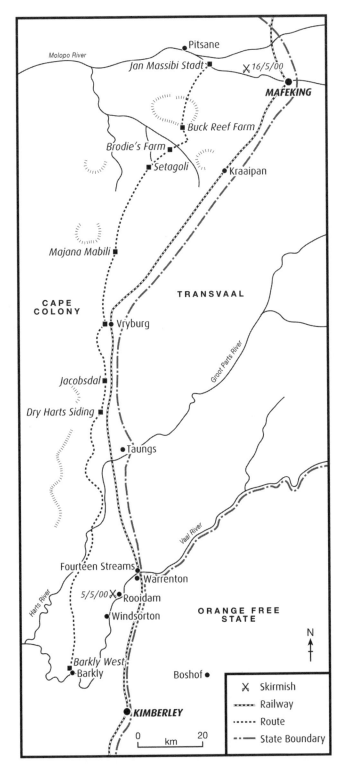

Molopo River

Pitsane

Jan Massibi Stadt   ✗ 16/5/00

MAFEKING

Buck Reef Farm

Brodie's Farm

Setagoli   • Kraaipan

Majana Mabili

TRANSVAAL

**CAPE
COLONY**

Vryburg

Jacobsdal

Groot Parts River

Dry Harts Siding

• Taungs

Vaal River

Fourteen Streams

Warrenton

5/5/00 ✗ • Rooidam

Harts River

• Windsorton

**ORANGE FREE
STATE**

N
↑

Barkly West
• Barkly

Boshof •

	Legend
✗	Skirmish
━━━	Railway
⋯⋯	Route
━·━·━	State Boundary

KIMBERLEY

0   km   20

Map 4 March of Colonel Mahon's Relief Column

another.'[45] There would be a settling of scores, too, as the officers included several Jameson raiders (Sir John C. Willoughby, Colonel Frank Rhodes, the brother of Cecil, and Major Walter Karri-Davies). Among the other officers were Prince Alexander of Teck;[46] Major Alfred H. M. Edwards (5th Dragoon Guards), who was temporarily the officer commanding the ILH with local rank of lieutenant-colonel; Major Baden Baden-Powell (Scots Guards); and Majors the Hon. Maurice Gifford[47] and Sam Weil, the brother of Benjamin, commanding the two detachments of Imperial Yeomanry. Finally, the exploits of the column received the maximum of publicity, albeit in retrospect, as the five war correspondents – Charles Hands (*Daily Mail*), A. W. A. Pollock (*The Times*), Filson Young (*Manchester Guardian*), Charles Falconer (*Daily Telegraph*) and John Stuart (*Morning Post*) – were sworn to secrecy at the outset.

Hunter had planned to divert Boer forces north and west of Kimberley from the 'flying column' by advancing northwards on the western side of the railway, part of the general advance ordered by Lord Roberts from Bloemfontein towards the Transvaal. Within two days of its departure, Hunter's Tenth Division outflanked about 1,500 Boers under General Sarel P. du Toit at Rooidam (5 May), and then pursued the retreating enemy, occupying Fourteen Streams on 7 May without opposition. As Corporal Robert McCaw (Royal Scots Fusiliers) recalled,

> We have accomplished our object and beaten back the enemy who were likely to harass the progress of the flying column . . . . We crossed the Vaal River at Windsorton Drift with transport and guns and took the enemy in the flank at Rooidam and Fourteen Streams, driving them from before us. We stayed at Warrenton a few days and assisted to build the railway . . . . Then we did a two days' march into the Transvaal, clearing all before us and hoisting the first British flag in the Transvaal.[48]

45 'In One Siege and at The Relief of Another', *Essex Herald*, 3 July 1900, p. 3; see also 'Return of Dr. Willie Davies', *Cambrian*, 19 October 1900, p. 5 and 'The Relief of Mafeking described by J. Emmerton, Imperial Light Horse', *Bedford and County Record*, 10 July 1900, p. 3.
46 Prince Alexander of Teck (1874–1957), was the brother of Queen Mary and later the 1st Earl of Athlone and Governor-General of South Africa (1923–31) and Canada (1940–6).
47 The Hon. Maurice Gifford (1859–1910), son of 2nd Baron Gifford, travelled widely in the Merchant Service and fought in Egypt (1882), the Red River Rebellion in Canada, and later in the First and Second Matabele Wars (1893 and 1896). He lost his right arm during the siege of Bulawayo (1896).
48 'Letters From The Front', *Kilmarnock Standard*, 23 June 1900, p. 5; see also NAM, Acc. 1971-01-23-110-2, f. 438, Roberts Mss. Lord Roberts to Lord Lansdowne, 8 May 1900.

While Hunter's division spent time repairing the railway and bridges, before resuming its forced march to Christiana, Taungs, Vryburg and on to Mafeking, Mahon's column had made haste further to the west. Leaving Barkly West on 4 May, it moved initially, as Gunner Brumfitt Atkinson ('F' Section, 1-pounder Maxims, South African Field Force), described,

> 25 and 30 miles [40–48km] a day over very rough ground – sometimes no road at all – and were going night and day. It was very hot in the day time, and just the opposite at night, when we could hardly keep ourselves warm. We had no tents, having to sleep out in the open, with two blankets and a waterproof sheet under us.[49]

As the marching rate dropped to 32 km a day, and lower after six days, that is, from Vryburg onwards, soldiers complained bitterly about the privations incurred. 'For the food during the last six days', wrote a Kimberley trooper, 'was something like one meal a day, and a small one at that, water being at a premium all the while.'[50] Trooper Dan A. Williams (KLH) added that 'we suffered considerably from veldt sores on our hands arising from insufficient food and absence of vegetables'.[51] Another gunner (RHA) summarized the ordeal: 'We did our march on biscuits and muddy water that we got by digging holes in the beds of rivers.'[52]

Nevertheless the column bypassed the Boers, who had been at Fourteen Streams, captured about forty rebels, burning their homesteads *en route*: 'It was a pantomime', wrote Private John Harris, somewhat callously, 'to see their houses all in flames.'[53] On 13 May, the column followed local intelligence and detoured westwards to Brodie's Farm, avoiding a possible ambush in the Koodosrand kopjes near Kraaipan. Lieutenant Charles John Eustace Moorson of Plumer's column made contact at the farm, where he received answers to Plumer's questions, using encoding devised by Colonel Frank Rhodes: 'Our numbers are the Naval and Military multiplied by ten; our guns, the number of sons of the Ward Family; our supplies, the O.C. 9th Lancers', that is, 940, six, and little respectively.[54] An engagement followed, nonetheless, when the

---

49 'An Addingham Soldier at the Relief of Mafeking', *Wharfedale & Airedale Observer*, 22 June 1900, p. 3.

50 'Only Just In Time', *Eastbourne Chronicle*, 7 July 1900, p. 3; on marching rates, see 'Mahon's March to Mafeking', *Morning Post*, 25 June 1900, p. 6.

51 'The Kimberley Light Horse. Dissatisfied Colonials', *South Wales Daily News*, 6 July 1900, p. 6.

52 'Hard Fare On The March', *Eastbourne Chronicle*, 7 July 1900, p. 3.

53 'With the Mafeking Relief', *South Wales Daily News*, 27 June 1900, p. 6.

54 As Filson Young explained, 'the Naval and Military Club is at 94, Piccadilly . . . the house of Dudley rejoices in six stalwart sons ... [and] the officer commanding the

ILH, moving through the bush as an advanced guard, encountered Boers in the late afternoon. Surgeon-Major William (Willie) Davies recalled that 'the enemy attacked our advanced squadron in the bush, and a very warm fight lasted about half an hour [*sic*: 45 minutes]'.[55] 'We came into action at about 800 yards [732 m]', wrote Gunner Atkinson, 'which is very close for us. Before we got into action', he added, two men of his section were shot, 'so we had to work with two men short. We shifted them out in quick time, however.'[56]

Although the 250 burghers under General Piet Liebenberg withdrew northwards, Trooper Patrick Maxwell (ILH) recognized that his unit had suffered relatively heavy losses: 'we never found any dead or wounded of theirs'.[57] Meanwhile Davies, in charge of the casualties, reckoned that 'we lost 5 killed and 25 wounded. Among the wounded was poor Major [Charles] Mullins', who was shot near the spine and partially paralysed. After bringing all the wounded back to Brodie's Farm, Davies rejoined the column, as it marched '22 miles [35 km], through heavy sand, with no water, to try to effect a junction with Col. Plumer's column from the north'.[58] The two columns met near Jan Massibi's kraal at 6 a.m. on 15 May.

After starting some 1,046 km apart and moving through largely hostile territory, with only one engagement apiece with the enemy, these two forces had achieved a remarkable rendezvous, but one dismissed by Gardner as merely reflecting 'the lack of control and determination shown by the Boers in that sector'.[59] Conversely, Hickman commended the fighting qualities shown by Plumer in moving southwards through the Bechuanaland Protectorate; the ability of Mahon to outmarch and largely evade his opponents; and the planning and physical effort required to affect the union in both time and place.[60] In a more rounded summary the *Official History* attributed the link-up to 'the enterprise of one belligerent and the supineness of the other' but also claimed that it reflected the 'vastness of the theatre of war', which accounted for both the peculiar difficulty and

---

9th Lancers is Colonel Little', F. Young, *Relief of Mafeking*, p. 237; see also TNA, WO 108/185, de Montmorency, diary, pp. 25–6.

55 'With Mahon To Mafeking', *South Wales Daily News*, 4 July 1900, p. 3. All other sources, including Mahon's report, indicate that the fight lasted 45 minutes: PP, *South Africa Despatches*, vol. 1, Cd 457 (1901), p. 126, Brigadier-General B. T. Mahon, report, 23 May, 1900; NAM, Acc. 1974-02-33, P. Maxwell Mss., Maxwell to Mamie, 20 May 1900, see also *Times History*, vol. 4, p. 219.

56 'An Addingham Soldier at the Relief of Mafeking', *Wharfedale & Airedale Observer*, 22 June 1900, p. 3.

57 NAM, Acc. 1974-02-33, P. Maxwell Mss., Maxwell to Mamie, 20 May 1900.

58 'With Mahon To Mafeking', *South Wales Daily News*, 4 July 1900, p. 3.

59 Gardner, *Mafeking*, p. 179.

60 Hickman, *Rhodesia Served The Queen*, vol. 1, p. 353.

relative immunity of conducting tactics in this campaign.[61] The columns had been sufficiently mobile and well supplied, with just enough artillery, to engage or disengage with the enemy where necessary, and to manoeuvre across a vast and inhospitable terrain.

Relief of Mafeking

As the senior commander, Mahon decided to rest the troops and horses for a day, which de Montmorency appreciated as not only 'pleasant' but also perfectly reasonable, since the southern column had 'covered 230 miles [370 km] in eleven days, encumbered with transport through that most inhospitable country known as the Great Thirst Desert'. The 'big gun-horses', he observed, 'had suffered more than the smaller troop-horses from want of water, besides, during the last two days, they had never had their harness removed'.[62] When the columns advanced on the following morning, William Wheeler, BSA Police and a former native of Cork, described how 'we heard the big guns firing at Mafeking which was about 10 miles [16 km] away'.[63]

Having halted for lunch at midday, a detachment of BSA Police scouting south of the river came under fire from an ambush, carefully prepared by General Jacobus (Koos) de la Rey. On the previous day he had deployed between 1,500 and 2,000 Boers with five guns and two pom-poms on both sides of the Molopo River at a junction known as Saane's Post. Liebenberg's burghers were on the ridges along the southern bank, Steenekamp with the Rustenburgers held positions on the ridges along the northern bank, while the Marico Commando defended the southern bank. The imperial columns advanced along the northern bank, with Plumer's brigade on the right and Edwards's on the left, the convoy with dismounted men in the centre, and part of the Kimberley Mounted Corps, under Lieutenant-Colonel Thomas Peakman, acting as a rearguard.[64]

At 1 p.m. on 16 May the fighting began, as the advanced guard and then the main convoy encountered rifle and artillery fire. Serving in Plumer's advance guard, a young trooper from Windsor recalled how

the 'band started playing', big guns, little guns, pom poms, Maxims, etc. on both sides. There being only sixteen of us left mounted in our

61 *Official History*, vol. 3, p. 203.
62 TNA, WO 108/185, de Montmorency diary, p. 28.
63 NAM, Acc. 1986-02-78, W. Wheeler letter to his mother, 30 May 1900.
64 For useful overviews of the engagement, see Pretorius, 'The Besiegers' and Lunderstedt, 'Relief of Mafeking' in Smith (ed.), *Siege of Mafeking*, vol. 1, pp. 102–3 and vol. 2, pp. 383–4 and *Times History*, vol. 4, p. 221.

squadron . . . . The remainder of our squadron, having no horses, were with the convoy, which the Boers shelled pretty freely.[65]

While the brigade under Colonel Edwards sought to outflank the enemy's right, with his horse artillery, as described by Gunner Atkinson, doing 'very good work',[66] the brunt of the enfilading fire and periodic attacks fell upon Plumer's brigade. Captain John Sampson, who had served with the scouts nearly 5 km in advance of the main body, and had exchanged shots with the enemy as early as 11 a.m., before galloping back to report 'the enemy in strength', observed that once the main fighting began:

> Our guns, both large and small opened at about 2,000 yards [1,829 m]. We were soon all engaged, our front being about a mile [1.6 km]. The Boers continued retiring and making flank attacks, but they would never let us get nearer than 800 to 1,000 yards [732 to 914 m]. So the fight ran along until the sun went down. I was galloping with orders all the time, and did not fire a shot . . . .[67]

Another Rhodesian, Trooper T. Watson acknowledged that the action evolved into a gunner's battle, with de Montmorency's 12.5-pounder opening fire on the Boer quick-firer in front, while 'the RHA battery got round on the right and the Canadian battery on the left'. When the enemy tried to 'get behind us', and attack the rear,

> E Squadron and our troop advanced towards their right flank . . . and, supported by the Canadian Artillery and the Queensland Mounted Infantry, we managed to get them cleared out in double-quick time. Our volleys were a bit too warm for them. After that we changed to our right front, where a lot of them had taken cover at a farmhouse [known as Israel's Farm or the White house]; but what between volleys and our guns they were forced to retire, and the Fusiliers took up position at the farm, and captured a waggon with a lot of ammunition.[68]

This somewhat compresses the sequence of events without doing justice to the decisive role of the Canadian artillery, which moved steadily forward and fired 106 rounds from three separate locations. As Sergeant A. J. Gorst,

---

65 'Relief of Mafeking', *Windsor Chronicle*, 13 July 1900, p. 10.

66 'An Addingham Soldier at the Relief of Mafeking', *Wharfedale & Airedale Observer*, 22 June 1900, p. 3.

67 'A Rhodesian Scout From Farnham', *Alton Mail*, 30 June 1900, p. 2.

68 'Last Fight For Mafeking', *(Dundee) Courier and Argus*, 3 July 1900, p. 3; see also TNA, WO 108/185, de Montmorency diary, pp. 30–4.

a Cestrian serving with the Queensland contingent, recalled, 'The Canadian artillery gradually silenced the Boer guns, but it was remarkable how so many escaped instant death, seeing the terrible fusillade from the Boer pompoms.'[69] 'The artillery did very good work', confirmed Lance-Corporal E. Field (Royal Welsh Fusiliers), and it was only at 5 p.m. that the infantry received an order to attack the farmhouse, which 'had received plenty of shells'. Having 'crept quietly towards it', they found it evacuated but, at about 7 p.m., the Irish Fusiliers heard the 'Boers coming down with their guns' and, after harrying them, seized the ammunition waggon.[70]

Those troopers who had been forced to fight dismounted found the action perplexing, especially the relatively few casualties (about forty, of whom ten were killed or died of their wounds, with one missing)[71] and a Boer withdrawal, which opened a route to Mafeking. Unaware of Steenekamp's fear that the British might enter the town from the north, and hence his decision to withdraw his Rustenburgers in a north-westerly direction to head them off,[72] they attributed the victory to superior will: 'It was Mafeking or bust for every one of us', wrote Rhodesian trooper, A. Fletcher, while the enemy 'cleared out pretty fast'.[73] On the other flank the brothers Maxwell, both ILH troopers, had differing opinions of the action: 'we had a good little fight . . . mostly artillery', wrote David,[74] whereas Patrick described it as 'a most soft affair', spending several hours pinioned to the ground firing at each other from 'about 2,000 yards [1,829 m] . . . & doing very little harm either side I imagine'. Then when ordered to advance, he added, 'the funks had cleared to a man taking their guns with them & we halted for the night'.[75]

In fact Major Karri Davis (ILH), with a sergeant major and eight troopers, set off for Mafeking directly. They saw no Boers and reached Mafeking at about eight o'clock at night, receiving a joyous reception from the pickets and townsfolk. The sergeant-major recalled 'shaking hands with Lady Sarah Wilson',[76] and Trooper Joseph Emmerton, being asked 'thousands of

69 'Chester Men With The Queenslanders', *Cheshire Observer*, 30 June 1900, p. 8; see also Miller, *Painting the Map Red*, pp. 185–6.

70 'A Lance-Corporal and the Relief of Mafeking', *Cheshire Observer*, 25 August 1900, p. 7.

71 Of the many estimates of casualty numbers, I have used the most recent in Lunderstedt, 'Relief of Mafeking' in Smith (ed.), *Siege of Mafeking*, vol. 2, p. 396n98.

72 Pretorius, 'The Besiegers' in Smith (ed.), *Siege of Mafeking*, vol. 1, p. 102.

73 'At Mafeking's Relief', *Scarborough Post*, 20 July 1900, p. 6.

74 NAM, Acc 1974-02-32, D. Maxwell Mss., Maxwell to father and mother, 18 May 1900.

75 NAM, Acc. 1974-02-33, P. Maxwell Mss., Maxwell to Mamie, 20 May 1900.

76 'The Gallant Dash to the Relief of Baden-Powell', *Eastbourne Chronicle*, 7 July 1900, p. 3.

questions', before being able to rub down the tired horses and consume a 'splendid meal . . . consisting of bully beef and biscuits, horse sausage, tinned fruit, and a box of cigars'.[77] After a message was flashed by lantern[78] that the route was clear, Mahon moved his force onto Mafeking, reaching the town about 4 a.m. and bivouacking near the Barolong stadt.

Although this was clearly the right decision, 'it was hard on my 16 wounded', wrote Surgeon-Major Davies,[79] and even harder on the ambulance and stretcher-bearers still collecting wounded on the battlefield, including Major Bird wounded severely in the arm, chest and three times in the leg. Trooper Herriot helped in the burying of Lieutenant E. Harland and three other men from the Rhodesia Regiment, and in bringing in the major and five others (two of whom died). They came under fire from the Boers, lost seven of their eight mules, and only reached Mafeking at 2 p.m. on 17 May. Herriot missed the rapturous reception that his comrades had received but then, as the column with its guns advanced on the eastern laagers of the enemy, he saw the 'Mafekingites . . . all out on the house tops – a place they had not been for months – watching the scrap, and they enjoyed it immensely'.[80]

Baden-Powell had only allowed the relief column a few hours' sleep before ordering troops to saddle up at about 8 a.m. to harry the remaining Boers. The armoured train under Captain More's direction ran up the line almost abreast of Game Tree Fort and, with co-ordinated firepower from its Maxim and the Nordenfeldt at Fort Rhodes, scattered about fifteen Boers.[81] The RHA with its 12-pounders, the ILH and Cape Police led a surprise assault on Snyman's headquarters at McMullin's Farm, where the burghers abandoned their breakfast and their wounded in retreating towards the Transvaal border. The looting, though officially banned, was prodigious: 'We got a lot of flour and potatoes', wrote Gunner Atkinson, 'also a quantity of clothing, the niggers clearing off the remainder of the stuff.'[82] Patrick Maxwell (ILH) recalled that the laagers provided 'a great haul' and all day waggons conveyed goods back to the town, with individual troopers 'riding home laden with flour meat jam etc. The poor ILH were not allowed in till the evening when the place was

77 'The Relief of Mafeking described by J. Emmerton, Imperial Light Horse', *Bedford and County Record*, 10 July 1900, p. 3.
78 'A Lance-Corporal and the Relief of Mafeking', *Cheshire Observer*, 25 August 1900, p. 7.
79 'With Mahon to Mafeking', *South Wales Daily News*, 4 July 1900, p. 3.
80 'Berwickshire Troopers in the Fight', *Berwickshire News*, 17 July 1900, p. 6.
81 *Mafeking Mail*, 18 May 1900, p. 2.
82 'An Addingham Soldier at the Relief of Mafeking', *Wharfedale & Airedale Observer*, 22 June 1900, p. 3. The Boers also abandoned their field hospital, with Boer patients, tents, livestock, and a valuable cache of letters and telegrams in Snyman's possession, Pretorius, 'The Besiegers' in Smith (ed.), *Siege of Mafeking*, vol. 1, p. 103.

pretty well cleared.'[83] In the afternoon, the relief column marched through 'the principal streets of the town, in review order, for the benefit of the inhabitants', who, as Private Wheeler described, 'cheered us enthusiastically'.[84]

Assessment of the Relief

'It was not such a big job', wrote Wheeler, capturing the sense of anti-climax that followed the relief.[85] In the absence of any major hand-to-hand engagements, the southern column had to take comfort from what Baden-Powell described as a 'march which would live in history', a 'record march' of about 404 km in fourteen days.[86] The soldiers would also exult in victory: 'Well, we defeated them that day', wrote Gunner W. Mayow (RHA) of the action at Saane's Post, 'and the next we marched into Mafeking'.[87] Just as satisfying, claimed Trooper Fletcher, was the sight of artillery shelling 'the Boers out of their main laager',[88] and then the spectacle as described by a sergeant of the BSA Police, of the enemy 'making their way towards the Transvaal at a pace unusually smart even for the mobile Boer'. The sergeant believed that they had reached Mafeking just in time: 'We found the inhabitants, many of them women and children, in a state of semi-starvation, living on horse flesh and bread made out of crushed oats.'[89] A Kimberley trooper agreed: 'We were only just in time, for the place could not have held out much longer.'[90]

These impressions were by no means uniform, and they varied with whom the troopers met and when they wrote. De Montmorency's deep cynicism about the siege, which so coloured the writing of Gardner, was stoked by a meal at the Weils on the evening of the 17 May. Over an elegant dinner the hosts regaled their guests with accounts of their own 'foresight in stocking

---

83   NAM, Acc. 1974-02-33, P. Maxwell Mss., Maxwell to Mamie, 20 May 1900.
84   NAM, Acc. 1986-02-78, Wheeler letter to his mother, 30 May 1900.
85   Ibid.
86   'Mafeking After The Siege', *Derby Mercury*, 6 June 1900, p. 6. There are varying estimates of the distance covered, some stopping at Jan Massibi's kraal, some at Mafeking, and some simply claim a 'record' see *Times History*, vol. 4, p. 222; 'Mahon's March to Mafeking', *Morning Post*, 25 June 1900, p. 6; 'An Addingham Soldier At The Relief of Mafeking', *Wharfedale & Airedale Observer*, 22 June 1900, p. 3; 'A Menston Soldier At The Front', *Wharfedale and Airedale Observer*, 29 June 1900, p. 3; 'In One Siege and at the Relief of Another', *Essex Herald*, 3 July 1900, p. 3.
87   'The Relief of Mafeking', *Abingdon Herald*, 28 July 1900, p. 7; see also 'Relief of Mafeking', *Windsor Chronicle*, 13 July 1900, p. 10.
88   'At Mafeking's Relief', *Scarborough Post*, 20 July 1900, p. 6.
89   'In A State of Semi-Starvation' and 'Boers On The Run', *Eastbourne Chronicle*, 7 July 1900, p. 3.
90   'Only Just In Time', *Eastbourne Chronicle*, 7 July 1900, p. 3; see also 'Chester Men with the Queenslanders', *Cheshire Observer*, 30 June 1900, p. 8.

their depots with provisions', which had 'contributed in no small measure to the stubbornness of the defence'. Meanwhile de Montmorency revelled in being able to sit 'at a table' after 'pigging it on the veld' and 'drinking out of a glass'.[91] While he was probably drinking something more potent than water, it was water, recalled Lance-Corporal Field, that was 'a great difference between Mafeking and Ladysmith': it was like 'drinking poison' when they relieved Ladysmith, 'while the water in Mafeking was as good as ever he (the writer) had at home in England'.[92] Mafeking itself hardly impressed; it was 'a miserable hole of a town', wrote Patrick Maxwell, but 'its few buildings' had been 'tremendously knocked about by shells' – an impression widely shared[93] – and the destruction, he reckoned, was 'far worse than Ladysmith', even if the rations were much better and tobacco readily available.[94]

Of those who remained in the town, enjoying the opportunity to buy clean shirts and tobacco, and have shaves in a barber's shop,[95] they soon encountered the opportunism of Mafeking's tradesmen. 'They charged extortionate prices for the tinned stuffs remaining', opined Trooper Dan A. Williams, 'and if many had had their way they would have fired the place. I was disgusted with the inhabitants, who were beneath contempt', and had not the place been

> the key to Rhodesia, they might have all gone to Pretoria for my part. Baden-Powell has made a grand defence no doubt, but to allow the coolies [Indian merchants] and Jews to price as they did is open to question. Our chief cry was, 'What price Kekewich?'[96]

At least this Kimberley veteran saw a purpose to the siege, both its 'grand defence' and the successful march of the relief column. Conversely, de Montmorency saw little purpose in defending 'a scattered collection of rather shabby-looking corrugated iron huts', an 'insignificant railway-depot'. He wondered about how a cavalry leader could begin the war by burrowing underground and then 'commence eating his horses'. He criticized further

---

91 TNA, WO 108/185, de Montmorency diary, p. 47.
92 'A Lance-Corporal and the Relief of Mafeking', *Cheshire Observer*, 25 August 1900, p. 7.
93 NAM, Acc. 1974-02-33, P. Maxwell Mss., Maxwell to Maime, 20 May 1900; see also 'Relief of Mafeking', *Windsor Chronicle*, 13 July 1900, p. 10; 'First Squadron In', *Eastbourne Chronicle*, 7 July 1900, p. 3 and 'Berwickshire Troopers in the Fight', *Berwickshire News*, 17 July 1900, p. 6.
94 NAM, Acc. 1974-02-33, P. Maxwell Mss., Maxwell to Maime, 20 May 1900.
95 'Relief of Mafeking', *Windsor Chronicle*, 13 July 1900, p. 10.
96 'The Kimberley Light Horse. Dissatisfied Colonials', *South Wales Daily News*, 6 July 1900, p. 6.

the burden that the defence of this 'not very important garrison' had placed upon Lord Roberts, particularly the 'necessity for detaching a column' and 'hazarding it in a dangerous march'. Finally, he speculated upon the failure of the Boers to capture the town and entered hearsay in his diary about how Kruger had not thought the place worth 'the lives of five Transvaal burghers', a nonsensical observation in light of his approval of Eloff's assault. Only later when he got to know Baden-Powell would de Montmorency acknowledge his 'geniality', 'lovable character' and 'generosity towards his subordinates'.[97]

Gardner could only find a quote from B-P's brother about 'the uselessness of investing places' in support of this cynicism, a quote that was directed primarily at the Boers as the investing forces.[98] Whatever their thoughts about the enemy, most of the relieving forces exuded pride in their own achievements: 'you would have been proud to call yourself English', wrote another RHA gunner, 'had you been in this column when we relieved Mafeking'.[99] They were also impressed, at least initially, by the stoicism and sufferings of the townsfolk; 'the people of Mafeking', wrote Trooper W. Adams, 'were overjoyed to see us; their delight knew no bounds. They have been having a rough time of it; they have been shut out from the outer world for seven months.'[100] Above all, they were impressed with Baden-Powell, who spoke generously about them after the relief. The Hon. Maurice Gifford, a military veteran, insisted that 'in all his experience he had seen nothing to equal the brilliancy of the work done by General Baden-Powell and his men'.[101] Many were impressed by B-P's appearance: Trooper Williams regarded him as a 'bit of a dandy, but with the appearance of a good fighter',[102] while Corporal Wood (BSA Police) described him as 'a very smart-looking man, about forty years of age . . . and rather good-looking, too'. With slight exaggeration, he continued, 'Tis marvellous how he managed to hold on so long, considering that he was outnumbered by almost ten to one. He is certainly the hero of the war.'[103]

---

97 TNA, WO 108/185, de Montmorency, diary, pp. 38–40 and 64.
98 Gardner, *Mafeking*, p. 179 and Baden F. S. Baden-Powell, *War in Practice* (London: Isbister & Co., 1903), pp. 24–5.
99 'Hard Fare On The March', *Eastbourne Chronicle*, 7 July 1900, p. 3.
100 'Trooper Adams with Plumer's Column', *Gorton, Openshaw and Bradford Reporter*, 21 July 1900, p. 6.
101 'Home From The Wars', *Bath Chronicle*, 26 July 1900, p. 5; see also a similar view from a soldier who arrived in Mafeking after the relief, 'Interesting Letters from South Africa', *Derbyshire Advertiser*, 27 July 1900, p. 6.
102 'The Kimberley Light Horse. Dissatisfied Colonials', *South Wales Daily News*, 6 July 1900, p. 6.
103 'The Relief of Mafeking. Letter From A County Antrim Man', *Belfast News-Letter*, 26 June 1900, p. 5.

Colonel Frank Rhodes, who had served in the defence of Ladysmith before joining Mahon's column, maintained that

> It is wonderful what he [B-P] did with so few men and guns . . .
> it made me blush for Ladysmith . . . . I should say [he is] the best
> man the country has produced. He is plucky, very quick, very slim,
> and makes up his mind and works indefatigably and sees others do
> their work. Of course he humbugged about the food, but he held
> Mafeking by his audacity and resourcefulness and it was really a
> wonderful show.[104]

Soldiers were also aware that the reputation of the siege had spread far and wide: as Hoël Llewellyn recognized months earlier, 'Nothing shows up so well during the whole campaign as Mafeking's defence. All papers, the British & other Powers talk of its wonderful defence. It certainly deserves a special clasp.'[105]

---

104 Col. F. Rhodes, letter, 1 June 1900, in Viscountess Milner, *My Picture Gallery*, p.194.
105 Hanbury-Tracy Mss., Llewellyn to Hanbury-Tracy, 16 January 1900.

Chapter 8

'Mafficking': The Celebrations and Their Significance

To 'maffick' (rejoice with hysterical boisterousness) passed into the English language soon after the scenes and celebrations that followed the relief of Mafeking. They began on the evening of Friday, 18 May 1900 ('Mafeking Night'), continued over several days, and engulfed most of Britain and the English-speaking empire. Both at the time and subsequently, the unprecedented outburst fascinated commentators, particularly the 'complete spontaneity' of the initial reactions, the lack of any official stimulus, and the celebratory nature of the occasion.[1] By likening the celebrations to Armistice Night (1918) or VE Night (1945), Richard Price distinguishes between the crowds on 'Mafeking Night' and the Jingo mobs that disrupted 'Stop the War' meetings, even if such distinctions were not so obvious to contemporary critics. He acknowledges, too, that the crowds on successive evenings were more confrontational in certain locations but there was nothing like the rioting and destructiveness of the eighteenth-century mobs.[2] London, where news of the relief was first published at 9.20 p.m., became the epicentre of the demonstrations, with scenes described by provincial writers as 'unexampled',[3] and the thousands on the streets as 'fairly mad with enthusiasm'.[4] The capital's response has attracted most analysis[5] but so too has recognition of Baden-Powell as the hero of the hour, a man whose image was displayed across the empire and whose exploits were extolled wherever the relief was celebrated. While this reaction, coupled with his self-advertisement, may have fuelled a degree of post-siege resentment within Mafeking among certain townspeople, and

---

1   Kruger, *Goodbye Dolly Gray*, p. 296; Gardner, *Mafeking*, p. 201; and Price, *An Imperial War*, p. 133.
2   Price, *An Imperial War*, pp. 133–7; Kruger, *Goodbye Dolly Gray*, p. 297; and Pakenham, 'Mafficking' in Smith (ed.), *Siege of Mafeking*, vol. 2, pp. 399–435.
3   'Scene in London', *Northern Echo*, 19 May 1900, p. 3.
4   'London Fairly Mad with Enthusiasm', *Sunderland Daily Echo*, 19 May 1900, p. 3.
5   Gardner, *Mafeking*, pp. 200–2, 204–5 and 207; Pakenham, 'Mafficking' in Smith (ed.), *Siege of Mafeking*, vol. 2, pp. 404–7, 410–12 and 430.

officers of the Mafeking garrison,[6] such feelings fail to capture the full range of emotions expressed in the wake of the siege.

This chapter will not in any way dispute the primacy accorded to the celebrations in London, and the adulation of B-P at home and in the colonies, but it will probe the range and nature of the emotions on display, particularly in the provinces. It will examine the eruption of feelings on 'Mafeking Night'; assess the rapid spread and character of the rejoicings on subsequent days and nights, including the remarkable response from across the empire; and review the debate about the meaning and significance of both 'mafficking' and the relief of Mafeking.

'Mafeking Night'

'Mafeking Night' did not happen in a vacuum. For months fears had been expressed about the fate of Mafeking, and Parliamentary questions about the possibility of its relief had been publicized in the press.[7] The promise of Lord Roberts to relieve Mafeking by 18 May was known so widely that it was the subject of a famous *Punch* cartoon, 'Eleventh Hour', printed on 9 May.[8] Anxiety mounted as the promised day approached, compounded by the pall of secrecy draped over the movements of Mahon's column.[9] Many communities, including those in Nottingham, Swindon and Bangor, tempted providence and planned their celebrations in advance of the impending relief,[10] and most remained, as the *Birmingham Daily Post* reported on the morning of 18 May, in 'a state of feverish expectation'.[11]

Even such expectations hardly anticipated the scale and nature of the subsequent response. Once the Reuter's telegram from Pretoria arrived in London, technically at 9.17 p.m.,[12] it was published a few minutes later on tapes in London clubs and institutions, on placards outside the newspaper offices of Fleet Street, and in a notice on the Mansion House. Despite the absence of

---

6   Jeal, *Baden-Powell*, pp. 301–11.
7   'Must Mafeking Fall!', *South Wales Daily Post*, 9 March 1900, p. 3 and 'Questions in Parliament. The Siege of Mafeking', *Belfast News-Letter*, 27 April 1900, p. 6.
8   'The Eleventh Hour', *Punch*, vol. 118, 9 May 1900, p. 335.
9   'Mafeking Relief Celebrations', *Woking Observer*, 23 May 1900, p. 1.
10 'Nottingham. Enthusiastic Demonstrations', *Nottingham Evening Post*, 19 May 1900, p. 4; 'The Relief of Mafeking', *Evening Swindon Advertiser*, 15 May 1900, p. 2; 'Preparing to Celebrate the Relief of Mafeking', *North Wales Chronicle*, 19 May 1900, p. 8; see also 'Is Mafeking Relieved?' *Daily Mail*, 17 May 1900, p. 4.
11 'Mafeking Relief Rumours', *Birmingham Daily Post*, 18 May 1900, p. 10; see also 'How The News Was Received In Middlesbrough', *North-Eastern Daily Gazette*, 19 May 1900, p. 3.
12 'How The News Was Transmitted', *Leeds Mercury*, 19 May 1900, p. 8.

official confirmation, people began cheering at these notices, attracting more and more people until tumultuous crowds gathered in the City, the Strand, Ludgate Circus and the thoroughfares of the West End. Commentators were amazed by the rapidity with which vast crowds assembled as the news flashed across London; the abundance of paper Union Jacks (pre-stocked by street traders or brought by people to work); and the extraordinary noise of the spontaneous cheering, singing, dancing and exultation: 'the cheering', recalled the *Daily News*, 'was intense, the tone deep and heartfelt, the vent of a long-pent anxiety'.[13] Just as astonishing was the collective reaction within the Royal Opera House, the theatres of London, and the music halls as announcements of Mafeking's relief were made. Audiences arose *en masse* to sing the National Anthem and other patriotic songs, and to cheer both the Queen and Baden-Powell, with the latter encored for eight times in the London Hippodrome.[14] The immense crowds, though boisterous and jubilant, were not conspicuously drunken: as the pro-Boer *Morning Leader* admitted, 'It was the honest, spontaneous outburst of a patriotic people, giving vent to their feelings after a prolonged period of anxiety which falls to the lot of few nations.'[15]

The telegraph ensured that the news reached the London suburbs, the provinces, Scotland, Wales and Ireland almost as soon as it did central London. Aberdeen reportedly learned of the relief about 9.30 p.m., and the *Evening Express* enjoyed record sales, while thousands paraded through the principal avenues, especially Union Street, singing 'Soldiers of the Queen' and other patriotic airs.[16] The news was spread by church bells, fog signals on railway trains, illuminations on public buildings, sirens on newspaper offices, newspaper sellers, choruses of foghorns on the Mersey and sirens and whistles on the Thames, mill and factory buzzers, and sirens and hooters at various coalfields.[17] Incalculable numbers of men, women and children left their beds,

---

13 'Reception of the News', *Daily News*, 19 May 1900, p. 5; see also 'Rejoicings in London', *Morning Post*, 19 May 1900, p. 7.
14 'In Theatre and Hall', *Daily Chronicle*, 19 May 1900, p. 5 and 'London's Roar of Jubilation', *Daily Mail*, 19 May 1900, p. 5.
15 'In The West-End', *Morning Leader*, 19 May 1900, p. 5.
16 'The War: Mafeking Relieved', *Elgin Courant*, 22 May 1900, p. 4; 'Saturday's Rejoicings in Aberdeen', *Aberdeen Weekly Journal*, 21 May 1900, p. 6.
17 'The Relief of Mafeking. Reception of the News in Ealing', *Middlesex County Times*, 19 May 1900, p. 6; 'Relief of Mafeking', *Abingdon Herald*, 26 May 1900, p. 8; 'Reception of the news in South Wales', *Western Mail*, 19 May 1900, p. 5; 'Nottingham. Enthusiastic Demonstrations', *Nottingham Evening Post*, 19 May 1900, p. 4; 'How the news was transmitted', *Liverpool Echo*, 19 May 1900, p. 3; 'Relief of Mafeking', *(Gravesend and Dartford) Reporter*, 26 May 1900, p. 5; 'Yorkshire', *Leeds Mercury*, 19 May 1900, p. 8; 'North Wales and the War', *North Wales Guardian*, 25 May 1900, p. 6; 'The Relief of Mafeking', *Consett Chronicle*, 26 May 1900, p. 8.

and night shifts, including those at the Royal Arsenal, Woolwich, abandoned
work. Huge gatherings assembled before public buildings, in the great
squares and parks, and at railway stations, with vast processions following as
onlookers crammed the principal streets of the major cities.

More evidence of commercial preparations diluted the myth of complete
spontaneity, once tradesmen, as in Ealing, hung out 'flags, which had been
kept in readiness', while in the East End street hawkers 'produced, as if
by magic, baskets and trays of Union Jacks, and rosettes, plus portraits,
and bunches of ribbons, which met with eager purchasers'.[18] Spontaneity,
nonetheless, remained the watchword for the *Croydon Express*, arguing
that after the 'the first shock of glad surprise', the town's unprecedented
rejoicing and impromptu torchlight procession only took place because the
news arrived so late at night (and in benign weather), when the streets
were at their least congested.[19] Similarly, in Newport and Nottingham,
prearranged demonstrations could not be mounted on 'Mafeking Night'
because the news of relief arrived too late.[20]

The news, however, failed to reach the entire hinterland, often on account
of post offices closing at 9.00 p.m., and so 'Mafeking Night' missed parts of
Sussex, Kent, Derbyshire, the West Country, Ulster and the Highlands, as well
as a cathedral city like Hereford and towns such as Mansfield, Loughborough,
Workington and Elgin. The process was quite random; while Lewes, the
county town of Sussex, missed the news, Brighton and Hastings did not.[21]
Nevertheless, the news penetrated the greater part of the country, prompting
congregations of amazing size in the principal cities of Birmingham,
Manchester, Glasgow, Belfast, and Leeds. Estimates of these night-time
turnouts were bound to be fanciful, but the 'hundreds of thousands' reported
in Liverpool, followed by crowds of 'gigantic proportions' on the following

18 'The Relief of Mafeking. Reception of the News in Ealing', *Middlesex County Times*,
19 May 1900, p. 6; 'The Relief of Mafeking. How the News was received in the South-
Eastern Districts', *Kentish Mercury*, 25 May 1900, p. 6; and 'The Relief of Mafeking',
Woolwich Herald, 25 May 1900, p. 5.
19 'At Last! Relief of Mafeking', *Croydon Express*, 19 May 1900, p. 1.
20 'Demonstrations at Newport', *South Wales Argus*, 21 May 1900, p. 2 and 'Nottingham.
Enthusiastic Demonstrations', *Nottingham Evening Post*, 19 May 1900, p. 4.
21 'The Relief of Mafeking', *East Sussex News*, 25 May 1900, p. 2; 'The Relief of
Mafeking', *High Peak News*, 26 May 1900, p. 6; 'Mafeking Rejoicings', *Cornishman*, 24
May 1900, p. 5; 'Relief of Mafeking', *North Devon Journal*, 24 May 1900, p. 3; 'The
Relief of Mafeking', *Hereford Journal*, 26 May 1900, p. 3; 'Nottingham. Enthusiastic
Demonstrations', *Nottingham Evening Post*, 19 May 1900, p. 4; 'Notes of the Week',
Workington Star, 25 May 1900, p. 2; 'The War: Mafeking Relieved', *Elgin Courant*, 22
May 1900, p. 4; 'Relief of Mafeking', *Brighton Gazette*, 19 May 1900, p. 5; 'Reported
Relief of Mafeking', *Hastings & St. Leonards Observer*, 19 May 1900, p. 7.

day, may have been eclipsed proportionately by the 40,000 revellers, if true, on the Outer Isle of Lewis.[22] Whatever the exact numbers all commentators agreed that the crowds dwarfed the celebrations, which had followed the reliefs of Kimberley and Ladysmith. Such comparisons appeared invidious even in Lancashire, where the county's regiments had fought tenaciously in the defence of both towns and in the relief of Ladysmith.[23] Just as remarkable was the rapidity with which the crowds gathered, their improvised activities, and their generally good behaviour on 'Mafeking Night'. Baden-Powell was unquestionably the hero of the hour, whether in the garrison town of Colchester, or Carlisle ready to celebrate a 'Boer official announcement', or Chichester awoken by its Cathedral Bells.[24]

Sustained Celebrations

Saturday, 19 May, began celebrations across mainland Britain and most of the dominions, an unprecedented phenomenon that lasted for several days with some events (as in Sheffield), coinciding with the commemoration of the Queen's Birthday on the following Thursday. The metropolis, bedecked in red, white and blue, set the tone with all parts of the town engaged, and an extraordinary display of flags, portraits of B-P and illuminations at night. Many thousands of people travelled up to town not to work but to celebrate. Every form of vehicle, horse and dog was festooned with patriotic colours, and the streets were packed with exultant crowds, singing the National Anthem, 'Rule Britannia' and 'Soldiers of the Queen'. The 'Te Deum' sung before a packed congregation at St Paul's Cathedral on Saturday afternoon set the tone for religious services on the following day, even if the Lord Mayor and his party could not pass through the multitude to attend.

From early morning to after midnight, processions – sometimes of many thousands – paraded through the streets, with student-led displays from King's College London and the Royal College of Art attracting widespread

---

22 'How the news was transmitted', *Liverpool Echo*, 19 May 1900, p. 3; 'The Rejoicings. Liverpool', *Liverpool Mercury*, 21 May 1900, p. 7; and 'In Lewis', *Glasgow Herald*, 22 May 1900, p. 5.
23 'The Relief of Mafeking' *Manchester Courier*, 21 May 1900, p. 8; 'The Relief of Mafeking', *Ashton-under-Lyne Reporter*, 26 May 1900, p. 7; 'Bolton and the Relief of Mafeking', *Bolton Chronicle*, 26 May 1900, p. 7; 'Manchester Mad with Joy', *Aberdeen Weekly Journal*, 21 May 1900, p. 6; see also John Downham, *Red Roses on the Veldt: Lancashire Regiments in the Boer War, 1899-1902* (Lancaster: Carnegie Publishing, 2000), Part 2.
24 'The Relief of Mafeking', *Essex County Standard*, 26 May 1900, p. 2; 'Mafeking Day', *Carlisle Journal*, 22 May 1900, p. 3; 'Chichester's Reception of the News', *Chichester Observer*, 23 May 1900, p. 5.

coverage. The latter included models of Kruger and Lord Roberts, and a colossal bust of Baden-Powell, made by M. Lanterie, one of the masters at the Royal College and his students. About 1.7 m high, the bust was a lifelike representation of the Colonel in his cowboy hat, flanked by towering palms and plants, and by his side a life-size replica of a lion. The procession from Knightsbridge wended its way through the West End and made a point of passing the home of Baden-Powell's mother in St George's Terrace, near Hyde Park, where a halt was made to cheer the hero of Mafeking. Similarly, when Mrs Baden-Powell, her two daughters and one man took a box that evening at the Alhambra Theatre, 'the party met with a splendid ovation'.[25]

The provinces more than compensated for any gaps in the jubilation of Friday night. The *Canterbury Register* maintained that every town, village and hamlet in Kent participated in the national rejoicings over the next few days with bell ringing, torch-like processions and bonfires with fireworks. Meanwhile the response in Scotland extended from Kirkwall to Kirkcudbright, Stornoway to St. Andrews, and across the populous central belt from Kilmarnock to Kirkcaldy.[26] Displays of flags, streamers and banners adorned public and private buildings, whether the Union Jack, Irish, Welsh and Scottish ensigns fluttering 'in the grimy smoke' of Birmingham, or Aberdeen 'practically swathed in bunting', or the decorations exhibited in 'the streets, the castle, the clubs, and the shipping in the harbour' at Carnarvon.[27] The celebrations engaged men, women and children and spread across class and political boundaries. In Nottingham, the national colours flew from 'dismal tenements and squalid slums, as from the private mansion', while in Glasgow the most conspicuous displays of 'outward loyalty' were in the wealthier working-class districts of Springburn, Shawlands, Cowcaddens, Trongate and Bridgeton and not the 'mansion houses' of Kelvinside nor 'the residences of the wealthy out by Pollockshields'.[28] Besides the bunting was a cacophony of noise from improvised minstrel troupes using tin whistles, penny trumpets, cornets, bugles, and all sorts of musical instruments; rockets fired from warships in Exmouth harbour; fireworks discharged at night,

25 'London's Carnival', *Daily News*, 21 May 1900, p. 4; 'The Relief of Mafeking', *Standard*, 21 May 1900, p. 8.
26 'Kent and Mafeking', *Canterbury Register*, 26 May 1900, p. 7 and 'Mafeking Relief', *Glasgow Herald*, 21 May 1900, p. 8.
27 'Saturday's Rejoicings in Aberdeen', *Aberdeen Weekly Journal*, 21 May 1900, p. 6; 'Rejoicings in Birmingham. A Day's Carnival', *Birmingham Daily Post*, 21 May 1900, p. 5; 'The Relief of Mafeking', *Carnarvon and Denbigh Herald*, 25 May 1900, p. 8.
28 'Nottingham. Enthusiastic Demonstrations', *Nottingham Evening Post*, 19 May 1900, p. 4 and 'Mafeking Rejoicings', *North British Daily Mail*, 21 May 1900, p. 5.

and a salvo of nineteen minute guns that concluded a pyrotechnic display at Alnwick Castle.[29]

Newspapers reminded readers that Mafeking was not simply a far-off outpost of empire, and that sometimes they had local connections with the siege. These included officers like Colonel Hore (Leamington Spa) or Major Panzera (Harwich), the seriously-wounded Sergeant-Major Poole (Winchester), and Troopers Josiah Tiffin, James and Ritchie (formerly of Carlisle). From Scotland John Fleming (Strathaven) and several railwaymen, Robert Coran (Troon), Alexander Moffat and David Campbell (Lochee), had been trapped in Mafeking.[30] Mrs Whiteley, the mayoress of Mafeking, attracted particularly effusive rejoicings outside her home, Lees House in the village of Thornhill, Yorkshire. Two nights and a day of exuberance culminated with the lighting of a 20-ton bonfire on Saturday night.[31]

Provincial town councils also sent a profusion of congratulatory telegrams to Mafeking, underscoring the bond they felt with their counterpart on the veld. Even more intense were the connections that communities claimed with Baden-Powell himself. Great crowds gathered to cheer the relief outside his Kentish home at Speldhurst, near Tunbridge Wells; outside the residence of a half-brother at Banbury; and outside The Croft at Crowborough, Sussex, home of his aunt. Liverpool had a longstanding connection with the family, as B-P's elder brother, Sir George, had represented the Kirkdale Division in Parliament until his death in 1898. Charterhouse School also had reason to celebrate, as Baden-Powell was a well-known Carthusian: the schoolboys so revelled in his achievements that the *Graphic* illustrated their merriment on its front page.[32]

As the hero of the hour, Baden-Powell was the subject of numerous biographical sketches, often accompanied by images of him in his distinctive

29 'In the West', *Trewman's Exeter Flying Post*, 19 May 1900, p. 8; 'Mafeking Relief Celebrations', *Alnwick Guardian*, 26 May 1900, p. 5.
30 'Local News', *Leamington Spa Courier*, 26 May 1900, p. 4; 'Harwich', *Essex Herald*, 22 May 1900, p. 5; 'Relief of Mafeking. Reception of the Good News in Winchester', *Hampshire Chronicle*, 19 May 1900, p. 4; 'Mafeking Day', *Carlisle Journal*, 22 May 1900, p. 3; 'Mafeking Relief', *Glasgow Herald*, 21 May 1900, p. 8; 'Troon Men in Mafeking', *Ayr Observer*, 22 May 1900, p. 1; 'State of Feeling in Lochee', *(Dundee) Evening Telegraph*, 19 May 1900, p. 5.
31 'Rejoicings Throughout the Country', *Dewsbury Reporter*, 26 May 1900, p. 6; 'The Provinces', *Standard*, 21 May 1900, p. 8.
32 'The Relief of Mafeking: Charterhouse Mad with Joy', *Graphic*, vol. lxi, 26 May 1900, p. 1 and 'Charterhouse Rejoicing', *Daily Mail*, 19 May 1900, p. 5; see also 'The Provinces', *Standard*, 21 May 1900, p. 8; 'Rejoicings in the Country', *Daily News*, 21 May 1900, p. 4; 'Liverpool', *Scotsman*, 19 May 1900, p. 10; and 'Crowborough', *East Sussex News*, 25 May 1900, p. 2.

cowboy hat. He became a household name, not only in Britain and across much of the empire but also in the United States. Writers emphasized that B-P was not an ordinary soldier but a man of many parts, with artistic, literary, theatrical and sporting accomplishments. As a commander in Mafeking, they insisted, he had found all these diverse skills, coupled with his geniality, energy and resourcefulness, utterly invaluable. Given his predicament at the outset of the siege, and lack of modern munitions throughout, the *Oban Telegraph* claimed that Baden-Powell knew that 'the ordinary mode of fighting' would not prevail, while 'in the hands of a less resourceful man, however brave', added Darlington's *Northern Echo*, 'Mafeking would hardly have held out for a month.'[33] Accordingly, B-P dominated the many ballads and poems about Mafeking, his portrait graced numerous parades (and a life-size version in oils appeared in Strathtay House, Dundee), and hawkers sold millions of B-P medallions (at least 2,000,000 manufactured in Birmingham).[34]

Mass hysterical gatherings, though, were by no means the only form of jubilation. In Scotland more sedate celebrations included a 'patriotic tea' by the Ladies' Club of Queen Mary's House, Inverness; traditional cake and wine banquets for select groups in Glenrinnes and Ayr; and a smoking concert on the Monday evening at the Gentleman's Club, Campbeltown, Argyllshire, after the opening of the club to ladies in the afternoon.[35] Mafeking's relief was also an opportunity for synagogues in Newport and Sunderland to profess their loyalty to the British state and support for the imperial cause.[36]

The processions, nonetheless, remained the more memorable features of the commemorative events, both in the United Kingdom and across the empire. If these events were opportunities to make parades of patriotic fervour, with tableaux about Mafeking, images of Lord Roberts and Baden-Powell, and effigies of Kruger, they varied considerably. Some seemed little more than carnivals, with people enjoying their half or full-day holidays, children

33 'The Hero of Mafeking', *Oban Telegraph*, 25 May 1900, p. 4; 'The Hero of the War', *Northern Echo*, 19 May 1900, p. 3; see also 'Mafeking Pictures', *Daily Mail*, 19 May 1900, p. 7; 'The Hero of the Hour', *Wharfedale & Airedale Observer*, 23 May 1900, p. 3 and 'The Hero of the War', *Liverpool Echo*, 19 May 1900, p. 3.
34 'The Relief of Mafeking' and 'Bravo Mafeking!', *Stockport Advertiser*, 25 May 1900, p. 5; 'A Tribute in Verse', *Morning Leader*, 22 May 1900, p. 3; 'Arthur Roberts at Southsea', *(Portsmouth) Evening News*, 25 May 1900, p. 2; Dundee Rejoices', *(Dundee) Courier & Argus*, 21 May 1900, p. 4; 'Millions of Medals', *Pudsey and Stanningley News*, 25 May 1900, p. 5.
35 'The Relief of Mafeking. Rejoicings in Inverness', *Inverness Courier*, 22 May 1900, p. 6; 'Glenrinnes', *Elgin Courant*, 22 May 1900, p. 4; 'Cake and Wine Banquet', *Ayr Observer*, 22 May 1900, p. 5; 'Relief of Mafeking. Celebrations at the Club', *Argyllshire Herald*, 26 May 1900, p. 3.
36 'Mafeking Day at Home and Abroad', *Morning Leader*, 21 May 1900, p. 5.

relishing a day off school, and people wearing all manner of fancy dress, even dressing up as Red Indians. Others were much more organized, involving 10,000 schoolchildren in Southampton or the torchlight procession through Edinburgh, led by students of Edinburgh University and watched by many thousands of onlookers.[37] Most represented the worthy elements of their localities, as in Northampton, where a procession of nearly fifty vehicles, led by mounted police, included the mayor, prominent councillors and their wives in landaus, the fire brigade, St John's Ambulance Brigade, local Volunteer and other bands, the Boys' Brigade, school children, carriages illuminated by Chinese lanterns and decorated by local sporting and political clubs, and members of friendly societies in their regalia (while forty of their number made collections for Lady Georgina Curzon's Mafeking Relief Fund).[38] The Windsor procession on Saturday, 19 May, was particularly notable. It was preceded by bands of the 1st Life Guards and the Grenadier Guards, and numbered in excess of 2,000, with 1,200 bearing torches, about half of whom were Eton College Volunteers and students, wearing their top hats. Granted the unique privilege of entering the castle's quadrangle, it marched twice past the Queen, before pausing to salute and serenade the Sovereign, whereupon she graciously acknowledged the display.[39]

Processions were a feature, too, of the colonial celebrations, including *inter alia* those in Quebec, Gibraltar, Durban, Adelaide, Melbourne (where the one on the public holiday of 23 May reportedly attracted 200,000 spectators), and an unprecedented crowd in Wellington, New Zealand.[40] Only in Cape Colony was there any reticence, where Cape Town and Kimberley awaited official confirmation of the relief before ecstatic celebrations ensued. The British press not only chronicled the colonial response but also recognized that the colonies had made a crucial contribution to both the defence and relief of Mafeking. Appropriately, recognition of this imperial theme found its most extensive airing in Chamberlain Square, Birmingham, on Saturday, 19 May. After an immense torchlit procession had reached the Bull Ring, and the concourse had moved onto the square, the organizers convened a 'monster

---

37 'Swindon's Celebration of the Relief of Mafeking', *Evening Swindon Advertiser*, 21 January 1900, p. 3; 'Monster Demonstration of School Children at Southampton', *Hampshire Advertiser*, 26 May 1900, p. 6; 'Students Torchlight Procession in Edinburgh', *Dumbarton Herald*, 23 May 1900, p. 5.
38 'Mafeking Rejoicing in Northampton', *Northampton Mercury*, 25 May 1900, p. 6.
39 'The Relief of Mafeking', *Windsor Chronicle*, 25 May 1900, pp. 2–3.
40 'Melbourne Rises to the Occasion', *(Melbourne) Argus*, 24 May 1900, p. 5; 'The Relief of Mafeking and of Wellington', *Wairarapa Daily Times*, 22 May 1900, p. 3; 'Jubilation Everywhere', *(Toronto) Globe*, 19 May 1900, p. 21; 'Mafeking Day at Home and Abroad', *Morning Leader*, 21 May 1900, p. 5; 'Empire's Joy', *Western Mail*, 21 May 1900, p. 5; 'Colonial Demonstrations', *Birmingham Daily Post*, 21 May 1900, p. 12.

meeting', with one of their number, the Unionist Councillor William E. Lovesey, lauding Baden-Powell as 'the man who had done more than any other man living to bring together the different parts of the empire, and to convince all nations that we were one united family, ready, if the time came, to present a united front to the world'.[41]

If the vast majority of crowds and processions were good-natured, and intent on simply enjoying themselves, a few had their darker side, when remnants of their number, usually after midnight, attacked the properties of reputed pro-Boers (as the anti-war protestors were popularly known). If most of these incidents occurred on the Saturday evening, when intoxication may have been a factor, there was a precedent in Leeds on 'Mafeking Night' when demonstrators attacked the house of Arnold Lupton, a prominent member of the South Africa Conciliation Committee, breaking three of his windows.[42] Several incidents occurred in the London suburbs, including stones thrown in Harlesden at the shop windows of a local greengrocer, said to have pro-Boer sympathies. Similar attacks were made on a baker's shop in West London and a hairdresser's shop which was set on fire in Tottenham; and assaults took place in North Finchley, where the windows of a draper's shop were not only broken but fireworks thrown in.[43] Writing in his diary the Socialist, John Burns deplored the mob passing his home, singing 'God save the Queen' on 'Mafeking Night', and exhibiting 'wild delirium over so small a victory' on the following night, when three of his windows were broken.[44] W. T. Stead, another prominent pro-Boer, suffered a similar fate when unruly roughs attacked his house and garden in Wimbledon, and then smashed two shops after one of their owners had thrown a bucket of water over the mob.[45]

Outside London minor incidents flared in places as diverse as Aspley Guise, Dorking and Morpeth but, in Dover, a near-riot occurred when a mob pelted the house of Mr J. F. Brown with stones, rotten eggs and 'every conceivable missile'. One hundred artillerymen and some 'red coats' had to assist the police in what proved a case of mistaken identity, as Mr Brown was not a pro-Boer but a Conservative, albeit one who had expressed pessimistic

41 'Rejoicings in Birmingham. A Day's Carnival', *Birmingham Daily Post*, 21 May 1900, p. 5.

42 'Mr. Arnold Lupton's Windows Broken', *Leeds Mercury*, 19 May 1900, p. 8.

43 'Rioting and Accidents', *Standard*, 21 May 1900, p. 8; 'The Relief of Mafeking. Disgraceful Scenes at Finchley', *Barnet Press*, 26 May 1900, p. 2; 'Pro-Boer's House set on Fire', *Worcester Herald*, 26 May 1900, p. 3; 'Mafeking Rejoicings. Cases at the Police Court', *West London Observer*, 25 May 1900, p. 5; *The Times*, 22 May 1900, p. 16.

44 BL, Add Mss 46,318, f. 21 John Burns diary, 18 and 19 May 1900; 'Rejoicings versus Rowdyism', *Reynolds's Newspaper*, 27 May 1900, p. 2.

45 'As we see Others', *Wimbledon News*, 26 May 1900, p. 1.

views about the course of the war in the local Chamber of Commerce.[46] Provocation contributed to several disturbances as at Splott, near Cardiff, when a local grocer both displayed a Transvaal flag, and pelted protesting celebrants with eggs and rice, before the mob compelled him to close his shop, lower the flag and raise a Union Jack in its place.[47] Even worse scenes occurred in Jersey, where a student-led procession passed through the French (and largely pro-Boer) quarter, whereupon a French lady threw dirty water over the students. A fracas followed in which hundreds of panes of glass were broken, principally in the houses of French residents.[48]

Outright hooliganism caused the most serious incident in Scotland, where youths in Galashiels tried to spread a bonfire onto a nearby corn mill. As the constabulary intervened, at least seven policemen, including the chief constable, and several civilians were injured, while the youths kept relighting the fire before the fire brigade extinguished it.[49] On the evening of 20 May blatant Jingoism surfaced in Aberdeen, when a crowd in excess of 20,000 protested round a hall prior to a pro-Boer rally. Police and sixty Gordon Highlanders had to intervene before the rally could take place, with the guest speaker, Samuel Cronwright-Schreiner, trying to mollify his critics by praising 'the cheeriness and good spirits and dauntless bravery' of Baden-Powell.[50]

In Ireland, omitted from most accounts of the Mafeking celebrations, the disturbances wore a distinctly sectarian hue. While the pro-Boer Nationalist community, which was primarily Catholic, though not exclusively so, appeared indifferent to the relief or contemptuous of the jubilation in England,[51] Loyalists, who were predominantly Protestant, gave vent to their feelings. The students of Trinity College, Dublin celebrated the news visibly and noisily on 'Mafeking Night', Belfast loyalists participated in massive parades on the Friday and Saturday, and Loyalist processions proliferated across the northern towns. Many were concluded without giving offence but Orangemen, marching through Armagh on Saturday evening, encountered 'a shower of stones and brick bats'. Only police intervention at the end of the

---

46 'Nota [*sic*] Bene' and 'The Riot. What began it?' *Dover Express*, 25 May 1900, pp. 5 and 6; see also '"Mafficking" at Aspley Guise', *Luton News*, 14 June 1900, p. 4; 'Dorking and the Relief of Mafeking', *Dorking Advertiser*, 26 May 1900, p. 5; 'Our Own Column', *Morpeth Herald*, 26 May 1900, p. 3.
47 'Flying the Boer Flag at Cardiff', *South Wales Daily News*, 23 May 1900, p. 6.
48 'Mafeking Day in Jersey', *Star (Saint Peter Port)*, 22 May 1900, p. 2.
49 'The Relief of Mafeking', *Border Advertiser*, 22 May 1900, p. 3 and 'The Mafeking Bonfire Riot at Galashiels', *Edinburgh Evening News*, 30 May 1900, p. 2.
50 The meeting was not broken up as claimed in Pakenham, 'Mafficking' in Smith (ed.), *Siege of Mafeking*, vol. 2, pp. 412–13, see 'Cronwright-Schreiner in Aberdeen', *Aberdeen Weekly Journal*, 21 May 1900, pp. 5–6.
51 'John Bull Jubilant', *(Dublin) Evening Herald*, 21 May 1900, p. 2.

march prevented a serious riot, when the Nationalists tried to rip up the drums and one of them was stabbed in the back, probably by accident.[52] A handful of other incidents occurred, notably in Newry and Lurgan, when Loyalist marchers tried to enter Nationalist areas or threw stones at the windows of Catholic clubs. Subsequent retaliation resulted in smashed Protestant windows in Edward Street, Lurgan, but the *Lurgan Times* concluded that 'on the whole we have reason to congratulate all concerned on the manner in which the relief rejoicings were carried out'.[53]

The celebrations continued until some merged with the birthday parades for the Queen on Thursday, 24 May, or lasted a week in certain colonies.[54] They added substantially to Lady Curzon's Mafeking Relief Fund, which eventually raised £24,000 (with another £5,267 in additional gifts), but did so at a price of several accidents, explosions and structural damage, even the odd fatality.[55] The Riot Act was not read but the Home Office approved the propriety of paying claims for compensation, where victims had suffered damage without provoking the mobs, which had 'riotously or tumultuously assembled' together.[56] Yet what did this mafficking delirium mean? As no one had foreseen its unprecedented scale, character and duration, and as it could not be measured by numbers engaged, monies raised, or the relatively few instances of mob violence, how did contemporaries interpret it?

Debates about 'Mafficking' and Mafeking

The entire spectacle had its critics, not least Charles F. G. Masterman, the radical, Cambridge-educated intellectual and man of letters, who was then living in south-east London. He described the Mafeking crowds as

> They surged through our streets, turbulent, cheerful, indifferent to our assumed proprietorship. . . . We gazed at them in startled

---

52 'The News in Dublin', *Irish Times*, 19 May 1900, p. 7; 'Belfast' and 'Ireland', *Belfast News-Letter*, 19 May 1900, p. 5 and 21 May 1900, p. 6; 'Mafeking Relieved', *Portadown News*, 26 May 1900, p. 5; 'The Relief of Mafeking. How it was celebrated in Armagh', *Armagh Guardian*, 25 May 1900, p. 3; 'Relief of Mafeking. Celebrations in Armagh. A Man Stabbed', *Ulster Gazette*, 26 May 1900, p. 3.
53 'How the news was received in Lurgan', *Lurgan Times*, 23 May 1900, p. 3 and 'Celebrating the Relief of Mafeking. Newry', *Newry Telegraph*, 22 May 1900, p. 3.
54 'Queen's Birthday', *Morning Leader*, 26 May 1900, p. 5; 'Mafeking Day', *Sydney Morning Herald*, 28 May 1900, p. 8; 'Mafeking Day', *Cape Times*, 29 May 1900, p. 7.
55 Lady Sarah Wilson, *South African Memories*, appendix 1, pp. 323–4; 'Rioting and Accidents', *Standard*, 21 May 1900, p. 8; 'Celebrating the Relief of Mafeking', *Newry Telegraph*, 22 May 1900, p. 3; 'Serious Accident', *Dorking Advertiser*, 26 May 1900, p. 5.
56 Price, *An Imperial War*, pp. 138–9.

amazement. Whence did they come, these denizens of another universe of being? . . . As darkness drew on they relapsed more and more into bizarre and barbaric revelry. Where they had whispered now they shouted; where they had pushed apologetically, now they shoved and collisioned and charged. They blew trumpets; they hit each other with bladders; they tickled passers-by with feathers; they embraced ladies in the streets, laughing genially and boisterously. Later the drink got to them, they reeled and struck and swore, walking, leaping, and blaspheming God.[57]

Masterman was by no means the only spectator astonished and alarmed by the Saturnalia. After watching these scenes French journalists, as their English counterparts noticed, expressed concern about the moral and mental welfare of the British nation; Francis de Pressensé, in *Le Temps*, even reflected upon the decadence of the English race.[58] National character was not the issue but a sense of proportion was: as Charles Williams of the *Morning Leader* reflected after the first two nights, this sense of proportion 'has been specially forgotten in these two days' demonstrations'.[59] Writing in his diary for 21 May, Wilfrid S. Blunt commented: 'This war has been so little glorious that our patriots are thankful for the smallest of small mercies. One would think that Napoleon and all the armies of Europe had been defeated by the British arms.'[60] Even the forms of celebration appalled radicals and pacifists: in Southampton Dr. Aldridge, a member of the school board, deprecated the closing of local schools, and the involvement of school children in the celebration of 'military exploits', while at a meeting of the Colchester and District Peace Association, Mr C. Howe denounced the burning of an effigy of Kruger, carrying a replica Bible.[61]

Yet it was the passion aroused by the war, and perceived as reaching a crescendo on 'Mafeking Night', that caused pro-Boers the greatest alarm. The Socialist *Reynolds's Newspaper* condemned the 'silly antics' of the mob and 'the sight of grey-haired gentlemen blowing penny hooters'. It deplored the attacks on the properties of pro-Boers, and asked 'If our Government must steal the goldfields and if we must lose our character for honesty, need we also

---

57   C. F. G. Masterman, *From the Abyss of its Inhabitants by One of Them* (London: R. Brimley Johnson, 1902), pp. 2–3.
58   'Occasional Notes', *Pall Mall Gazette*, 21 May 1900, p. 2 and 'French Opinion of the Relief', *Northern Echo*, 21 May 1900, p. 3.
59   'Change in National Character', *(Dundee) Courier & Argus*, 22 May 1900, p. 6.
60   Wilfrid S. Blunt, *My Diaries: Being a Personal Narrative of Events 1888-1914*, 2 vols (London: Martin Secker, 1929), vol. 1, p. 453.
61   'Mafeking Day and the School Children', *Hampshire Advertiser*, 9 June 1900, p. 5. and 'Colchester Peace Association', *Essex County Standard*, 7 July 1900, p. 5.

lose our dignity and become a laughing stock to other people.'[62] Concerned Liberals saw these passions as rooted in the war, fanned by the coverage of an imperialist press. In his famous Cambridge speech John Morley, having praised the moral qualities involved in the successful defence of Mafeking (see Chapter 1), later referred to the 'hellish panorama' of the war, fuelled by feelings of 'revenge' (over Majuba), and described the 'language of England' as not a 'moral language' but a 'language of pride, of force, of violence, of revenge'.[63] The Reverend Lord William Cecil, brother of Lord Edward, preached in Gray's Inn Chapel that 'popular enthusiasm should make us cautious, for nothing, as history both sacred and profane, had shown, was more dangerous than popular enthusiasm'.[64] A year later the veteran Liberal Sir W. Vernon Harcourt hoped that peace would 'inspire a soberer sentiment in the people of this country, and that the time will come when the melodies of the music halls and the Mafeking mobs will not be regarded as the true exponents of English statesmanship'.[65]

This criticism of 'mafficking', whether expressed by foreigners or British radicals, with the latter denounced as coming from 'a few superior – and cynical – persons',[66] provoked a vigorous rebuttal. Lord Hugh Cecil, another brother of Lord Edward, and the Conservative MP for Greenwich, defended 'our great rejoicings', which 'had excited no little surprise abroad'. Neither the surrender of Cronjé and 4,000 Boers at Paardeberg (27 February 1900), nor the humiliation of the enemy at Mafeking had prompted the exultation, only 'the relief and protection given to our countrymen'. The national enthusiasm, he maintained, merely illustrated 'how much more keenly we felt the sorrows and anxieties of individuals than was the case abroad'.[67] In toasting the 'Hero of Mafeking' at the Constitutional Club, Scarborough, Sir Charles Legard, JP, reminded his audience that Mafeking was where the war had begun, and that, unlike any other aspect of the war, it had been a focus of attention (or anxiety) for the previous seven months.[68]

Apart from the effects of this anxiety, and of the build-up to 18 May, the significance of the siege divided commentators. Only a minority accepted the importance of diverting Cronjé and his commandos at the outset of the

---

62 'Rejoicings versus Rowdyism', *Reynolds's Newspaper*, 27 May 1900, p. 2.
63 'Sir John Morley, MP at Cambridge', *Cambridge Independent Press*, 25 May 1900, p. 8.
64 'Pulpit References', *Standard*, 21 May 1900, p. 8.
65 *Parliamentary Debates* [*Parl. Deb.*], Fourth Series, vol. 90 (14 March 1901), col. 1,640.
66 *Nottingham Evening Post*, 3 July 1900, p. 2.
67 'Lord Hugh Cecil, M.P., at Greenwich', *Kentish Mercury*, 25 May 1900, p. 6.
68 'Patriotic Scarborough', *Scarborough Post*, 26 May 1900, p. 3.

war from either pressing onto Rhodesia or driving south into Cape Colony.[69] A majority reckoned that Paardeberg, the relief of Kimberley and Ladysmith, and the occupation of Bloemfontein, were much more important events, but as the *Blackpool Times* explained, 'It is just because it had no material, strategic advantage, but only pure glory and honour that we went mad over Mafeking on Saturday, and why we are semi-delirious even yet!'[70]

Many Liberal and pro-Boer newspapers agreed that Mafeking was worth celebrating simply because of the drama of the siege, the moral qualities displayed and the national honour involved. The *Northern Echo* declared that the 'rejoicings over Mafeking have their spring in higher feelings than mere vulgar exultation over a defeated enemy'.[71] Nor were such feelings, claimed Dundee's *Courier & Argus*, merely a case of revenge for Majuba: 'the demonstrators were thinking more of that splendid example of British gallantry and determination shown by the Mafeking garrison against overwhelming odds than of the revenge Mr. Morley, the philosopher, so glibly talks about'.[72] Moral qualities had prevailed, insisted the *Western Morning News*:

> We were holding high holiday, were festive and gay because, in a trial
> of strength and endurance, a handful of our countrymen had held
> out against an overwhelming force of the enemy, because British
> pluck has triumphed over shot and shell and hunger, because a band
> of noble men and women had saved England the humiliation of a
> surrender to a determined foe.[73]

'Mafficking' and the siege itself exacerbated divisions among Liberals, if not the Liberal press, which largely applauded Mafeking's relief and supported the popular reaction. A leading Liberal Imperialist, Richard B. Haldane MP, distinguished between the Mafeking celebrations and the Jingoism, he detested: 'All London', he wrote on 19 May, 'is a ferment with delight at the relief of Mafeking. The defence is one of the finest things in our military records.'[74] Two days later, Ernest J. Soares, the Liberal candidate for

---

69 'Celebrating the Relief of Mafeking', *Bury and Norwich Post*, 29 May 1900, p. 2 and *Nottingham Evening Post*, 3 July 1900, p. 2.

70 'Mafeking', *Blackpool Times*, 23 May 1900, p. 4; see also 'Relieved!' *Morning Leader*, 19 May 1900, p. 4; 'Is our National Character Changed?' *Sheffield and Rotherham Independent*, 22 May 1900, p. 5.

71 *Northern Echo*, 22 May 1900, p. 2; see also 'Relieved!' *Morning Leader*, 19 May 1900, p. 4.

72 'The Mafeking Rejoicings', *(Dundee) Courier & Argus*, 22 May 1900, p. 4.

73 *Western Morning News*, 21 May 1900, p. 4.

74 NLS, MS 5,963, f. 156, Haldane Mss., Haldane to his mother, 19 May; see also 'Mr. Haldane, M.P., on the War', *Haddingtonshire Advertiser*, 8 June 1900, p. 2.

Barnstaple, aroused cheers by describing Mafeking's relief as 'the best and brightest spot in the whole of the war so far'.[75] Meanwhile on Saturday, 19 May, at the height of the celebrations, the Liberal leader, Sir Henry Campbell-Bannerman, who was struggling to hold the fractious wings of his party together, conspicuously failed to utter a single word about Mafeking at the unveiling of a Gladstonian bust in the House of Commons.[76]

The Liberal press proved much more perceptive than the leader of the parliamentary party; it realized that if the war had proved the graveyard of military reputations, Mafeking had proved the exception. The siege had caught the public imagination because it had demonstrated that a small British garrison, without modern artillery, could fight against the odds; beat the Boers at their own 'slim' (underhand) game; and restore a sense of national pride. 'Thank God we can still appreciate', intoned the *Northern Echo*, 'courage, self-sacrifice, endurance, patient cheerfulness amid trying circumstances . . . virtues which we can still recognise, and we have recognised them in Col. Baden-Powell'.[77] The voluntary ethic underpinned these qualities, argued the *Kilmarnock Standard*: 'Every Briton in Mafeking was a volunteer in defence of Queen and country, and it is because the glory is shared by soldier and civilian alike that all creeds and classes of British men and women indulged in such a frenzy of joy last Saturday.'[78]

Needless to say numerous commentators interpreted these virtues as peculiarly British, carrying racial overtones in certain accounts,[79] and hailed the importance of pluck in defying the odds (see Chapter 2). Such views resonated across the empire: the *Sydney Morning Herald* agreed that the relief of Mafeking was 'a moral rather than a military triumph', and that on this account, 'we may discover the whole secret and explanation of the burst of jubilation, which has convulsed the Empire'.[80] These moral virtues resonated through many of the thanksgiving services held during the celebrations, but Canon Scott Holland, speaking in St. Paul's Cathedral, set these qualities within an imperial context and siege history. 'Never has the flood of emotion run deeper or stronger', he claimed, and this 'little band of imperial officers and Colonial troops' have 'by their gallant conduct purged it [Mafeking] of its ill fame [the Jameson Raid] and it now ranks with Chitral and Lucknow . . . as a name at which

---

75 'Liberal Meeting at Woolfardisworthy', *North Devon Journal*, 24 May 1900, p. 2.
76 'Occasional Notes', *Pall Mall Gazette*, 21 May 1900, p. 2.
77 'The Mafeking Rejoicings', *Northern Echo*, 22 May 1900, p. 3; see also 'Mafeking', *Blackpool Times*, 23 May 1900, p. 4; and 'Is our National Character Changed?' *Sheffield and Rotherham Independent*, 22 May 1900, p. 5.
78 *Kilmarnock Standard*, 26 May 1900, p. 4.
79 'Mafeking', *Hampshire Advertiser*, 23 May 1900, p. 2.
80 *Sydney Morning Herald*, 21 May 1900, p. 6.

English hearts will thrill for many a long year'.[81] Within this imperial identity and historical memory, *The Times* detected that the 'defence of Mafeking' had excited something more, namely a 'touch of romantic devotion'. This romantic element, it argued, set Mafeking aside from the sieges of Kimberley, with its abundance of riches, and Ladysmith, with its embarrassing thousands of regular soldiers.[82]

In a subsequent editorial it used this notion to explain 'the exuberance of popular delight', since the 'man in the street' did not suppose for a moment that he was celebrating a decisive victory. 'He was simply overjoyed because a handful of his fellow countrymen who had fought a long and desperate fight, and whose fortunes he had been watching for months, had been succoured by British troops.' More fundamentally, it reckoned that Mafeking was

> an affair of the people rather than of the Army. The man in the street pictures the garrison – and quite correctly – as being largely civilians like himself, called upon to do their best to fill the place of Regular troops. He feels a special pride in their success and a special delight in their rescue, because they are representative of the race and show him the reserves of courage, energy, resource, and endurance, which lie behind all the paraphernalia of the War Office.[83]

This populist feeling explained how the relief of Mafeking had provoked a spontaneous reaction of hysterical delight across the empire. If the rejoicings of 1900, so soon after the Diamond Jubilee (1897), represented a pinnacle of populist feelings about the empire, the defenders of Mafeking, argued *The Times*, represented

> the common man of the Empire, the fundamental stuff of which it is built, with his back to the wall, fighting overwhelming odds without a thought of surrender . . . and at long last coming out proud, tenacious, unconquered, and unconquerable. The story of Mafeking has all the elements of a romance.[84]

Assessment

The debate carried its share of emotional baggage about the state of the garrison and Mafeking's white citizens surviving in a 'half-starved'

---

81 'Pulpit References', *Standard*, 21 May 1900, p. 8.
82 *The Times*, 19 May 1900, p. 11.
83 *The Times*, 21 May 1900, p. 11.
84 Ibid.

condition, scant coverage of the contribution from black people, whether armed or unarmed, and unwarranted assumptions about the determination of the enemy. It had nonetheless tried to explain the shock of the euphoric scenes that had convulsed London, most of the provinces, and the English-speaking empire. Celebrations were always likely after the precedent set by Ladysmith but the scenes of 'Mafeking Night', and its aftermath, exceeded all expectations, and would never be repeated even after the ending of the two world wars. Whether in the press, pulpit or Parliament, commentators sought to interpret the reaction despite considerable uncertainty about what had actually happened in the final days. When Arthur J. Balfour, as Leader of the House of Commons, was pressed on 'Mafeking Night' about the unofficial report of the relief, he could only answer: 'we hope and trust, and have good reason to think that it may be true'.[85] Even if people were certain that the relief had occurred, the reportage from Mafeking had only partially covered the events of March, April and May, and full accounts of Eloff's attack and the relief operations had yet to appear.[86]

Whether further information would have modified the exultant response in any way seems doubtful. People celebrated the relief because it extinguished their anxiety over a siege that had lasted from the outset of the war for 217 days. In the early months of the war when feelings of humiliation and despair followed the unexpected series of defeats and surrenders, Baden-Powell by issuing a series of resolute, laconic and amusing statements had proved both reassuring and inspirational. 'Colonel B-P', wrote Pakenham, 'had given back the other BP, the British Public, its faith in itself.'[87] Mafeking, too, as a small, isolated outpost on the frontier of the empire, holding out against superior odds and modern artillery, seemed emblematic of all the imperial sieges of the past fifty years, and much more so than either Kimberley or Ladysmith.

Undoubtedly the hysteria had exaggerated B-P's achievements and the significance of Mafeking's survival. Yet it seems harsh to characterize the pandemonium as 'pathetic, the relieved reaction of a nation fed on grandiose notions of imperial might but underneath all the glitter, pomp and circumstance, insecure, resentful of international hostility, and embarrassed at the war's early fiascos'.[88] 'Splendid isolation' may not have felt so splendid at the turn of the century, especially in the wake of the national humiliations in the early months of the war, but this conclusion does scant justice to the depth and character of popular imperialism, which was then at the height of its appeal. It was rooted in the diffusion of martial values, manly Christian

85 *Parl. Deb.*, 4th Series, vol. 83, 18 May 1900, col. 672.
86 Beaumont, 'Reporting the Siege' in Smith (ed.), *Siege of Mafeking*, vol. 2, pp. 339–40.
87 Pakenham, *Boer War*, p. 417.
88 Judd and Surridge, *Boer War*, p. 182.

virtues and the cult of the Christian soldier in schools, Sunday schools, Boys' Brigades and their Anglican, Jewish and Catholic equivalents. It found reflection in the pervasive imperial imagery in the cards and scraps for children's albums, illustrated weeklies, school texts, juvenile fiction and books of heroes. It also found dramatic reproductions of soldiers and imperial war in battle art, the engravings and photographs of war artists, advertising, theatrical melodrama, regimental histories, music hall songs, pyrodramas and military tournaments.[89]

If some of this material may have served as 'escapist narcotics' for its audience, who would neither rush to the colours in peacetime nor emerge as ardent imperialists,[90] it confirmed popular stereotypes and contributed, as Dave Russell argues in respect of popular patriotic songs, towards a 'positive acquiescence' in imperial sentiments, thereby constructing or reinforcing popular attitudes.[91] Jeffrey Richards has taken this analysis further in his massive study of the British ballad, hymn, music-hall song and marches – the staples of popular music – to assert that the empire at this time was 'above all the People's Empire, a major element in their sense of identity and national pride'.[92] Undoubtedly memories and myths about imperial siege histories contributed to this sense of identity.

'Mafficking', however excessive in form and distasteful in instances of mob violence, makes more sense within this context. The popular rejoicing, following the period of heightened anxiety and preparatory planning (in some places), was not only a massive relief in itself but also a confirmation of so many imperial assumptions. If, like most successful sieges, Mafeking was seen as a triumph of moral virtues – endurance, resolve, tenacity, self-sacrifice and pluck (in its Victorian sense) – it was even more of a triumph for ordinary colonists, displaying such virtues, in the absence of regular troops. Ordinary men and women, led by a charismatic commander and his able staff, had distinguished themselves over 217 days – a grinding, often monotonous ordeal – but one that reflected fully the romantic element that *The Times* had detected.

---

89 John M. MacKenzie, 'Introduction Popular imperialism and the military' in MacKenzie (ed.), *Popular Imperialism*, pp. 1—24; Jeffrey Richards (ed.), *Imperialism and Juvenile Fiction* (Manchester: Manchester University Press, 1989); John O. Springhall, *Youth, Empire and Society: British Youth Movements, 1883-1940* (London: Croom Helm, 1977); Spiers, *Scottish Soldier and Empire*, pp. 113–18.
90 Jonathan Rose, *The Intellectual Life of the British Working Classes* (New Haven: Yale University Press, 2001), pp. 8, 331–5 and 341.
91 Dave Russell, *Popular Music in England, 1840-1914* (Manchester: Manchester University Press, 1997), pp. 124–9, 239, 250.
92 Richards, *Imperialism and Music*, p. 523.

Chapter 9

Mafeking: Aftermath and Assessment

Any notion that Mafeking had an aftermath contradicts much of the literature about the siege. Rayne Kruger memorably described how the nation in its rejoicing had experienced a 'single orgiastic moment', before falling 'back limp';[1] Jeal regarded Baden-Powell, who had been promoted major-general after the relief over 200 more senior officers, as such a dominating presence that no-one was interested in the relief columns;[2] and Jacqueline Beaumont reckoned that 'events' overtook the press: 'Most papers published a letter or two describing the attack by Eloff and the relief, a month or more later, and left it at that.'[3] Superficially this seems plausible. Within a few weeks, on 5 June, the army of Lord Roberts occupied Pretoria, lending credence to the assumption that the war would soon be over. Reportage dwindled, as the vast majority of reporters, like Lord Roberts at the end of the year, left South Africa and went home.[4] Mafeking, nonetheless, had an enduring appeal, for several months it continued to attract a remarkable degree of popular interest, fed by written and illustrative material from South Africa.

Quite apart from the books written by the Mafeking journalists, all of which appeared in the second half of the year, with Major Baillie's appearing in print as early as 2 July 1900,[5] the vast majority of the letters, diary extracts and an entire diary, as used in this volume, appeared after the siege. Written by ordinary soldiers and citizens, they found a willing outlet in the provincial press by virtue of the local associations of the authors and the populist appeal of the siege. The diary of Corporal Oscar Hulse (Bechuanaland Rifles) appeared in serialised form over eleven issues of the *Penistone, Stocksbridge, Hoyland Chapeltown Express* from 20 July to 12 October 1900. If this was a major

---

1   Kruger, *Goodbye Dolly Gray*, p. 297.
2   Jeal, *Baden-Powell*, p. 301.
3   Beaumont, 'Reporting the Siege' in Smith (ed.), *Siege of Mafeking*, vol. 2, p. 340.
4   Stephen Badsey, 'The Boer War as a Media War' in Peter Dennis and Jeffrey Grey (eds), *The Boer War Army, Nation and Empire, The 1999 Chief of Army/Australian War Memorial Military History Conference* (Canberra: Army History Unit, 2000), pp. 70–83, at p. 81; see also 'The War drawing to a Close', *Derbyshire Times and Chesterfield Herald*, 23 June 1900, p. 8.
5   'The Siege of Mafeking, Published To-Day', *Morning Post*, 2 July 1900, p. 6.

coup for a South Yorkshire newspaper, the *Leamington Spa Courier* carried the letters and diary extracts of Mrs Gustavus Simmonds over the period from 19 May to 1 September, the *Berwickshire News* devoted five columns to the diary of the 'Eyemouth Man', and the *Armagh Guardian* published extracts from the Nun's diary over three weeks from 27 July to 3 August. Dozens of major letters, particularly from soldiers, appeared in the press from June to September. Some had been written during the siege but had taken months to arrive;[6] others were written after the relief but still took months to appear in print.[7]

The numerous reports of Eloff's defeat appeared soon after news of the relief, as did the reports of the generous speeches by Baden-Powell at the parade, the words of appreciation by Colonels Plumer and Mahon, and the speech by Mayor Whiteley at the farewell dinner. The mayor not only commended B-P for imbuing Mafeking with 'his own dogged spirit and determination', but also revealed that a Boer newspaper, having read captured letters from the town, containing accounts of the hardships and the diet endured, revealed that 'there had never been in them one word of surrender'.[8] By mid-June the illustrated weeklies and the odd evening newspaper published more photographs and sketches of events during the siege, and of the dilapidated state of the town.[9] All accounts of Mahon's column, whether by accredited correspondents or by officers and men, appeared in the weeks and months after the relief. Far from any lack of interest in the relief, at least fifty-seven letters from the two columns, as used in this volume, were published and only thirteen from Plumer's column appeared before the relief. So insatiable was the interest about the marching and fighting of Mahon's column that at least thirty-two eyewitness accounts, including a couple reproduced in differing newspapers,[10] appear in this volume, and the *Cambrian* reported the return

6   'A Bradford Man in Mafeking', *Bradford Daily Telegraph*, 14 June 1900, p. 3; 'At the Siege of Mafeking', *Scarborough Post*, 15 June 1900, p. 5.

7   'Life in Mafeking under the Siege', *Nottingham Evening Post*, 25 June 1900, p. 4; 'Inside Mafeking', *Newbury Weekly News*, 12 July 1900, p. 2; 'An Eyemouth Man in Mafeking', *Berwickshire News*, 17 July 1900, p. 5; 'The Siege of Mafeking', *Ayr Advertiser*, 23 August 1900, p. 5.

8   'Mafeking After The Siege', *Derby Mercury*, 6 June 1900, p. 6; 'Mutual Congratulations at Mafeking', *Dewsbury Reporter*, 2 June 1900, p. 5; 'The Last Scene at Mafeking', *Newcastle Weekly Courant*, 23 June 1900, p. 3.

9   For example, see images in the *Graphic*, 16 June 1900, p. 868; 30 June 1900, pp. 937, 943 and 951 and 7 July 1900, p. 4; 'Aberdeen Plumber in Mafeking', *(Aberdeen) Evening Express*, 4 July 1900, p. 2.

10   Gunner Atkinson's letter appeared in the *Wharfedale and Airedale Observer*, 22 June 1900, p. 3 and the *Craven Herald*, 22 June 1900, p. 2 and Gunner Mayow's letter in the *Abingdon Herald*, 28 July 1900, p. 7 and *Jackson's Oxford Journal*, 28 July 1900, p. 8.

of the column's doctor as late as 19 October 1900. Just as soldiers wanted to describe their experiences, so recipients of these letters passed them on to editors of their local newspapers, who knew that popular interest in all facets of the Mafeking siege and relief had not abated. The editor of *Blackwood's* agreed; he published articles by a trooper from Plumer's column and by an English doctor pressed into service with the Boers.[11]

In the post-siege correspondence several Mafekingites raised issues above and beyond the siege itself. The Nun concluded her diary extracts by claiming that 'It is extraordinary to hear of the devotion of the Irish Catholics to the Boers, if they were out here for a while they would form a very different opinion of them.' The Boers, she insisted, 'hate everything Catholic', and 'some of the Relief Column said to us they were not fighting in this war for their Queen, but their Religion, as the fact of being a Catholic was sufficient to prevent a man getting a situation of any importance under Government', despite possessing appropriate qualifications.[12] J. R. Algie, the town clerk, and a former resident of Newport, wrote to the chief agent for the Conservatives in the south Wales boroughs, commending the imperialist credentials of a local Conservative parliamentary candidate, Dr. Rutherfoord Harris. The latter, he affirmed, knew that the Rand had to be freed from 'the tyranny of Oom Paul and his Hollanders' crowd'. Great Britain, he added, depended on her colonies:

> It is only by developing her vast dominions under a wise Administration that she will retain and secure the respect and love of her pioneer sons and afford an outlet for her industrial products and for her surplus population and capital. Coming out from a seven months' siege you can quite understand I feel a bit strongly . . . . We in Mafeking are thoroughly imperialistic, and we all want England to be the same.[13]

Other letters were more personal and poignant. Arthur G. Holley, 37th Squadron of the Imperial Yeomanry, arrived in Mafeking after the relief to find 'poor Elkington, not dead as reported, but in a pitiful state – totally blind, and half his face blown away. They gave him £1,000 out of the Mafeking fund, and made him a full pensioner for life.' Elkington, though, 'says he does not

---

11 'With Plumer to the Relief of Mafeking', *Blackwood's Edinburgh Magazine*, vol. 168 (1900), pp. 804–16 and 'With the Boers round Mafeking, 1899-1900', *Blackwood's Edinburgh Magazine*, vol. 171 (1902), pp. 16–27.
12 'A Nun's Diary in Mafeking', *Armagh Guardian*, 3 August 1900, p. 3.
13 'Mafeking speaks to Newport', *Western Mail*, 11 August 1900, p. 5.

want to return to England; in fact he says he does not want to live'.[14] While Holley tried to cheer up his friend, Mrs. E. C. McMullin wrote of how her husband had died of heart disease in Mafeking on 30 January, and of how 'the Boers have destroyed our home'. This was a farm about 4 km to the east of Mafeking, which Snyman had used as his headquarters throughout the siege, but in the process the Boers had destroyed 'everything movable and immovable'. Left with six children to support, Mrs. McMullin could not get the place repaired and did not know when she would receive compensation.[15] Unfortunately her plight was not unique; when Gunner S. Wilkinson visited Mafeking, 'the only place in Cape Colony worth seeing' in early July 1900, he found that nearly every house 'shows the effect of Boer fire – some blown down altogether; others with large holes through them'.[16] Ironically, in late August, a cyclone blew through Mafeking, uprooting trees, demolishing roofs and verandahs, and wrecking a nearby military camp. It reportedly caused more destruction in a few hours than 'the Boer shells' achieved 'during the seven months' siege'.[17]

However harrowing these tales of post-siege Mafeking, the siege still commanded attention, especially as the Pekin delegation was enduring a 55-day investment and Kumase, the so-called 'northern Mafeking', was awaiting relief. Although these sieges both ended successfully, and much more quickly than Mafeking, the press compared them: 'the miseries of Mafeking', wrote the *Standard*, 'were as nothing to those of the five hundred in Pekin'.[18] These fears reflected the atrocities already committed by the Boxers, and the perceived fears of the 'Yellow Peril', but, by 14 August 1900, the siege was over without arousing anything like the jubilant scenes that followed Mafeking's relief. Doubtless distance failed to lend enchantment, as did the multi-national composition of the diplomatic community and the relief force, even if British forces were first to enter the Legation Quarter.[19] The British people appreciated the resilience demonstrated in both sieges, as well as the risks run, but had less to identify with in either case, not least Kumase, where

---

14 'Letter From Mafeking', *Bedford and County Record*, 16 October 1900, p. 3; see also 'The War. A Mafeking Sufferer', *Luton News*, 6 September 1900, p. 4.
15 'Pathetic Letter From A Mafeking Woman', *Derbyshire Times and Chesterfield Herald*, 11 August 1900, p. 6.
16 'A Sandgrounder in Mafeking', *Southport Guardian*, 4 August 1900, p. 7.
17 'Cyclone at Mafeking', *(Newcastle) Evening Chronicle*, 31 August 1900, p. 3.
18 'The War in North China', *Standard*, 28 August 1900, p. 3 and *Daily News*, 14 August 1900, p. 4.
19 Peter Fleming, *The Siege at Peking* (Edinburgh: Birlinn, 2001), pp. 206–7 and Diana Preston, *The Boxer Rebellion* (New York; Berkley, 2000). On the risks in China, see 'Terrible Experiences of an Essex Lady', *Essex County Chronicle*, 7 September 1900, p. 6.

Hausa troops both defended the fort and comprised the bulk of the relief force.[20]

So the metropolitan and provincial press continued their reporting on Mafeking, interviewing returning soldiers and citizens over several weeks. Some of these interviews, as used in the text, were excellent, especially the reflections of Corporal Rose, which filled two columns of the Aberdeen *Evening Express*, the wide-ranging commentary of Mayor Frank Whiteley published in several West Yorkshire newspapers, the memories of a crippled George Green in Penzance, and specialist evidence on the making of £1 notes (Edward J. Ross), nursing (Sister Gamble), newspaper production (Tom Morse), the role of religion (Reverend W. H. Weekes), the making of a gun carriage (Charles Clucas, an ex-mayor of Mafeking), the use of the Nordenfeldt gun (J. W. S. Lowe), and improvisation in the making of chemical supplies (J. E. Jones).[21] Interviews with returning railwaymen proved less useful but, like many others, they heaped accolades upon Baden-Powell.[22] Ben Weil was more self-serving; he insisted that his firm had saved the town, although he generously commended 'the conduct of the natives who behaved splendidly' throughout, not least during Eloff's attack.[23] Local communities honoured the return of their own celebrities with a 'smoker' (for Theodore Mathias in Newport), dinners (for Charles E. Congdon, a well-known Devonian footballer, in Exeter and Colonel Hore in Leamington Spa), and a banquet (for Mayor Whiteley with Reverend Weekes in attendance at Bradford).[24]

Of all these returning individuals none made a more positive contribution to the memory of the siege than the tall, commanding presence of the Reverend W. H. Weekes. Having returned to Bristol on 20 July where he was an old boy of Bristol Grammar School (and his father had been one of the masters), he gave interviews there before speaking on behalf of Whiteley

---

20 'Ashantee Rising', *Western Morning News*, 14 August 1900, p. 8.

21 Interviews were published on the following dates, *(Aberdeen) Evening Express*, 28 August 1900, p. 5; *Dewsbury Reporter*, 21 July 1900, p. 8; *Leeds Mercury*, 23 July 1900, p. 3; *Cornishman*, 26 July 1900, p. 5; *Alton Mail*, 8 September 1900, p. 2; *South Wales Daily News*, 24 July 1900, p. 5; *Belfast News-Letter*, 1 August 1900, p. 7; *Devon Evening Express*, 21 July 1900, p. 1; *Lloyd's Weekly Newspaper*, 21 October 1900, p. 2; *Stroud Journal*, 10 August 1900, p. 3 and 17 August 1900, p. 3; *Penistone Express*, 13 July 1900, p. 5.

22 See Chapter 6 and 'Mafeking Besieged Welcomed to Portobello', *Edinburgh Evening News*, 4 August 1900, p. 2 and 'A Portobello Man in Mafeking', *Edinburgh Evening News*, 15 August 1900, p. 2; 'Home From Mafeking', *(Dundee) Courier & Argus*, 20 July 1900, p. 5.

23 'Mafeking' and 'The Man who fed the Town', *Cape Times*, 26 May 1900, p. 5.

24 These events were recorded by the *Western Mail*, 24 July, p. 5; *Devon Evening Express*, 18 August 1900, p. 3 and *Western Times*, 21 August 1900, p. 2; *Leamington Spa Courier*, 13 October 1900, p. 5; *Bradford Daily Telegraph*, 27 July 1900, pp. 2–3 and *Bradford Daily Argus*, 27 July 1900, p. 4.

at his banquet in Bradford a week later. Thereafter he toured the country, conducting services and lecturing on Mafeking. He used lantern slides and displayed siege mementoes in places as diverse as Exeter, Cardiff, Sheffield, Cambridge, Wickford and Bath. Raising funds to restore the Anglican church in Mafeking, Weekes spoke not only about his hospital work, and the challenges of conducting funerals under shellfire, but also of living in shelters, avoiding shells and surviving on rations. A strong defender of the siege on account of its 'strategical position', and its value in retaining the loyalty of the local Barolong, he praised the volunteering spirit of the Town Guard, the resourcefulness of manufacturing a gun under siege conditions and the cheerful leadership of Baden-Powell. Speaking at Christ Church Hall, Bath, in late December, he said that the 'highest praise' he could give Baden-Powell was to say 'that what was thought of him at home was quite true'.[25]

By illustrating his talks with siege artefacts, Weekes underscored another aspect of the siege's popularity, namely its material history. He displayed 'pieces of Boer shells, specimens of siege bread and polony, a full set of Mafeking siege stamps, siege money, and Boer bullets'.[26] The Clucas brothers presented an even larger collection, including 113 soldiers' badges and numerals, many gathered by the ex-mayor's brother, Albert, who had survived the siege in Kimberley. They also had shoulder straps purportedly taken off Eloff's uniform, shells and shell fragments, Mauser bullets, photographs and curios of a non-warlike character.[27] Even relatively small collections attracted publicity, like the pieces of siege bread brought home by Mathias, 'as well as some bullets, stamps, paper money, and other curios of the siege'.[28] Some of this material had a growing collectable value: on 26 July, Christie's sold a complete set of Mafeking siege notes and an envelope with three 3*d*. and two 2*d*. Mafeking siege stamps for 20 guineas. By mid-August, a complete set of 'Mafeking besieged" siege stamps realized £36 in Covent Garden.[29]

Yet Baden-Powell and Mayor Whiteley, the leading personalities of the siege, left the greatest marks on its aftermath. On 19 June, Baden-Powell

---

25 'The Rev. H. J. [*sic*: W. H.] Weekes on Mafeking', *Bath Chronicle*, 20 December 1900, p. 6; see also 'The Rector of Mafeking', *Devon Evening Express*, 21 July 1900, p. 1; 'Rector of Mafeking at Bristol', *South Wales Daily News*, 24 July 1900, p. 5; 'The Rector of Mafeking in Cardiff', *Western Mail*, 3 September 1900, p. 6; 'Rector of Mafeking in Sheffield', *Sheffield & Rotherham Independent*, 9 October 1900, p. 9; 'The Siege of Mafeking Described', *Cambridge Independent*, 2 November 1900, p. 2; 'The Rector of Mafeking speaks at Wickford', *Essex County Chronicle*, 7 December 1900, p. 6.
26 'Rector of Mafeking at Bristol', *South Wales Daily News*, 24 July 1900, p. 5.
27 'The Ex-Mayor of Mafeking in Douglas', *Isle of Man Weekly Times*, 4 August 1900, p. 6.
28 'Back from Mafeking', *Western Mail*, 24 July 1900, p. 5.
29 'Mafeking Siege Notes', *Nottingham Evening Post*, 27 July 1900, p. 2 and 'Sale of South African Relics', *Morning Post*, 22 August 1900, p. 6.

gave a widely reported interview in Pretoria to Winston Churchill, special correspondent of the *Morning Post*, and another highly ambitious rising star of the war, whose escape from a Pretoria prison had burnished his political credentials. It was not an interview that reflected well on either party. While Churchill almost certainly muddled the action at Game Tree Fort with the trench warfare in the brickfields, B-P exaggerated by claiming that 'nearly 9,000' Boers faced them initially (a precursor to even greater exaggerations in later writings),[30] and by a display of false modesty, asserting that 'We are all astonished to find so much interest taken in the defence of Mafeking.'[31] In fact, he had received a letter from his sister, Agnes, in early April, describing the widespread interest in the siege (Chapter 6). He had also publicized this knowledge on 11 May, when interviewed by the Press Association's correspondent in Mafeking, claiming that the morale of the garrison had been boosted by 'the praise of the English people' and by the 'knowledge that the whole Empire is watching with appreciation the good fight which they have fought . . .'.[32]

To Churchill, though, he revealed an interesting choice of anecdotes, particularly the unhelpful attitude of the Cape government pre-war, and the importance of deterrence in the early days by laying dummy minefields, which were made more credible when the Boers blew up the truck filled with dynamite. Manufacturing cartridges, cannon, shells, fuses, paper money and stamps he described as simply keeping 'us busy and made life less monotonous'; extending the lines, pushing out the trenches, and capturing forts secured 'grazing and breathing space'; and the darkest hour came when he received news about the disaster at Spion Kop, which he had to keep to himself 'and look cheerful'. If Eloff's storming party proved the most serious challenge to the defending forces, B-P was only quoted as praising the convicts in the nearby jail, when Murchison led them in shooting at the Boers.[33] Whether he praised anyone else was not printed in the interview, but oversights then, as in subsequent commentary, doubtless compounded the resentments among those with whom he had served in Bulawayo, Mafeking, and on the relief columns.

More immediately Mayor Frank Whiteley blundered into the general election campaign of September and October 1900. Having spent most

---

30 'Baden-Powell Interviewed', *Morning Post*, 27 June 1900, p. 7 and Gardner, *Mafeking*, p. 230.
31 'Baden-Powell Interviewed', *Morning Post*, 29 June 1900, pp. 3 and 5, at p. 3.
32 'The Siege of Mafeking. Baden-Powell on his Experiences', *Liverpool Echo*, 23 May 1900, p. 4.
33 'Baden-Powell Interviewed', *Morning Post*, 27 June, p. 7, 28 June 1900, p. 7 and 29 June 1900, pp. 3 and 5.

of the previous twenty-seven years as an explorer, hunter and later an affluent merchant when settled in Mafeking,[34] he had returned to England two months after the 'mafficking' celebrations, unaware (possibly) of the bipartisan, populist support for the siege and its relief. Despite being a scion of a Bradfordian Liberal family, he chose to support J. Leslie Wanklyn, the Liberal Unionist M.P. for Central Bradford. In appearing on his platform on 26 September, Whiteley declared that the people of South Africa were looking upon this election 'with an absorbing interest'. While he castigated the 'deplorable Jameson Raid', he asserted that the 'vacillating policy of 1881' was fresh in the mind, and so both the 'Dutch' and the colonists were watching for any sign of 'weakness in your policy'. Consequently, he declared that 'every loss to the Government will be a distinct gain to the Boers', a phrase later modified as 'Every Government seat lost would be regarded by the Boers as a gain to themselves.'[35]

A huge gift to the Conservative and Unionist cause, this phrase was repeated in Conservative newspapers across the country. Their editors lauded the intervention as a 'clarion cry' by a 'gallant mayor', who had 'actual knowledge' of living in South Africa as distinct from Liberal theories.[36] While a high-minded Tory like Henry T. Anstruther in St. Andrews Burghs disavowed this rhetoric (and just held his seat),[37] Joseph Chamberlain had no such inhibitions. He employed the phase repeatedly on the hustings, endorsed it in party advertisements, and exhorted party candidates to repeat it.[38] The phrase appeared on party placards and billboards across the country, in a full-page advertisement in the *Bradford Daily Argus* on the eve of Bradford's voting, and gained cheers whenever Conservative candidates referred to it.[39]

---

34 'The Mayor of Mafeking', *Bridlington Free Press*, 25 May 1900, p. 8 and 'The Mayor of Mafeking', *(Dundee) Evening Telegraph*, 23 May 1900, p. 4.

35 'The Mayor of Mafeking on the Election Issues', *Yorkshire Post*, 27 September 1900, p. 8 and 'A Voice from Mafeking', *Bradford Daily Argus*, 27 September 1900, p. 4.

36 *Royal Cornwall Gazette*, 4 October 1900, p. 3 and *Huddersfield Daily Chronicle*, 29 September 1900, p. 5; see also 'Remember Mafeking!', *Derbyshire Times and Chesterfield Herald*, 29 September 1900, p. 6; 'Election Notes', *Grantham Journal*, 29 September 1900, p. 6; 'What Mafeking's Mayor said at Bradford', *(Hull) Daily Mail*, 1 October 1900, p. 5; and *Nottingham Evening Post*, 2 October 1900, p. 2.

37 'St Andrews Burghs', *(Dundee) Courier & Argus*, 29 September 1900, p. 6.

38 'Empire before Party', *Bradford Daily Argus*, 28 September 1900, p. 7; 'Mr. Chamberlain to the Men of Yorkshire', *Glasgow Herald*, 1 October 1900, p. 3; 'The Mayor of Mafeking's Warning', *Bradford Daily Argus*, 1 October 1900, p. 4; 'The County Contests', *Standard*, 6 October 1900, p. 2 and 'Mr. Chamberlain at Stourbridge', *Standard*, 10 October 1900, p. 2.

39 'The Mayor of Mafeking's Warning', *Bradford Daily Argus*, 1 October 1900, p. 4; 'Mr. Younger at Claypole', *Grantham Journal*, 6 October 1900, p. 6; 'Heywood Division' and 'Hyde Division', *Manchester Courier*, 9 October 1900, p. 7; 'Mr. Austen Chamberlain at Kenilworth', *Leamington Spa Courier*, 13 October 1900, p. 3.

The Liberal Imperialists, who supported the war, were incensed. Speaking in Oldham on 29 September, Sir Edward Grey questioned whether Whiteley could have said these words, which bore all the hallmarks of a 'Birmingham' slur.[40] Unable to resist the bait, the mayor wrote to Sir Edward, affirming that he had made the quote since he believed it represented the 'view of the vast majority of both loyal and disloyal elements in South Africa'.[41] Grey then led the counter-attack, brandishing the credentials of the Liberal Party as a party of empire,[42] while H. H. Asquith, in referring to Whiteley's charge, doubted that he had heard 'more offensive or misleading language' and denounced the Tories for 'descending to the lowest depths of political degradation'.[43] Even towards the end of the campaign Liberal 'Imps', such as George Whiteley (Pudsey) and Hunter Craig (Govan), contested the barb, which had circulated within their constituencies. They defended the patriotism of Liberals like themselves, doubted Whiteley's sanity, and deplored his 'abominable assertion' (and both held their seats).[44]

Whether the mayor's calumny had any influence is impossible to prove. The *Bradford Daily Telegraph*, the town's leading organ of Liberalism, originally discounted it as an 'unnecessary intrusion' but not one that would affect the issue one way or the other.[45] It reconsidered this view after the Unionists retained all three seats in Bradford with vastly increased votes, and attributed these results and similar Conservative triumphs in Birmingham, Glasgow, Manchester, Leeds and Sheffield, to a pro-war or 'khaki' vote in the big cities and towns. These votes increased the Unionist majority overall, despite Liberal gains in smaller boroughs and counties. Meanwhile Frank Whiteley compared the Bradfordian results to 'three reliefs of Mafeking', and so the *Telegraph* reminded him that 'the city did right to "maffick" when the news came of the relief of Baden-Powell and his gallant band, but politicians cannot expect to live and move and have their being in that event forever'.[46]

This was a fair riposte since the mayor, by adopting a high profile and exploiting his Mafeking links for party political purposes, had damaged

40 'Sir Edward Grey at Oldham', *Manchester Courier*, 1 October 1900, p. 9.
41 The Ex-Mayor of Mafeking and the General Election', *Essex County Standard*, 6 October 1900, p. 4 and 'Mafeking's Mayor', *Oldham Standard*, 6 October 1900, p. 3.
42 'The Contest in Bishop Auckland Division', *North-Eastern Daily Gazette*, 4 October 1900, p. 2.
43 'Speech by Mr. Asquith', *Glasgow Herald*, 6 October 1900, p. 10 and 'Mr. Chamberlain at Stourbridge', *Standard*, 10 October 1900, p. 2.
44 'The Pudsey Division Election', *Leeds Times*, 6 October 1900, p. 12 and 'Candidature of Mr. R. Hunter Craig', *Glasgow Herald*, 11 October 1900, p. 9.
45 'The Tory Farce', *Bradford Daily Telegraph*, 27 September 1900, p. 2.
46 'The Polls' and 'Black Thursday', *Bradford Daily Telegraph*, 3 October 1900, p. 2 and 5 October 1900, p. 2.

the memory of Mafeking. The damage was not catastrophic; the Reverend Weekes still found audiences, with one in Sheffield during the middle of the election; Mafeking notes and stamps fetched even more extraordinary prices in auctions; and people celebrated the siege by buying prints, photographs and other memorabilia of B-P, some of which had had 'an enormous sale'.[47] They enjoyed, too, a profusion of light music: 'The Mafeking Waltz', 'The Mafeking Grand March', 'Our Hero B.-P.' and the 'Baden-Powell March by Algrette', among others.[48] Mafeking, though, had never carried party-political overtones, so Whiteley's intervention remained deeply controversial. Critics of the mayor found malcontents from Mafeking, willing to claim that he had favoured surrender during the siege, and had hidden in the bombproof shelter of the women's laager. In replying to these canards, Whiteley revealed that 'a small section of the townspeople' had wished to surrender and had wanted him to apprise the Colonel of their wishes. He had refused to do so but referred the matter to B-P and Lord Edward Cecil, who both regarded it as a joke. As regards his personal safety, he retorted that apart from his weekly inspections of the women's laager, he 'was the only European in Mafeking who had no bomb-proof'. A letter of support from Baden-Powell was also published, which confirmed that the mayor kept 'flying about the place on his bicycle under fire', and working from an office 'draughty with shell holes'.[49] Yet the revelation of internal dissent punctured B-P's post-siege mythology that 'the whole community was pervaded by a spirit of loyal endurance and cheery good feeling'.[50] Even more sadly, the mayor's political partisanship had damaged the memory of 'mafficking' when people of all classes and parties had identified with the defenders of Mafeking. Both the memory and mythology of Mafeking had suffered.

Assessment

How far then have the 154 letters, diary extracts, interviews and lectures by eyewitnesses from Mafeking, as used in this volume, contributed to the understanding of the siege, its relief, and overall significance? This correspondence

---

47　'Mafeking Pictures', *Daily Mail*, 19 May 1900, p. 7 and "Mafeking Number of the "Illustrated Mail"', *Daily Mail*, 25 May 1900, p. 5; see also 'The Rector of Mafeking in Sheffield', *Sheffield & Rotherham Independent*, 9 October 1900, p. 9; 'Sale of War Stamps', *Standard*, 11 October 1900, p. 8 and 'High Prices for Stamps', *Morning Post*, 13 October 1900, p. 8.
48　Gardner, *Mafeking*, p. 225; and Peter B. Boyden, Alan J. Guy & Marion Harding (eds), *ashes and blood: The British Army in South Africa 1795-1914* (London: National Army Museum, 1999), p. 467.
49　'The Mayor of Mafeking and his Critics', *Daily News*, 22 October 1900, p. 7.
50　'B-P report', p. 903.

covers the entire period of the siege from the pre-war preparations through the early days of investment, the Cronjé period, the disaster of Game Tree Fort, rationing, shellfire, the Eloff attack and the eventual relief. The material reflects the impressions of citizens, soldiers and refugees in Mafeking, civic and military leaders, and the interest of the metropolitan, provincial and colonial press in a siege that spanned 217 days. The material has its shortcomings – errors of detail not least about enemy casualties, and limitations of perspective – but it indicates what the participants believed and how they sustained their morale in testing circumstances. It reveals that the participants did not separate their social conditions and inter-relationships from the strategic and military aspects of the siege, and recognized that these factors were inextricably linked together. It also reflects first-hand, uncensored evidence about the pivotal issues of the siege, insights on the Boer 'way of warfare', or at least siege warfare, and an awareness of many that they were contributing to the history of imperial sieges. So this is a substantive body of material, different from the perspectives of individual diarists, but often complemented and contextualised by those diaries and their knowledge of specific issues.

Although the experiences were far from uniform, they provide scant support for revisionist theories about how the siege began, how it slumped into mere monotony and boredom, and how it became little more than a vehicle for the vanity and ambition of its commanding officer. They show how the Mafekingites realized the strategic significance of their town before the war erupted, its value in retaining the loyalty of local, pro-British black communities, and its vulnerability on account of the town's recent history (Jameson Raid) and exposed location. Frustrated by the pusillanimity of the Cape government, they wanted to defend their town almost as much as Baden-Powell, bereft of modern artillery and mobile support services, saw its defence as the best way of fulfilling his orders. If luring 5,600 Boers with a powerful array of modern artillery into a siege operation met B-P's requirements, local citizens realized that this was a siege and not a picnic (however grateful they were for Sundays without shellfire), and that their boredom and monotony hardly offset the destructive threat and the psychological anxiety from the Boer shelling and Mauser rifle-fire. They suffered far less than the much larger black communities from the effects of shelling and rationing, and certainly not from starvation, but they suffered nonetheless, as evidenced by the mounting toll of sick, the complaints about the quantity and quality of rations, and the protracted periods of convalescence. As the *Daily Chronicle*'s correspondent observed, 'The siege is no picnic, but we can joke and keep in good temper, notwithstanding it all.'[51]

---

51 'The Relief of Mafeking', *Hampshire Chronicle*, 12 May 1900, p. 6.

Of these siege eyewitnesses Colonels Hore and Vyvyan, and Majors Godley and Hanbury-Tracy, worked with Baden-Powell in a professional capacity, but everyone knew him or had opinions about his command. They delighted in his pithy ripostes to Boer diplomacy, praised his ingenuity in finding ways to deter or deceive the enemy, and admired his conscientiousness in inspecting military, medical and civilian facilities. They praised, too, his prominence on look-out duties during the day and his monitoring of enemy positions at night, earning his sobriquet: 'the wolf who never sleeps'.[52] Eyewitnesses appreciated that B-P, whatever his personal ambitions, had many gifts as a siege commander: he was energetic, resourceful, focused on key tasks (like reducing the demand for rations and extending the defensive perimeter), and, in his public persona, cheerful and confident about the future. Above all, in a peculiarly small and isolated community, he regarded civil-military relations as a priority and exploited the Sunday interludes to bolster morale through sports, concerts, dances, gymkhanas and a major siege exhibition. As a consummate showman, he excelled in these recreations, a leadership role that was widely appreciated. Many soldiers and citizens professed complete confidence in his command, and Bernard Short was by no means alone in stating that he was 'very proud of being through the siege of Mafeking with Colonel Baden-Powell'.[53]

Tensions arose over the course of 217 days, amidst all the uncertainty, rumour, false or misleading information, and fitful communications with the outside world. Although communications improved during 1900, the letters of these eyewitnesses, mainly sent after the relief, demonstrate that the siege was never as porous as the revisionists imagined. Inevitably B-P bore the brunt of any 'grousing' that occurred, even if he drew a veil over it in post-siege reports. He also accepted responsibility for the defeat at Game Tree Fort, and the disappointment that followed, not least the realization, as Lieutenant Gemmell observed, that 'After this affair . . . there were no more movements of an offensive nature made by us, and we settled down to play a purely waiting game.'[54] Undoubtedly this passivity added to the tensions within the tiny garrison and fuelled B-P's determination to push the defensive perimeter outwards over the next three months to obtain more grazing land and place the town beyond aimed, rifle fire. Whether this prudent approach appeased all his officers may be moot, as Lord Roberts subsequently alleged 'that those who were with him at Mafeking do not look upon him as a great

---

52 'B.-P.'s Vigil: A Last Look Round at Night in Mafeking', *Graphic* (30 June 1900), p. 1.
53 'A Forest Hill Man in Mafeking', *Kentish Mercury*, 13 July 1900, p. 3; see also 'With B.-P. in Mafeking', *Lloyd's Weekly Newspaper*, 21 October 1900, p. 2.
54 'The Siege of Mafeking', *Ayr Advertiser*, 23 August 1900, p. 5.

commander'.[55] Such a charge did not apply to Godley, who remained a staunch supporter of the Colonel.

So too did Vyvyan. He may have disagreed with B-P latterly over working parties but generally they worked closely together, regularly exchanging notes about matters as diverse as hospital sanitation, pathways, the erection of dummies, newly-built forts, and trenches in the brickfields. They agreed upon the strategic rationales for the siege (protecting Rhodesia and valuable railway property in Mafeking, as well as 'keeping a large force occupied in watching us'), and shared a mutual disdain for the press. Vyvyan also knew where credit lay for the successful outcome: 'we have held our own', he insisted, due to 'B.P.', that is, 'British Pluck' and 'Boer Pusillanimity' but first and foremost, 'Baden Powell'.[56]

Many of the eyewitnesses, both civil and military, who criticised the Colonel, even obliquely and so fed the revisionist critique, were those who felt a sense of propriety and responsibility towards the Barolong and the black refugees. 'The Native question', as Baden-Powell informed Lord Roberts, 'has been a difficult one', but the 'native refugees', including 'about a thousand' from Johannesburg, had proved 'a blessing in disguise'. They had done 'invaluable service on our defence works', digging wells, trenches and bombproof shelters.[57] He also advised Lord Kitchener that he had armed and paid 'about 200 natives to act as cattle-guards and as guards over our commissariat food and forage stores about the place'. The Barolong had taken up arms to defend 'their suburb of the town, and the Afrikanders and Fingoes [*sic*] took up arms in defence of their location near the Brickfields'. Yet B-P refused Barolong requests to 'organize a native force',[58] that is, a body paid and disciplined in support of the imperial cause, so preserving the veneer of a 'white man's war'.

Writing in this vein betrayed the quasi-accounting approach of B-P, whenever he assessed the contribution of blacks to the siege. He had either paid for their services as labourers, guards and messengers, or simply expected them to act in their own self-interest. This attitude contrasted with that of his

---

55 TNA, PRO 30/57/20, Kitchener Mss. Lord Roberts to Lord Kitchener, 4 May 1901; see also 'B-P's report', p. 892.
56 Brent. L., Vyvyan Mss., MS. 147/3/3/2, MS. 147/5/2/36 and MS. 147/5/2/49 on notes between B-P and Vyvyan; MS. 147/1/1/21 on Vyvyan's contempt for Stent and Hamilton, Vyvyan to his aunt, 6 May 1900; and MS. 147/1/1/22 on Vyvyan's strategic thinking and commendation of B-P, Vyvyan to Mollie, 21 May 1900.
57 NAM, Acc. 1971-01-23-6, R6/1, Roberts Mss., Baden-Powell to Lord Roberts, 20 February 1900.
58 NAM, Acc. 1971-01-23-1, R6/2, Roberts Mss., Baden-Powell to Lord Kitchener, 2 March 1900. As an interim total, this may explain the difference with the 300 cattle-guards mentioned in B-P's evidence before the *RCWSA*, vol. 2, p. 427.

intelligence officer, Major Hanbury-Tracy, who debriefed all the black runners after their hazardous missions, and Vyvyan, who remarked after following orders to cut his working parties to ten (244 labourers) that 'reducing the number of employed boys will mean more starving natives to be fed & so no return for it'.[59] B-P wanted many 'starving natives' to leave the siege, and his lack of emotionalism over the policy (Chapter 6) contrasted with the passionate pleas of Major H. Goold-Adams, the Resident Commissioner, Bechuanaland Protectorate. On 5 May Goold-Adams wrote:

> Numbers of men, women, and children have been killed either by shot and shell, in the ordinary course of the bombardment, or in a most cold-blooded manner when trying to escape from the town, or when out foraging for food, or when carrying letters, as this letter itself must be carried, through the enemy's lines. Added to these trials they have suffered from starvation and distress . . . . Through all these trials the Barolongs have never flinched and have taken part in resisting the efforts of the enemy to take the town.[60]

Lieutenant Gemmell also acknowledged the 'excellent work' done 'for us' by the Barolong 'all through the siege'. Once rationing was introduced, he described how 'The natives were given horse soup made out of bones from which nearly all the meat had been removed, and filthy-looking stuff it was; but it just managed to keep body and soul together in a number of them.'[61] As regards B-P's plan to eject refugees to conserve stocks of grain, Algie agonized over how it would be implemented. On the dark night when Magistrate Bell, assisted by Sol T. Plaatje, tried to organize a mass breakout, Algie asserted that

> most white people were anxiously wondering how many of the poor wretches would be shot down by the heartless Boers; in fact, many of us felt conscience-stricken to think that we were permitting these refugees – women and children, British subjects – to go out to face such risks. It is true many of them were willing, and wanted to go . . . but that notwithstanding, we could not help thinking that it would be a lasting disgrace and a stigma to British rule in South Africa if these natives met with any mishap.

59   Brent. L., Vyvyan Mss., MS. 147/5/2/50 Vyvyan to Colonel Commanding, 4 April 1900 and see the debriefs in the Hanbury-Tracy Mss.
60   'The Barolongs in Mafeking', *The Times*, 2 July 1900, p. 10.
61   'The Siege of Mafeking', *Ayr Advertiser*, 23 August 1900, p. 5.

A few hours later, he added, 'we were almost pleased' to learn that the breakout had failed and the refugees had returned.[62]

However squeamish his feelings, Algie, like Bell, conceded that B-P's logic was impeccable, and that the success of the siege, in view of the uncertainties about stocks of food and likelihood of relief, depended upon significantly reducing the demand for food. Just as a civil-military board, including Goold-Adams, Whiteley and Bell, had endorsed the policy as 'the best in the circumstances', so Algie agreed that Mafeking needed to rid itself of several hundred blacks.[63] Feelings of guilt were not eased by the successful escape of about 1,200 blacks to Kanye, since the black communities bore the brunt of the non-combatant casualties throughout the siege, namely an estimated 446 out of the 487 officially recorded as dead and wounded.[64]

Undoubtedly Baden-Powell differed from his critics, and even his staunch supporters, like Whiteley and the Reverend Weekes, by his famous lack of outward emotion and sentimentality. Whereas most of the eyewitnesses testified to the loyalty, sacrifice and multiple services of the Barolongs, B-P demurred on such matters (save in his General Order, which commended their exceptional scouting and fighting assistance during Eloff's incursion). Just as he characterized the Barolongs as merely taking up arms to defend their homes and cattle against a traditional enemy, so he described his own officers and men, who incurred 233 of the 316 combatant casualties,[65] as simply doing 'their duty'. In his final speeches at Mafeking he lavished praise neither on his own trained forces nor the armed blacks defending their homes, but upon the Town Guard. The guardsmen, he described, as all volunteers, who had submitted themselves to martial law and served as sentries, performing arduous night work throughout the siege.[66]

Nevertheless, most eyewitnesses including those like Edward Ross, who believed that B-P courted publicity (Chapter 6), recognized that the Colonel was a man who had brought his many-sided talents to bear upon a complex command. They respected the way in which he had conducted himself through a protracted and enervating siege, and how he had risen to the challenge of Eloff's attack. Lord Roberts applauded this 'grand success', and before his disappointment with B-P as a field commander, and as an organizer of the

---

62 'The Native Problem at Mafeking', *Liverpool Echo*, 5 May 1900, p. 4.
63 Ibid and NAM Acc.1968-10-42, B-P staff diary, 14 March 1900.
64 'B-P's report', p. 893.
65 Ibid.
66 'Mafeking After the Siege', *Derby Mercury*, 6 June 1900, p. 6 and 'The Last Scene at Mafeking', *Newcastle Weekly Courant*, 23 June 1900, p. 3.

South African Constabulary, he recognised that Baden-Powell in Mafeking had 'nobly upheld the honour of the British flag'.[67]

Where there was more unanimity among the eyewitnesses was in their perception of the enemy. Baden-Powell was convinced that the Boers should have been able to capture Mafeking at the outset 'after a fight', but that the series of 'kicks' at several points in the perimeter 'seemed to demoralize them'. In the intervening period the upgrading of the town's defences both increased the costs of any assault (as Eloff discovered) and blunted the effects of shell and rifle fire by establishing a 10-mile (16 km) perimeter and constructing 'over 4 miles [6.4 km] of covered ways, and bombproofs innumerable'. Thereafter the Boers simply wasted 'force, ammunition, and lives in watching Mafeking'.[68]

The colonists, both in Mafeking and the relief forces, claimed to know the enemy, or at least know him better than their British counterparts. The Mafeking defenders had engaged the enemy over an unprecedented period, fraternized with some of them on Sundays, and conversed with prisoners after Eloff's débâcle. As Algie remarked, the enemy were 'a cautious lot of warriors', preferring to fight from cover and at long range, but 'in low cunning and in Generalship for their own style of warfare . . . the Boers are adept'. They might not be 'as plucky as the Englishman understand it, but they are not fools'; they had benefited from foreign training, particularly in gunnery, and understood 'the fearful destructive power of modern weapons'.[69] Algie, like Bell, believed that the imperial authorities had severely underestimated the Boers, and that this had been the cause of their early disasters.[70]

Throughout the siege, many regarded the Boers as essentially craven, and even worse as 'curs' (B-P) or 'heartless' (Algie) in their shooting of black women and children,[71] and made little allowance for possible errors in night-time combat. They interpreted messages from the Boers as a form of psychological pressure and their various ruses, including the despatch of ambulance waggons at crucial moments in skirmishes as a 'slim' or underhand form of combat. Convinced that the Boer press was unreliable, and acted as an organ of propaganda, defenders mocked claims of minimal casualties after each skirmish (whereas these claims appear to be true, with the defenders only

---

67 Compare NAM, Acc. 1971-01-23-6, R6/1, Roberts Mss., Lord Roberts to Baden-Powell, 21 May 1900 with TNA, PRO 30/57/20 Kitchener Mss., Lord Roberts to Lord Kitchener, 20 July 1901.

68 NAM, Acc. 1971-01-23-6, R6/1, Roberts Mss., Baden-Powell to Lord Roberts, 20 February 1900.

69 Algie, 'Diary', 17 November 1899 and 6 January 1900, pp. 45 and 94.

70 Ibid., 6 January 1900, p. 94 and Bell, 'Diary', 31 January 1900, p. 63.

71 NAM, Acc. 1971-01-23, R6/2, Roberts Mss., Baden-Powell to Lord Kitchener, 2 March 1900 and 'The Native Problem at Mafeking', *Liverpool Echo*, 5 May 1900, p. 4.

able to confirm the number of Boer casualties after Eloff's attack). Above all, the Mafekingites deplored the killing of women and children by the supposedly 'deliberate' shelling of the women's laager, for which the evidence seems to be circumstantial and some of it may have been in error. Nevertheless, those who encountered the Boers directly appreciated their assistance with casualties after Game Tree Fort, and their honourable treatment of Lady Sarah Wilson and other white captives, including wounded soldiers like Captain Kenneth McLaren.

Eyewitnesses rejoiced at signs of Boer weakness. They lauded the Cape Boys for engaging the enemy directly and successfully in the brickfields, where the sapping and counter-sapping proved a labour-intensive and exacting form of combat. They noticed divisions within the Boer ranks, characterized by Reverend Weekes as 'rich Boers' living 'lazily and safely in the laagers', while poorer Boers and foreign volunteers manned the forts and trenches.[72] Such divisions seemed magnified after Eloff's abortive attack, which revealed a Boer command riven with doubts and dissension. Finally, Mafeking celebrated the rapid flight of the Boers once they came under fire from the Royal Horse Artillery.

How important then was the siege of Mafeking? Most of the eyewitnesses thought that the town was either strategically important in itself or worth defending once it was under investment. Captain de Montmorency, whose cynicism so infected the writing of Gardner, was the odd exception but the vast majority were proud to have been part of the siege and regarded its relief as a great achievement. The importance of the siege, though, was not at issue during the 'mafficking' response; even those who doubted that the town had any importance were just as ready to rejoice at its long-awaited relief. 'Mafficking' was an opportunity to identify with its defenders, to applaud their moral values, to hail B-P as one of the war's more accomplished commanders, and to celebrate the upholding of the nation's honour.

Fundamentally the siege derived its importance from the willingness of the Boers to invest the town. For the two republics, facing the might of the British empire, they could ill afford to squander scarce resources on an unimportant objective at the outset of the war. Yet they devoted significant numbers of men and guns to secure the capture of Mafeking, and raised the profile of the siege by sending Cronjé to conduct the investment. Once they had done so, they could not abandon the commitment altogether, even if willing to reduce

---

72 'Rector of Mafeking in Sheffield', *Sheffield & Rotherham Independent*, 9 October 1900, p. 9; see also Pretorius, 'The Besiegers' in Smith (ed.), *Siege of Mafeking*, vol. 1, pp. 84, 98, 100.

the quantity and quality of the forces engaged. Mafeking remained a thorn in the side of the Boers, and its relief a matter of abject humiliation.

In effect, the importance of Mafeking evolved over the course of the 217-day siege. During a war that had shocked the imperial consciousness by the scale and nature of the early British defeats, the spectacle of a small, isolated garrison holding out against a much larger and better-armed enemy evoked traditional siege memories and resonated across the empire. The predominant role of colonial troops in both the siege and the relief forces assumed more than a purely symbolic importance, as the dominions began sending forces to support the imperial cause. Ultimately, the prospective relief of Mafeking became increasingly important as confirming that the tide of war had changed irreversibly. Eyewitnesses understood some of these points better than others, but they professed a fierce imperial commitment and a belief that British prestige was inextricably linked to the outcome. While Mafeking cannot be compared with the great sieges of the twentieth century, Kut-Al-Amara (1915–16) and Singapore (1941–2) where the losses were catastrophic, and the damage to British prestige in India and East Asia of long-standing consequence, the reflection of the Eyemouth man on Mafeking remains instructive. In defending Mafeking, he was proud to have 'upheld the name of the British Empire', and to have served under 'such a worthy General as our Commander and his willing staff of officers'.[73]

---

73 'An Eyemouth Man in Mafeking', *Berwickshire News*, 17 July 1900, p. 5.

Appendix A

The Protectorate Regiment

Average age: 27 years

Nationalities:

English	217
Scots	45
Irish	47
Colonial born	121
Foreigners	17
TOTAL	447

Previous trades and occupations:

No trades (younger sons)	60
Clerks	55
Labourers	29
Farmers	26
Engineers (electrical & mining)	17
Carpenters	16
Engine drivers	12
Masons	12
Storemen	11
Others (less than 10 apiece)	209

N.B. 112 had served in regular imperial army, imperial militia, imperial yeomanry, English yeomanry, colonial volunteers, colonial permanent corps as well as various police forces, including the Indian police and the Royal Irish Constabulary.
Source: 'The Protectorate Regiment', *Pall Mall Gazette*, 10 July 1900, p. 8.

Appendix B

Notice: 11 February 1900

The Commander-in-Chief has asked us to make every effort to hang on here, if possible, till the middle of May.

This no doubt is a great disappointment to many who were looking forward to an early release, but I feel sure that on seeing the necessity for it everyone will join cheerfully in sacrificing personal comfort for a few more weeks, to make the siege a complete success.

We have supplies sufficient – with careful economy – to keep the white people and Barolongs, but not for all the outside Natives as well, consequently every effort must be made to get these people away.

All extra servants and hangers-on should be dismissed without delay and advised to make their way to Kanya [*sic*: Kanye] where supplies are laid down for them. The grain shops in town will close on 20th instant.

The middle of May is given as an outside limit up to which we must be prepared to last out, but if other plans come off successfully in the meantime, we shall get relief before then.

In the meantime I feel confident that the patience and courage which have been so conspicuously shown by all, and which have gained the admiration of our fellow countrymen at home, will continue to carry the siege out to a triumphant finish.

R.S.S. Baden-Powell, Colonel
Source: B.L. Add. Mss. 46,848, f. 89, Weil Mss.

Appendix C

The Colonel on 'Grousing'

I hear that again wiseacres are busy in town, informing people as to what I am doing and what I am leaving undone. As their deductions are somewhat inaccurate I wish to state that the condition of affairs is in no way altered since my last general notice, which stated we must be prepared to remain besieged all that time. Indeed I hope that we may be free within the next fortnight or three weeks, but it would be folly on our part not to be prepared against possible unforeseen delays. Had we not been prepared in the first instance we should all have been prisoners in Pretoria by the beginning of January, and the Boers would have now been enjoying the use of our property in Mafeking.

I am, I suppose, the most anxious of anybody in Mafeking to see a Relief Column here and the siege at an end; all hope that can be done, for our relief, from both North and South, is being done, but the moves of troops in the face of the enemy must necessarily be slow, and we have to sit in patience until they develop.

As regards the smallness of our rations, we could, of course, live well on full rations for a week or two and then give in to the 'women slaughterers' and let them take their vengeance on the town, whereas by limiting our amount of daily food we can make certain of outlasting all their efforts against us. The present ration, properly utilized, is a fairly full one as compared with those issued in other sieges – in fact I and my staff have, during the past few days, been living on a far smaller ration without any kind of extras to improve it – and we still live.

There are, by the way, two hints I should like to give for making small rations go further – hints derived from personal experience of previous hungry times – and these are:

1. To lump your rations together as much as possible for cooking and not every man to have his little amount cooked separately.
2. To make the whole into a big thick stew, from which, even three quarter lbs. of ingredients per man, three good meals can be got per day.

It is just possible that we may have to take 2 ozs. off the bread stuffs, but otherwise our supplies will last well over the period indicated. It has been objected that we are feeding horses on oats, but the oats so used are a lot (of Colonial oats) that have been found quite useless for making flour for human consumption.

I am told that I keep back news from the public. This is not in accordance with the facts, for I make a point of publishing all news of general interest as soon as possible after receipt, first by telephone, then by notices posted about, and lastly through Mr. Whales, in the Mafeking Mail Slips; I have no object whatever in keeping news back. Occasionally, of course, items of military information have to be kept quiet because, as we all know, their publication in Mafeking means their transmission within a few hours to the enemy's camp.

Although it may have been somewhat out of my province, I have been writing to the High Commissioner as strongly as I could put them, the claims which the citizens and refugees have for consideration in the matter of compensation, pressing for very early settlement on some more satisfactory basis than was the case on a former occasion. And there is no doubt that the good part they have borne in the defence of the place will add great force to their claims.

I have no feeling of doubt whatever that the large majority of the townspeople have sufficient confidence in me to know that I am working, as far as possible, for their good, but there are always busybodies in every assemblage to cavil at whatever is done, and I should like just to remind these gentlemen of the order issued early in the siege about 'grousing'.

I am always, not only willing, but anxious to personally hear any reasonable complaints or suggestions, and those who have them to make, need only bring their grievances to me to get what redress is in my power, but veiled hints and growlings cannot be permitted; at such times as these they are apt to put people 'on edge' and to alarm the ladies, and for these reasons they must be suppressed. 'Grousing' is generally the outcome of funk on the part of the individual who grouses, and I hope that every right-minded man who hears any of it will shut it up with an appropriate remark, or the toe of his boot. Cavillers should keep quiet until the siege is over and then they are welcome to write or talk until they are blue in the face.

By these remarks I do not wish for one instance to suggest that this 'grousing' is widespread. On the contrary the patience and loyal obedience of the main body of inhabitants under the restrictions of Martial Law, form one of the conspicuous features of the siege. But there are a few individuals – most of whom are known to me (as they will find when their claims for compensation come up for adjudication) – and it is these gentlemen that I desire to warn to keep as quiet as otherwise I shall have to take more stringent steps against them, but I should be ashamed if the fame of Mafeking and its heroic defence should be marred by any whisper among various outsiders, that there was any want of harmony or unity of purpose among us.

R.S.S. BADEN-POWELL
Colonel.

Source: *Mafeking Mail Special Siege-Slip*, 29 March 1900, pp. 1–2.

Bibliography

Manuscript Sources

Bodleian Libraries, University of Oxford,
    The papers of Alfred Milner, Viscount Milner, 1824-1955

Brenthurst Library, Johannesburg,
MS. 147/1/–147/11	Courtenay B. Vyvyan Collection
MS. 407/1/1	Lionel Cooke, 'Game Tree'

Brighton & Hove City Libraries, Brighton & Hove City Council,
    Lord Wolseley Collection

British Library,
Add. Mss 46,848 – 46,852	Benjamin Weil Mss.
Add. Mss. 46,318	John Burns diary

National Army Museum,
1968-10-42	R. S. S. Baden-Powell, Mafeking Diary
1971-01-23	Lord Roberts Mss.
1974-01-138	K. Francis diary
1974-02-32	D. Maxwell letters
1974-02-33	P. Maxwell letters
1986-02-78	W. Wheeler letter
1997-02-13	H. Llewellyn Mss.

National Library of Scotland,
MS 5,963	R. B. Haldane Mss.

Richard H. Nicholson Collection, Woodcott House, Upper Woodcott, nr. Whitchurch, Hampshire,
    Hon. A. Hanbury-Tracy Mafeking Mss.

The National Archives,
CO 417/275	
PRO 30/57/20	Lord Kitchener Mss.
WO 32/7849	
WO32/7852	
WO 105	Lord Roberts Mss.

WO 108/185   Maj. H. de Montmorency diary
WO 108/284   Lt.-Col. C. B. Vyvyan, 'The Defence of
                  Mafeking', n.d.

Parliamentary Papers

Minutes of Evidence before Royal Commission of the War in South Africa, vol. 2, Cd
   1791 (1904), XLI
South Africa Despatches, Vol. 1, Cd 457 (1901), including Brigadier-General
   B. T. Mahon, report, 23 May 1900

Mafeking Printed Sources and Autobiographies

Algie, J. R., 'The Mafeking siege diary of John Ronald Algie (Town Clerk) 1899-
   1900', t/s copy in Brenthurst Library, original in Mafikeng Museum
Baden-Powell, Major-General R. S. S., *Sketches in Mafeking and East Africa*
   (London: Smith, Elder & Co., 1907)
Baden-Powell of Gilwell, Lord, *Lessons From The 'Varsity of Life* (London:
   C. Arthur Pearson, 1933)
Baillie, Major F. D., *Mafeking. Diary of The Siege* (London: Archibald Constable
   & Co, 1900)
Bell, C., 'The Mafeking siege diary of Charles Bell, magistrate, 1899-1900',
   t/s copy in Brenthurst Library, original in Cory Library, Rhodes University,
   Grahamstown
Blunt, W. S., *My Diaries: Being a Personal Narrative of Events 1888-1914*, 2 vols
   (London: Martin Secker, 1929)
Bottomley, J. (ed.), 'The Siege of Mafeking and the Imperial Mindset as Revealed
   in the Diaries of T. W. P. (Tom) Hayes and W. P. (William) Hayes, District
   Surgeons', *New Contree*, no. 41 (1997), pp. 25–161
_____, 'A Scots "Salvationist" Perspective of the Siege of Mafeking. The
   Diary of Thomas A. Young', *New Contree*, no. 45 (1999), pp. 217–51
Butler, Sir W. F., *An Autobiography* (London: Constable, 1911)
Christison, G. (ed.), '*Lord of Hosts on our Side*': *Mafeking Siege Diary of Sarah
   Dixon Gwynne* (Pietermaritzburg: Little Oribi Press, 1996)
Cock, A., *Petticoat in Mafeking: The Letters of Ada Cock*, ed. by J. Midgeley
   (Kommetjie, C. P.: private, 1974)
Comaroff, J. L. (ed.), *The Boer War Diary of Sol T. Plaatje: An African at Mafeking*
   (London: Cardinal, 1976)
Crauford, A. M., 'A Nurse's Diary in Besieged Mafeking', *Crampton's Magazine
   of Fiction*, vol. 16 (1900), pp. 57–68 and vol. 17 (1901), pp. 37–42, 109–19,
   245–7, 285–92, 396–401 and 488–94.
Creswicke, L., *South Africa and the Transvaal War*, 6 vols (Edinburgh: T. C. & E.
   C. Jack, 1900)
Davey, A. (ed.), *The Defence of Ladysmith and Mafeking: Accounts of two sieges, 1899
   to 1900, being the South African War experiences of William Thwaites, Steuart*

Binny, Alfred Down and Samuel Cawood (Johannesburg: The Brenthurst Press, 1983)

Drooglever, R. (ed.), *'A Monument to British Pluck': Captain Herbert Greener's Journal of the Siege of Mafeking* (Honiton, Devon: Token Publishing, 2009)

Godley, General Sir A., *Life of an Irish Soldier* (London: John Murray, 1939)

Godley, Lieutenant-Colonel R. S., *Khaki and Blue: Thirty-Five Years' Service in South Africa* (London: Lovat Dickson & Thompson Ltd., 1935)

Hamilton, J. A., *The Siege of Mafeking* (London: Methuen, 1900)

Headlam, C. (ed.), *The Milner Papers*, 2 vols (London: Cassell, 1933)

'Major-General Baden-Powell's official report on the Siege of Mafeking', *London Gazette*, 8 February 1901, pp. 890–903.

Neilly, J. E., *Besieged with B.-P.: A Full and Complete Record of the Siege* (London: C. Arthur Pearson, 1900)

Pollock, Major A. W. A., *With Seven Generals in the Boer War: A Personal Narrative* (London: Skeffington & Son, 1900)

Saunders, F., *Mafeking Memories*, ed. by P. Thurmond Smith (Cranbury, N.J.: Associated University Presses, 1996)

Sinclair, D., *The White Tide* (Gweru, Zimbabwe: Modern Press, 2002)

Weir, C. J., *The Boer War: A Diary of the Siege of Mafeking* (Edinburgh: Spence & Phimister, 1901)

Willan, B. P. (ed.), *Edward Ross, Diary of The Siege of Mafeking October 1899 to May 1900* (Cape Town: van Riebeeck Society, 1980)

Wilson, Lady S., *South African Memories: Social, Warlike & Sporting* (London: Edward Arnold, 1909)

Young, Filson, *The Relief of Mafeking; How It was Accomplished by Mahon's Flying Column: with an Account of Some Earlier Episodes in the Boer War of 1899-1900* (London: Methuen, 1900)

Other Printed Primary Sources

Booth, B. A. and E. Mehew (eds), *The Letters of Robert Louis Stevenson*, 8 vols (New Haven and London: Yale University Press, 1995)

Power, F., *Letters from Khartoum* (London: Sampson Low et al, 1885)

Preston, A. (ed.), *In Relief of Gordon: Lord Wolseley's Campaign Journal of the Khartoum Relief Expedition 1884-1885* (London: Hutchinson, 1967)

Spiers, E. M. (ed.), *Letters from Ladysmith: Eyewitness Accounts from the South African War* (Barnsley: Frontline Books, 2010)

_____(ed.), *Letters from Kimberley: Eyewitness Accounts from the South African War* (London: Frontline Books, 2013)

Wessels, A. (ed.), *Lord Kitchener and the War in South Africa 1899-1902* (Stroud, Glos.: Sutton Publishing for the Army Records Society, 2006)

Wolseley, Gen. Viscount, *The Soldier's Pocket Book for Field Service* (London: Macmillan, 1886)

Newspapers

(Aberdeen) Evening Express
Aberdeen Weekly Journal
Abingdon Herald
Alnwick Guardian
Alton Mail
Armagh Guardian
Ashton-under-Lyne Reporter
Ayr Advertiser
Ayr Observer
Barnet Press
Bath Chronicle
Bedford and County Record
Belfast News-Letter
Berkshire Chronicle
Berwickshire News
Birmingham Daily Post
Blackpool Times
Bolton Chronicle
Border Advertiser
Bradford Daily Argus
Bradford Daily Telegraph
Bridlington Free Press
Brighton Gazette
Bucks Herald
Bury and Norwich Post and Suffolk Journal
Cambrian
Cambridge Independent
Canterbury Register
Cape Times
Carlisle Journal
Carnarvon and Denbigh Herald
Cheltenham Chronicle
Cheshire Observer
Chichester Observer
Consett Chronicle
Cornishman
Craven Herald
Daily Chronicle
Daily Mail
Daily News
Derby Daily Telegraph
Derby Mercury

Derbyshire Advertiser and North Staffordshire Journal
Derbyshire Times and Chesterfield Herald
Devon Evening Express
Dewsbury Reporter
Doncaster Gazette
Dorking Advertiser
Dover Express
(Dublin) Evening Herald
Dumbarton Herald
Dumfries and Galloway Courier and Herald
(Dundee) Courier & Argus
(Dundee) Evening Telegraph
East Anglian Daily Times
Eastbourne Chronicle
East Sussex News
Edinburgh Evening News
Elgin Courant
Essex County Chronicle
Essex County Standard
Essex Herald
Essex Newsman
Essex Standard
Evening Swindon Advertiser
Falkirk Herald
Glasgow Herald
(Gloucester) Citizen
Gorton, Openshaw and Bradford Reporter
Grantham Journal
Graphic
(Gravesend and Dartford) Reporter
Hampshire Advertiser
Hampshire Chronicle
Hastings & St. Leonards Observer
Hereford Journal
Huddersfield Daily Chronicle
(Hull) Daily Mail
Huntingdonshire Post
Illustrated London News
Inverness Courier
Irish Times
Isle of Man Weekly Times
Jackson's Oxford Journal
Kentish Mercury
Kilmarnock Standard
Leamington Spa Courier and Warwickshire Standard

Leeds Mercury
Leeds Times
Leicester Chronicle and Leicestershire Mercury
Lincoln, Rutland and Stamford Mercury
Liverpool Echo
Liverpool Mercury
Lloyd's Weekly Newspaper
Lurgan Times
Luton News
Macclesfield Courier and Herald
Mafeking Mail: Special Siege Slip
Manchester Courier
Manchester Evening Chronicle
Manchester Guardian
Mansfield Chronicle
(Melbourne) Argus
Middlesex Chronicle
Middlesex County Times
Morning Post
Morpeth Herald
(Newcastle) Evening Chronicle
Newcastle Weekly Courant
Newbury Weekly News
Newry Telegraph
Northampton Mercury
North British Daily Mail
North Devon Journal
North-Eastern Daily Gazette
Northern Echo
North Star
North Wales Chronicle
North Wales Guardian
North Wilts Herald
Nottingham Evening Post
Nuneaton Chronicle
Oban Telegraph
Oldham Standard
Pall Mall Gazette
Penistone, Stocksbridge Hoylund Chapeltown Express
Penny Illustrated
Perthshire Advertiser
Poole, Parkstone and East Dorset Herald
Portadown News
(Portsmouth) Evening News
Pudsey and Stanningley Observer

Punch
Reynolds's Newspaper
Royal Cornwall Gazette
Sale and Stretford Guardian
Scarborough Post
Scotsman
Sheffield and Rotherham Independent
Sheffield Daily Telegraph
Shrewsbury Chronicle
Somerset County Gazette
Southport Guardian
South Wales Argus
South Wales Daily News
South Wales Daily Post
Standard
Star (Saint Peter Port)
Stockport Advertiser
Strathearn Herald
Stroud Journal
Sunderland Daily Echo
Sydney Morning Herald
The Times
(Toronto) Globe
Trewman's Exeter Flying Post
Tunbridge Wells Gazette
Ulster Gazette
Wallasey and Wirral Chronicle
Western Gazette
Western Mail
Western Morning News
Western Times
West London Observer
Westminster Gazette
Wharfedale & Airedale Observer
Wiararapa Daily Times
Wigan Observer and District Advertiser
Wiltshire Telegraph
Wimbledon News
Windsor Chronicle
Woking Observer
Woolwich Herald
Workington Star
Yorkshire Herald and York Herald
Yorkshire Post
Yorkshire Telegraph and Star

Secondary Sources

Aitken, W. F., *Baden-Powell, The Hero of Mafeking* (London: S. W. Partridge & Co., 1900)

Amery, L. S. (ed.), *The Times History of The War in South Africa 1899-1902*, 7 vols (London: Sampson, Low, Marston and Co., 1900–9), particularly vol. 4 ed. by B. Williams (1906)

Baden-Powell, B. F. S., *War in Practice* (London: Isbister & Co., 1903)

Begbie, H., *The Story of Baden-Powell: The Wolf that Never Sleeps* (London: Grant Richards, 1900)

Bennett, Ian, *A Rain of Lead: The Siege and Surrender of the British at Potchefstroom 1880-1881* (London: Greenhill Books, 2001)

Boyden, P. B., A. J. Guy & M. Harding (eds), *ashes and blood: The British Army in South Africa 1795-1914* (London: National Army Museum, 1999)

Brendon, P., *Eminent Edwardians* (Harmondsworth, Middlesex: Penguin, 1981)

_____, *The Decline and Fall of the British Empire 1781-1997* (London: Vintage, 2008)

Callwell, Col. C. E., *Small Wars: A Tactical Textbook for Imperial Soldiers* (London: H.M.S.O., 1906, third edition reprinted by Greenhill Books, 1990)

Cammack, D., *The Rand At War 1899-1902: The Witwatersrand & the Anglo-Boer War* (London: James Currey, 1990)

Carruthers, J. et al (eds), *The Jameson Raid: A Centennial Retrospective* (Johannesburg: Brenthurst Press, 1996)

Carver, Field Marshal Lord, *The National Army Museum Book of The Boer War* (London: Pan Books, 2000)

Cecil, H. and M. Cecil, *Imperial Marriage: An Edwardian War and Peace* (London: John Murray, 2002)

Changuion, L., *Silence of the Guns: The History of the Long Toms of the Anglo-Boer War* (Pretoria: Protea Book House, 2001)

Cromer, Earl of, *Modern Egypt*, 2 vols (London: Macmillan, 1908)

David, S., *The Indian Mutiny 1857* (London: Penguin, 2003)

Davitt, M., *The Boer Fight for Freedom* (New York: Funk and Wagnalls, 1902)

Dawson, G., *Soldier Heroes: British adventure, empire and the imagining of masculinities* (London and New York: Routledge, 1994)

Dennis, P. and J. Grey (eds), *The Boer War Army, Nation and Empire, The 1999 Chief of Army/Australian War Memorial Military History Conference* (Canberra: Army History Unit, 2000)

Downham, J., *Red Roses on the Veldt: Lancashire Regiments in the Boer War, 1899-1902* (Lancaster: Carnegie Publishing, 2000)

Doyle, A. Conan, *The Great Boer War* (London: Smith, Elder & Co., 1900)

Faught, C. B., *Gordon: Victorian Hero* (Washington, D. C.: Potomac Books, 2008)

Flower-Smith, M. and E. J. Yorke, *Mafeking: The Story of a Siege* (Welrevredenpark; Covos Bay, 2000)

Fremount-Barnes, G., *The Indian Mutiny 1857-58* (Oxford: Osprey, 2007)

French, P., *Younghusband: The Last Great Imperial Adventurer* (London: HarperCollins, 1994)

Fuller, J. F. C., *The Last of the Gentleman's Wars: A Subaltern's Journal of the War in South Africa, 1899-1902* (London: Faber & Faber, 1937)

Gardner, B., *Mafeking: A Victorian Legend* (London: Cassell, 1966)

Girouard, M., *The Return to Camelot: Chivalry and the English Gentleman* (New Haven and London: Yale University Press, 1981)

Grinnell-Milne, D., *Baden-Powell at Mafeking* (London: Bodley Head, 1957)

Harrington, P., *British Artists and War: The Face of Battle in Paintings and Prints, 1700-1914* (London: Greenhill Books, 1993)

Hichberger, J. W. M., *Images of the Army: The Military in British Art, 1815-1914* (Manchester: Manchester University Press, 1988)

Hickman, Colonel A. S., *Rhodesia Served The Queen*, 2 vols (Salisbury: Government Printer, 1970), vol. 1 'Rhodesian Forces in the Boer War'

Hillcourt, W. and Olave Baden-Powell, *Baden-Powell: The Two Lives of a Hero* (London: Heinemann, 1964)

Hobson, J. A., *The Psychology of Jingoism* (London: Grant Richards, 1901)

Hunter, A., *Kitchener's Sword-Arm: The Life and Campaigns of General Sir Archibald Hunter* (Staplehurst, Kent: Spellmount, 1996)

Jackson, T., *The Boer War* (London: Channel 4 Books, 1999)

Jeal, T., *Baden-Powell* (London: Hutchinson, 1989)

Judd, D. and K. Surridge, *The Boer War* (London: John Murray, 2002)

Keown-Boyd, H., *A Good Dusting: A Centenary Review of the Sudan Campaigns 1883-1899* (London: Leo Cooper, 1986)

Kruger, R., *Goodbye Dolly Gray: A History of the Boer War* (London: NEL MENTOR, 1963)

Lehmann, J., *The First Boer War* (London: Buchan & Enright, 1985)

MacKenzie, J. M. (ed.), *Popular Imperialism and the Military 1850-1950* (Manchester: Manchester University Press, 1992)

Masterman, C. F. G., *From the Abyss of its Inhabitants by One of Them* (London: R. Brimley Johnson, 1902)

Matthew, H. C. G., *Gladstone 1875-1898* (Oxford: Clarendon Press, 1995)

Maurice, Major-General Sir F. B. and M. H. Grant, *History of the War in South Africa 1899-1902*, 4 vols (London: Hurst & Blackett, 1906–10)

Miller, C., *Painting the Map Red: Canada and the South African War, 1899-1902* (Montreal & Kingston: Canadian War Museum and McGill-Queen's University Press, 1993)

Milner, Viscountess, *My Picture Gallery 1886-1901* (London: John Murray, 1951)

Morris, D. R., *The Washing of the Spears* (London: Sphere Books, 1968)

Nasson, B., *The South African War 1899-1902* (London: Arnold, 1999)

Nicoll, F., *Gladstone, Gordon and the Sudan Wars: The Battle over Imperial Intervention in the Victorian Age* (Barnsley: Pen & Sword, 2013)

Pakenham, T., *The Boer War* (London: Weidenfeld and Nicolson, 1979)

Peck, J., *War, the Army and Victorian Literature* (Basingstoke: Macmillan Press, 1998)

Porter, A. N., *The Origins of the South African War: Joseph Chamberlain and the Diplomacy of Imperialism* (Manchester: Manchester University Press, 1980)

Powell, G., *Plumer – The Soldier's General* (London: Leo Cooper, 1990)

Preston, D., *The Boxer Rebellion: The Dramatic Story of China's War on Foreigners That Shook the World in the Summer of 1900* (New York: Berkley Books, 2000)

Pretorius, F., *The A to Z of the Anglo-Boer War* (Lanham, Md.: Scarecrow Press, 2009)

Price, R., *An Imperial War and the British Working Class: Working-Class Attitudes and Reactions to the Boer War 1899-1902* (London: Routledge & Kegan Paul, 1972)

Reynolds, E. E., *Baden-Powell: A Biography of Lord Baden-Powell of Gilwell* (London: Oxford University Press, 1942)

Richards, J., (ed), *Imperialism and Juvenile Fiction* (Manchester: Manchester University Press, 1989)

————, *Imperialism and Music: Britain 1876-1953* (Manchester: Manchester University Press, 2001)

Ricks, C. (ed.), *The Poems of Tennyson* (London and Harlow: Longmans, Green & Co., 1969)

Robertson, W., *The Defence of Mafeking* (London: Oxford University Press, 1941)

Rose, J., *The Intellectual Life of the British Working Classes* (New Haven: Yale University Press, 2001)

Rosenthal, M., *The Character Factory: Baden-Powell and the Origins of the Boy Scout Movement* (London: Collins, 1986)

Russell, D., *Popular Music in England, 1840-1914* (Manchester: Manchester University Press, 1997)

Smith, I. R., *The Origins of the South African War, 1899-1902* (London: Longman, 1996)

———— (ed.), *The Siege of Mafeking*, 2 vols. (Johannesburg: Brenthurst Press, 2001)

Spiers, E. M., *The Victorian Soldier in Africa* (Manchester: Manchester University Press, 2004)

————, *The Scottish Soldier and Empire, 1854-1902* (Edinburgh: Edinburgh University Press, 2006)

Springhall, J. O., *Youth, Empire and Society: British Youth Movements, 1883-1940* (London: Croom Helm, 1977)

Symons, J., *England's Pride: The Story of the Gordon Relief Expedition* (London: Hamish Hamilton, 1965)

Trench, C. C., *Charley Gordon: An Eminent Victorian Assessed* (London: Allen Lane, 1978)

Warwick, P. (ed.), *The South African War: The Anglo-Boer War 1899-1902* (Harlow: Longman Group, 1980)

————, *Black People and the South African War 1899-1902* (Cambridge: Cambridge University Press, 1983)

Wilson, H. W., *With The Flag To Pretoria: A History of the Boer War of 1899-1900*, 2 vols. (London: Harmsworth, 1901)

Yorke, E., *Mafeking 1899-1900* (Stroud, Glos.: History Press, 2014)

Articles and Chapters

Beaumont, J., 'The British Press during the South African War: The Sieges of Mafeking, Kimberley and Ladysmith' in M. Connelly and D. Welch (eds), *War and the Media: Reportage and Propaganda, 1900-2003* (London: I. B. Tauris, 2005), pp. 1–18

Hill, R., 'The Gordon Literature', *The Durham University Journal*, vol. XLVII, no. 3 (1955), pp. 97–103

Morgan, K. O., 'The Boer War and the Media (1899-1902)', *Twentieth Century British History*, vol. 13 (2002), pp. 1–16

Pretorius, F., 'Boer Propaganda During the South African War of 1899-1902', *Journal of Imperial and Commonwealth History*, vol. 37, no. 3 (2009), pp. 399–419

_____, 'Welcome but Not That Welcome: The Relations between Foreign Volunteers and the Boers in the Anglo-Boer War of 1899-1902' in C. G. Krüger, S. Levsen (eds), *War Volunteering in Modern Times* (London: Palgrave Macmillan, 2010), pp. 122–49

Smerdon, G., 'An Apprentice at Mafeking', *Journal of the Society for Army Historical Research*, vol. 74 (1997), pp. 46–50

Spiers, E. M., 'Military correspondence in the late nineteenth-century press', *Archives*, vol. 32, no.116 (2007), pp. 28–40

Surridge, K., '"All you soldiers are what we call pro-Boer"; The Military Critique of the South African War, 1899-1902', *History*, vol. 82 (1997), pp. 582–600

Tighe, G., 'How we defended Mafeking' in W. Woods (ed.), *Marvellous Escapes from Peril, as told by survivors* (London: Blackie & Son, 1915), pp. 166–79

'With Plumer to the Relief of Mafeking by One of his Troopers', *Blackwood's Edinburgh Magazine*, vol. 168 (1900), pp. 804–16

'With the Boers round Mafeking, 1899-1900', *Blackwood's Edinburgh Magazine*, vol. 171 (1902), pp. 16–27

Unpublished Works

Cooper, A. A.,'The Origins and Growth of Freemasonry in South Africa, 1772-1876' (University of Cape Town: unpublished MA thesis, 1980)

On-Line Material

U.S. Scouting Service Project, The Siege of Mafeking A Diary kept by Trooper William Robertson Fuller, Protectorate Regiment, Frontier Force, Mafeking, www.usscouts.org/usscouts/history/siegediary.asp (accessed 3 September 2018).

Index